World
War One
A Chronological
Narrative

Other books by Philip Warner:

THE MEDIEVAL CASTLE
THE SPECIAL AIR SERVICE
THE CRIMEAN WAR
DERVISH
THE JAPANESE ARMY OF WORLD WAR II
THE SOLDIER
THE BATTLE OF LOOS
THE FIELDS OF WAR (ED)
PANZER
ALAMEIN
THE D-DAY LANDINGS
INVASION ROAD
AUCHINLECK
PHANTOM
THE SPECIAL BOAT SQUADRON
THE BRITISH CAVALRY
HORROCKS
THE SECRET FORCES OF WORLD WAR II
PASSCHENDAELE
FIREPOWER: FROM SLINGS TO STAR WARS
WORLD WAR II
THE VITAL LINK: THE STORY OF THE ROYAL SIGNALS, 1945–1985
THE BATTLE OF FRANCE, 1940
FIELD MARSHAL EARL HAIG

WORLD WAR ONE

A Chronological Narrative

Philip Warner

ARMS AND
ARMOUR

Arms and Armour Press
A Cassell Imprint
Wellington House, 125/130 Strand, London WC2RR 0BB

Distributed in the USA by Sterling Publishing Co. Inc.,
387 Park Avenue South, New York, NY 10016-8810.

Distributed in Australia by Capricorn Link (Australia) Pty.
Ltd, 2/13 Carrington Road, Castle Hill, NSW 2154.

British Library Cataloguing-in-Publication Data: a catalogue
record for this book is available from the British Library

ISBN 1-85409-294-4

Designed and edited by DAG Publications Ltd.
Designed by David Gibbons; edited by Gerald Napier;
indexed by Hilary Bird; printed and bound in Great Britain.

Contents

Preface

In general the pattern of the book has been to describe events as they were happening. However, when certain developments were remote from the main theme or did not last for the entire period the outcome has been given in the text even though it meant taking the narrative into a later period.

Hundreds of books have been written about various aspects of the First World War: official and unofficial histories, specialist books in medicine, artillery, logistics, etc., personal reminiscences, and novels which were often autobiographical. Most of them are long out of print.

In the 1990s we encounter the eightieth anniversaries of the outbreak and its ending. In hindsight we can see the achievements and mistakes of the time. Many conflicts of the present decade may be traced to origins in the 1919 peace settlements: it is, of course, easy to be wise after the event.

With the mass of material available, the writer and reader of today may see the war in perspective and form judgements which were previously impossible.

The last word, the final summary, the ultimate definitive view can never be made, but the student in the 1990s is probably in a better position to see the war in its proper perspective than any of his predecessors have been.

The Causes
of the First World War

Although the immediate cause of the First World War was the assassination of the Austrian Archduke, Franz Ferdinand on 28 June 1914 in Sarajevo, this merely precipitated a conflict between the major powers which had become inevitable. The main reasons were the ambitions, apprehensions, and miscalculations of Germany, Russia, France and Britain. All, in their different ways, considered that their vital interests were threatened.

Austria felt that the stability of her territories, which contained 23,000,000 Serbs, was threatened by Serbia, which saw herself as the leader of a Pan Slav movement. The assassination of the Archduke, who was heir to the Austrian throne, was thought to have been encouraged by the government of Serbia. Austria therefore attacked Serbia.

Austria was already allied to Germany, who saw her as a reservoir of valuable manpower for any conflict in which Germany might herself become involved; Austria was a useful stepping stone to Germany's aspirations for influence (and perhaps possessions) in the Mediterranean and the Middle East. Germany had colonies in Africa and the Pacific, with which her communications were extremely vulnerable. Germany also felt she was encircled and contained by France and Russia on land, and Britain by sea.

Russia felt she was under an obligation to support Serbian aspirations, as a fellow Slav state. She also hoped to use her connections with Serbia to gain influence on the Mediterranean seaboard.

France was allied to Russia because both were apprehensive of German ambitions. Their defensive treaty meant that Germany would be deterred from attacking either, as this would immediately lead to a war on both east and west, which Germany dreaded. France was highly suspicious of Germany's alliance with Austria and Italy.

Britain noted that Germany was making great efforts to expand her navy, building submarines and large ships in an effort to challenge Britain, whose navy was so large that peace had been maintained at sea for nearly a hundred years with the exception of a battle between Russia and Japan in 1905.

However Britain was not immediately drawn into the war by a challenge to her seapower but by a guarantee she had given to defend Belgian neutrality. When Germany attacked France she violated Belgian neutrality as part of her strategic plan. In the longer term German naval expansion was seen as threatening the British Empire, which included Canada, South Africa, Australia, New Zealand, India, and many other territories. In 1917 America, outraged by Germany's ruthless submarine warfare, often directed against neutral ships, joined the Allies. Turkey had joined Germany and Japan had joined the Allies, both in 1914.

Although one bullet had killed the Austrian Archduke and effectively started the war it was later estimated that for every man subsequently killed 50,000 rifle bullets were fired.

By 11 November 1918, Germany and her allies (known as the Central Powers) had had 3,500,000 killed and the Allies 5,250,000. These are minimum figures. At least another 11,000,000 had been wounded and probably incapacitated for life.

CHAPTER 1

1 9 1 4

4 August was a blazingly hot day in Britain. It was also a Bank Holiday. For many people these official holidays were the only free days they ever had apart from Sundays, for at that time there was no statutory right to a holiday. In consequence, vast numbers rushed to the seaside or the country, although that day there was an inexplicable shortage of trains. When they came back late that night, hot, tired, but probably happy, they learned that Britain was about to go to war with Germany and that other countries, such as France and Russia, were in it too.

It was a bewildering piece of news, but rather exciting. Nobody expected the war to last long. Britain always won and although Britain had never fought the Germans before there was no reason to believe that they would be any more of a problem than the Russians, the French, the Spanish, the Turks, the Chinese and all those other countries which had mistakenly tried to check the advance of the British Empire.

No one had the faintest idea of the fact that the world would never be the same again and that millions of able bodied men would be slaughtered or disabled for life in unimaginably sordid circumstances, that women would suffer appallingly when their husbands or sons, or the men whom they might have married, were remorselessly wiped out. Nobody visualised that by 1918 the status of women would have changed so much that it was possible that one day they might even be allowed to vote. (Until 1918 only male householders had the vote.)

Although the newspapers had been talking of a crisis in the Balkans, or of German military and naval ambitions, these reports had no more effect on the average reader than the reports there had been of floods in China or earthquakes in South America, where that sort of thing was to be expected. But suddenly the situation had changed. The searchlight, instead of picking out distant objects for a moment or two, had swung round and focused on them and stayed there. Twenty-five years later, when Britain once more found herself at war with Germany, there was a much clearer view of why this had happened. Most people had a radio (which they called a wireless)

11

in 1939, and they had also seen a lot of menacing newsreels in the cinemas, which were attended by hundreds of thousands of people every week. But even in 1939 there was a sense of bewilderment, of why, and what it would be like, and how would it all end. Today, when television and hourly radio news bulletins overwhelm everyone with facts about events at home and abroad, there is no reason why anyone should fail to understand the causes of a conflict. Yet if small wars should spread and a third world war seem imminent, the same bewilderment would shock people again, perhaps with even more sense of foreboding. All it needs is for some fanatical leader of a small, belligerent state, perhaps, to acquire enough modern highly lethal weapons, nuclear, chemical or bacteriological, to challenge the western world. For a while, no doubt we would be as bemused as our ancestors in 1914 at this threat to our ordinary, orderly existence.

Of course, some people knew very well what was happening in 1914 and were in a position to influence events, though not necessarily responsibly. There was the German High Command, there was the government of the Austro-Hungarian Empire, there were the watchful, opportunist, leaders of Russia, there was the apprehensive government of France which had been trounced by the Russians 43 years earlier, and there was the British Foreign Office, whose mission was to hold the Empire together and thwart attempts by other nations to obtain advantages in the Middle East. The Foreign Office stressed that sacrifices might have to be made in one area in order to prevent larger, more vital, concessions being made in another. It hoped that war could be avoided by clever diplomacy: unfortunately, games of chess, however brilliantly played, end suddenly when someone tips up the board and scatters the pieces on the floor.

In hindsight we all know that war was probably inevitable. For years Germany had been building an army and navy, and working out plans to expand its empire. The Germans had come too late into the field of imperial expansion and had to accept what other countries did not want. Germany also had apprehensions about Russia and France, suspecting that one day the latter would seek revenge for the crushing defeat and humiliating peace of the Franco-Prussian War of 1871.

In 1895 Germany had completed the construction of the Kiel Canal, thus giving the Baltic fleet clear entry to the North Sea. Five years later, the German Navy had stipulated that Germany must build a fleet capable of challenging (and defeating) the mightiest naval power, that is Britain. For years German officers had been drinking toasts to 'Der Tag' – the day when they would wrest control of the oceans from the Royal Navy. The French

Secret Service also knew of a complex military plan by which Germany expected to win a victory over France before France's ally, Russia, could come to her assistance. The French response was to build a series of frontier forts. Nobody expected Britain to become involved in a war on the Continent. There were contingency plans, of course, there always are. But the French suspected that British sympathies inclined more towards Germany than France. After all, the British royal family was of German extraction and the Kaiser was Queen Victoria's nephew, even though Edward VII had been a Francophile.

As always, there were forces under the surface which were likely to upset any neat diplomatic solution to a crisis.

By 1914 the leading countries of the world had gradually grouped into two main camps. Britain, though principally concerned with the maintenance of her vast empire, was well aware of the growing power and ambition of Germany, which now had a well trained army, a disconcertingly strong navy, and a powerful industrial base. Germany was also unpredictable. Just before the outbreak of the South African (Boer) war in 1899, the Kaiser had shown considerable friendliness to the Boers, who had been adequately supplied with excellent guns from Krupps of Essen: those guns had caused great damage to British troops when the conflict had begun. And that was when Queen Victoria was still on the throne. Edward VII (1901–1910) felt considerably less affection for his German cousins: he preferred France and its way of life; he liked the French aristocracy and he could converse fluently in their language. Edward VII did not concern himself with trying to influence foreign policy, but the personal Entente Cordiale which he established paved the way for certain political agreements in 1904; these defined spheres of influence and therefore helped to remove possible sources of friction between Britain and France.

Rather surprisingly Britain entered into a similar arrangement with Russia in 1907. In spite of its crushing defeat by Japan in 1905, Russia still seemed to entertain expansionist ambitions. Its vast size – eight million square miles – did not appear to satisfy it so much as to fuel its imperial ambitions, or so it seemed to people outside Russia. Inside Russia, matters looked somewhat different. Vast areas of the country were totally unproductive, whereas just beyond its borders lay territories which contained all the materials which Russia coveted, and also warm-water ports. Several attempts to force a way through the Dardanelles into the Mediterranean had been made during the nineteenth century, but all had ended in frustration, of which the Crimean War in 1854–6 had probably been the most humiliating. Persia, along its south-western frontier, was a tempting prospect, but this was an independent country under British influence. India, also to the south, was an even more alluring prize, but that was part of the British Empire and any attempts to invade it would encounter formidable resistance. So far Russian attempts to probe at India had been limited to stirring up trouble in Afghanistan and on the North-West Frontier. Britain already had enough trouble with turbulent tribesmen who were always on the alert for a swift raid on towns on the plains. However, in 1907 Britain had joined the Entente Cordiale with Russia and France. The agreement gave Russia a large, exclusive trading zone in northern Persia on the understanding that there would be no more Russian interference in Afghanistan or Tibet. The south and east (on the Persian Gulf) were to be in the British Zone, and the central zone would be neutral. Persia would still be an independent country.

These non-military arrangements seemed innocuous enough to Britain, France and Russia: to Germany they looked like deliberate and successful attempts to encircle her.

Germany was undoubtedly highly sensitive in this matter, a fact which becomes more understandable when one reflects that it had only been a united country for less than a hundred years. But, having been transformed by Bismarck into a dynamic, industrial state, Germany was now looking for a place in the sun. Unfortunately for this ambition, all the best sunny spots were already occupied by its European neighbours, rather like bathers placing their towels on the best places on the beach with the intention of denying them to any later arrivals.

To Germany there appeared to be two ways out of this deadlock, as they saw it. The first was to strengthen her position in Europe itself, by a close alliance with Austria and later with Italy, then by giving Britain so much cause for concern in her maritime Empire that there might be opportunities to acquire colonies by bargaining.

'Austria' was, of course, the Austro-Hungarian Empire, a ramshackle collection of states in southern Europe, of which Austria and Hungary were the largest. It was the successor to the former Holy Roman Empire (described by Voltaire as neither holy, Roman, nor an empire) and contained a number of small, turbulent peoples, many of whom had been driven there, or left behind as earlier conquerors had ravaged through the area. However, in 1879, Austria looked a very promising partner for Germany, with its huge resources of manpower. Bismarck therefore linked Germany with Austria in the secret Dual Alliance of that year, the basis of the alliance being that each country would assist the other if either was attacked by Russia. On the surface this did not seem a very likely possibility but both were well aware that Russia had ambitions to reach the Mediterranean, which would involve breaking through Austro-Hungarian territory and that, if she were successful, she would create an effective bar to German ambition to expand into the Persian Gulf and the Indian Ocean.

Italy had been united even more recently than Germany but Italy too occupied an immensely important strategic position. With her new-found status as an independent power, with no foreign armies now on her soil, Italy soon joined in the fashionable clamour for colonies. The obvious and easy place for Italy to acquire one was in North Africa and her eyes fell on Tunis. Unfortunately for this intention, France acquired Tunisia in 1881 on the basis that the disturbances there were endangering the next door territory of Algeria, which was already a French colony. This immediately provoked a wave of hostility against the French, although the latter had been very helpful to Italy at the time of Italian unification. Bismarck therefore had no difficulty over drawing Italy into the Dual Alliance, which in consequence became the Triple Alliance in 1882. Italy might regret her hasty decision later, for she was really much more at ease with France than Austria, her new ally. But the Triple Alliance remained in force until 1914, although it did not develop quite as Bismarck had wished.

France, seeing herself isolated by Germany, realised she must make new friends quickly. She mollified Italy by an agreement that neither country would interfere with each other's intentions in North Africa. She also persuaded Italy that her future welfare lay with France, not Austria or Germany, although Italy would have to help defend the latter two if they were attacked, provided the attacker was not France. Subsequently in both the First and the Second World Wars Italy began as the ally of Germany but finished up as an ally of the Allies.

In hindsight it is clear that only a miracle could prevent this clash of interests and tangled diplomacy ending in war. Ironically all this was happening when philosophers were seriously contending that wars could never happen again because civilisation had now reached a point at which such barbaric methods of solving problems were now obsolete.

In spite of her flirtation with Italy, France knew very well that the country whose help she really needed against the growing power of Germany was her traditional enemy, Britain. Although Britain had defeated France in the 22-year-long Napoleonic Wars a century earlier, and the two countries had fought side by side against the Russians in the Crimean War (1854–6), there were several occasions in the late nineteenth century when France and

Britain nearly came to blows. The huge underground forts inland from Portsmouth and many other British coastal defences date from that period. But by the turn of the century the French knew where their best interests lay. The 1904 Dual Entente gave evidence of that.

However, behind these genteel diplomatic moves were some crude driving forces, which may be euphemistically described as national interests. Britain's national interest was to control the sea lanes of the world, the North and South Atlantic, the Indian Ocean, and the Pacific. In order to safeguard British interests in the Far East, where Russia might be thought to have designs, Britain had signed a treaty with Japan in 1902. It was a dangerous move for it was directed against Russian expansion in the Far East, and Britain needed to cultivate Russian friendship (as she did, later, in 1907). Britain also gave Japan help with shipbuilding, a move she would regret later.

France's national interests were to keep Germany under control in Europe, maintain a strong naval presence in the Mediterranean, develop interests in the Middle East and colonise Indochina. The increasing demand for oil would soon bring her into rivalry with Britain in the Middle East.

Russia's national interests have already been mentioned. Although Communist propaganda always described pre-1914 Russia as a backward country which was only transformed into a modern state by the miracle of Marxism, this, like most other Communist claims, is untrue. Before 1914 Russia was one of the leading industrial powers: it was seventy years of Communist domination which reduced it to chaos. It was Russia's industrial strength which made a warm-water port such a necessity. One means of achieving this was to back the Serbs, who might then gain access to the Adriatic. Serbia, which is featuring strongly in the news at the time of writing (1992), is a Slavic state which gives her much common ground with Russia (as with many other countries). In the fourteenth century Serbia had controlled a small empire, but this successively fell, first under the domination of the Turks and then of the Austrians. By 1882, after various wars, it became an independent kingdom again. Austria's annexation of Bosnia and Hercegovina in 1908 both incensed Serbia and fired her ambitions, and she promptly formed a Balkan League with Bulgaria, Montenegro, and Greece. This declared war on Turkey in 1912 and again in 1913, on a flimsy pretext, but with the intention of acquiring territory from the moribund Turkish Empire. After various bitter conflicts Serbia, Greece and Romania gained territory and Bulgaria (who had quarrelled with the League) lost some. This victory encouraged the Serbs in their ambition to wrest further territory from the more powerful Austro-Hungarian Empire, whom she felt, probably rightly, was determined to thwart her plans.

These incessant, bitter, and apparently petty conflicts in the Balkans (as the area was known) were observed by the governments of the Great Powers, who occasionally wondered whether they might be utilised for their own interests: Germany hoped that her ally Austria might gain some advantage if Russia pondered how to encourage her Slav kinsfolk the Serbs, and further her own ambitions in the process. Italy hoped that these squabbles might enable her to gain control of the Adriatic and perhaps wrest some territory from Austria. Although Austria was scarcely in control of her cumbersome empire she had ambitions to expand it, mainly at the expense of Turkey, whose empire was in an even worse state than her own. Austria was already in control of Dalmatia on the Adriatic coast, which contained two useful ports, Spalato and Cattaro: these were coveted by landlocked Serbia. Albania, which was also former Turkish territory, also had two ports but these were not likely to become available to Serbia.

Although these conflicts of interests, and consequent tensions, eventually led to the outbreak of the First World War, it needs to be remembered that there were also a host of other minor rivalries as well as projects which were bound to upset neighbours.

Now that the First World War has been pushed into the background of memory by the Second, one occasionally encounters people who claim that the First could have been avoided, though not the Second. Certainly it seems incredible that thousands of young men could have been killed on the Somme and at Passchendaele because of nationalists squabbling in countries they had probably never heard of, or if they had heard of, would not be able to place on a blank map. Unfortunately, as we have learnt by bitter experience, events in distant countries can have dramatic repercussions on events at home. Czechoslovakia and Poland had no significance for the ordinary inhabitants of Britain until Chamberlain went to Munich to resolve the Czech 'crisis' in 1938, and Germany invaded Poland in 1939. Similarly, few people had heard of Korea in 1950 but the conflict when the North invaded the South subsequently saw the deaths of many British soldiers and at one point looked like developing into the Third World War.

Doubt about another country's intentions has often resulted in war. In 1982, the Argentine government decided that the British withdrawal of the survey ship *Endurance* signified that Britain had lost interest in the Falkland Islands. In consequence Argentine forces invaded, only to find that they were ejected after a brief but bloody war. In 1991 Saddam Hussein of Iraq decided that he could invade his neighbour Kuwait and the Western Powers would shrug their shoulders at the 'fait accompli'.

Similar miscalculations precipitated the First World War. Germany assumed that she could knock out France with a devastating blow long before Russia could assist her Entente partner. She also assumed she could violate neutral territories with impunity. Britain assumed that her sea power would easily overwhelm the German navy, and that the Turks were opponents who could easily be brushed aside in the Dardanelles and Mesopotamia (Iraq). France thought she could hold Germany on her frontiers. War seems to begin with miscalculations and continue with mistakes.

Russia assumed that the steamroller effect of her massive armies would soon overwhelm the Germans. She learnt otherwise, at appalling cost, and three years later the unimaginable occurred, the Tsar and his family were deposed and murdered and a Marxist oligarchy put in their place.

In times of peace it is difficult to forecast the future; in times of war it seems impossible. Although it is sometimes said that war settles nothing and the peace treaties always contain the seeds of the next war, neither statement is entirely true. The First World War prevented Germany conquering and occupying France. In the Second, Nazi Germany occupied France and inflicted the horror of the Gestapo and the holocaust on that nation. She was only ejected by a supreme effort using all the resources of modern technology. It has been said that Germany could have been defeated by a naval blockade alone in the First World War. This is nonsense. By occupying France, Germany could have defied any naval blockade.

War, unfortunately, is the only means by which powerful tyrants can be defeated.

CHAPTER 2

The First Shot

The events which precipitated the outbreak of war in 1914 seem, in retrospect, as bizarre as they were tragic. On 28 June 1914 the Archduke Franz Ferdinand of Austria-Hungary, nephew of the Emperor Franz Josef (who had been Emperor since 1848 but was still alert and healthy), decided to pay a state visit to Sarajevo, the capital of Bosnia. Bosnia was a former Turkish province which, in the peace treaty after the Russo-Turkish war of 1877–8, had been put under Austro-Hungarian administration although still nominally a Turkish province. In 1908 Austria had formerly annexed the province, an act which caused less annoyance to the Turks than to Serbia, which was Bosnia's neighbour.

The Austro-Hungarian Empire was the twentieth century survivor of the medieval Holy Roman Empire and had been created by a mixture of conquests and marriage contracts. During its turbulent history it had acquired a population of minorities, speaking different languages and having little in common. Nevertheless it had been a great power for many centuries. The complexities of the Austro-Hungarian Empire are too numerous to be explained here, but the upshot was that the empire was precariously held together by the prestige of the Emperor, who, it is said, could speak all the languages of the minorities. However, even without the effect of the First World War, nationalism would probably have fragmented the empire soon after the Emperor's death in 1916. As we have subsequently seen, the experiment of creating new states by the post-1918 peace treaties has not produced the harmonious development which had been hoped for. It is said that the assassinated Archduke was a man of liberal ideas who would have done much to satisfy the aspirations of some of the minority groups. This may be so but his behaviour in 1914 prior to his death does not suggest either wisdom or foresight.

The chief thorn in the flesh of the Austrian government was the small but hyperactive state of Serbia, whose turbulent history has already been described. In order to impress the Serbians that Austria was in no mood to stand any nonsense in Bosnia, the Archduke first of all held some military manoeuvres in Bosnia and then decided to pay an official visit, the first since the country had been annexed six years earlier. Rather unwisely he chose 28 June although he must have known that this was a national holiday for Serbs, celebrating the day Serbia had gained her own independence. It was also a Serbian saint's day, their patron saint being St Vitus.

The Archduke's arrival had been greeted by some inaccurately thrown bombs and he was most dissatisfied with the reception. When he was leaving, his chauffeur took a wrong turning and drove into a cul-de-sac. As he reversed the car to drive out, he was spotted by a young student sitting in a café. Although a Bosnian, the student was a member of a Serbian secret society called the Black Hand, which had supplied him with a gun. In a flash he had rushed out of the café, jumped on the running board and shot the Archduke and his morganatic wife who was accompanying him. The young man, whose name was Gavrilo Princip, had hoped to shoot the Archduke earlier in the day but had been unable to get near him. He escaped, survived, and later became a museum curator. The vehicle in which the Archduke was travelling is now in the Heeresgeschichtliches (military) Museum in Vienna, where its very convenient running boards along the side may be inspected, though there are no visible bloodstains.

The assassination of the heir to the Austro-Hungarian Empire was an event which seemed likely to have unpredictable consequences. Although Serbia was not officially involved, there was considerable suspicion as to how far she had encouraged this dramatic killing. The 'Great Powers' (Britain, France, Germany, and Russia) watched the situation with interest and apprehension; it seemed unlikely that Austria would let slip the opportunity to demand some sort of recompense from Serbia, perhaps in the form of territory, probably that which Serbia had recently wrested from the Turks. In the event of the Serbs being defiant, it seemed likely that Austria would declare war and take revenge and compensation by force; it offered an excellent opportunity to cripple the Serbs, one way or another. As a centre of Slav nationalism, Serbia was an inspiration to Slavs in the Austrian empire, and the Great Powers could hardly believe that such a golden opportunity to cripple her would be missed by the Austrians: they were therefore astonished when there was no immediate reaction.

But Austria was cunningly biding her time. She knew that a premature and rash step could easily bring Russia into the struggle, in support of Serbia. If that happened, Austria could be in a very difficult position; she therefore made approaches to Germany to discover whether she would have German support if Russia came into the war. With the possibility that attacking Austria in support of her Serbian protégé might bring Germany into the war, Russia might decide it was in her best interests to leave the Serbs to their fate. Somewhat rashly the Germans gave their assurance.

Austria now had all the cards in her hand. She could draw up demands which would hold down the Serbs for the foreseeable future, and if this was refused she could go to war, backed by her powerful ally Germany, and gain by force what she had failed to gain by diplomacy. During the three weeks in which Austria was perfecting her plans, the other European powers optimistically assumed that the crisis was gently drifting away. Then on 23 July Austria suddenly delivered an ultimatum to the Serbs, which they thought would be unacceptable, with the proviso that, if all ten demands were not conceded within forty-eight hours, Austria would launch a full scale war. As this ultimatum required Serbia to suppress all anti-Austrian societies and propaganda, remove from the Serbian army and Civil Service all those whom Austria specified were anti-Austrian, and to allow Austrian officials to be present in Serbian courts at the trials of those suspected of complicity in the murder of the Archduke, it seemed unlikely that Serbia would concede them. To general surprise, she accepted eight, within the specified forty-eight hours, and suggested that the remaining two should be referred to the Hague Tribunal for arbitration. (Conferences had been held at the Hague in 1899 and 1907 with a view to limiting armaments and had established a Permanent Court of Arbitration.)

This conciliatory reply had no effect on Austria: she decided it was unacceptable and began to mobilise her army. This belligerent attitude surprised even Germany, who suggested restraint. Germany's head of state was Kaiser William II, not noted for his tact or caution, and his hesitation at this point should have restrained Austria. However, it did not. On 28 July Austria declared war on Serbia and began shelling Belgrade, the Serbian capital. The Kaiser continued to advocate restraint, but Austria did not listen. (When, at the end of the war in 1918, Austria disintegrated and her former empire was divided into several independent states in the peace settlement, it was thought by some that she had been harshly treated others thought she had deserved her fate.)

From then on events moved rapidly. Russia, however unwilling, could not stand by and see her Serbian Slav friends crushed: on 31 July she proclaimed general mobilisation. Russia is a huge country and could initially mobilise six million men (in the end it was thirteen million). Germany could only mobilise four and a half million, so she felt that if Russia was going to put into the field larger numbers, the sooner they were confronted the better. She therefore sent Russia an ultimatum on 31 July, demanding that this hostile act of mobilisation must be stopped. Needless to say, the ultimatum was ignored. The same day, Germany enquired what France would do in the event of war between Germany and Russia. France had no choice: she was Russia's ally, so on 1 August she too ordered a general mobilisation. Germany felt that this put the issue beyond doubt and therefore on 3 August declared war on France.

The German fighting machine was already on the move. On 2 August German troops had overrun Luxembourg. The same day, somewhat optimistically, Germany demanded permission of the government of Belgium to send her troops through Belgian territory into France. She promised that Belgium's status as an independent country would in no way be compromised and that she would be paid an indemnity if she cooperated. With considerable courage, Belgium refused and at the same time appealed to Britain for help.

Britain also had little choice in the matter. She was a signatory to a treaty drawn up seventy-five years earlier which guaranteed Belgium's independence and territorial integrity. The treaty was so ancient that the German government assumed that even if it had not lapsed it could scarcely be regarded as a reason for going to war. In fact in a remark usually attributed to the Kaiser, but certainly quoted by von Bethmann Hollweg, German attitudes were expressed in the words: 'Just for a scrap of paper Britain is going to war'. This dismissive statement shows how greatly Germany had misread the situation. The original treaty had come into existence because in 1830 Belgium had broken away from Holland, to which it had been joined by the Treaty of Vienna in 1815. There was much sympathy for her position and in 1839 the Treaty of London (signed by Britain, France, Austria, Prussia and Russia) recognised Belgium's independence and guaranteed it. On 31 July 1914 Sir Edward Grey, the British Foreign Secretary, had asked France and Germany whether they would respect Belgian neutrality. France immediately gave that assurance, Germany refused to do so. In view of what was soon learnt about German war plans, it would have been impossible for her to accept the principle of Belgian neutrality. On 4 August, German troops crossed the frontier into Belgium. Britain issued an ultimatum and as it was ignored, she formally declared war on Germany the same day.

CHAPTER 3

The Schlieffen Plan

For many years Germany had considered that she might have to fight France again and had therefore planned accordingly. She was only too well aware that France was now allied to Russia and therefore war with France on the western front was going to coincide with war on the eastern front. This was a strategic nightmare. However, the Chief of the German General Staff between 1891 and 1907 was a dedicated, totally unscrupulous, military thinker named Count von Schlieffen. He noted that France had fortified the Swiss border, but had omitted to build fortifications opposite Belgium and Luxembourg on the basis that these were neutral countries and would remain so. This latter fact appeared to von Schlieffen to offer a magnificent opportunity to defeat France in a single crushing blow (spread over six weeks), while the Russians were still mobilising their full strength. Then, with France out of the war, Germany could turn to the conscripted, ill-equipped, Russian armies and tear them to bloody shreds.

(In spite of its experience in the First World War, Belgium did not learn that being neutral and defenceless is merely an invitation to an unscrupulous aggressor, and in the Second World War was invaded and occupied again. The only countries which manage to preserve their neutrality are those which are not in the path of the aggressor or whose neutrality gives an opportunity for trading, spying, or other activities. Switzerland preserved its neutral status because its banking facilities as a neutral made it more valuable than it would have been as a vassal state.)

Schlieffen's plan was to deploy five separate armies, in a line of which the left flank pivoted on Metz, moving forward like a swinging door. The two armies on the extreme right would arrive in France on the western side of Paris (as they described their arc) and having done so would come up behind the French armies which would have rushed east to protect their frontier against the two German armies advancing from Lorraine. Some troops from the army on the extreme right of the German First Army would meanwhile occupy the Channel ports in Belgium.

Schlieffen had emphasised that the essence of the plan was to keep the right wing strong and, in fact, is believed to have repeated this with his dying breath in 1912, two years before his infamous plan was launched. However, the plan was so bold that many German Staff officers became distinctly nervous that instead of producing overwhelming victory it might produce chaotic disaster. The Commander in Chief by this time was von Moltke (the younger) and he, aware that the Russians might mobilise more quickly than expected, *weakened* the right wing by detaching two army corps from it and sending them to bolster the defence against the Russians on the eastern front.

However, initially the plan went well. The Allies had assumed that the great Belgian forts at Liège and Namur would hold up the Germans and enable Britain and France to meet them on Belgian soil. But the weight of the German artillery, notably their siege howitzers (guns which launch shells upwards at about 45°) was too much for the defences. Liège was the first to fall, Namur soon followed. The German juggernaut looked unstoppable.

Even before the outbreak of war the British Grand Fleet had been ordered to its war stations: in the event, it would take a surprisingly small part in this war. The heaviest part of the conflict would be in France, although there would also be severe fighting in Poland, Italy, Mesopotamia (Iraq), and Palestine. There would also be minor campaigns in Africa and the Far East.

It was, however, the desperate four-year struggle in France which gave the First World War its horrific character. Even today, the battlefields and cemeteries of northern France and Belgium convey a sense of chilling horror with their rows and rows of graves, some with pathetic headstones with the name of an only son, perhaps aged 19, some with no name at all, just the inscription 'A Soldier. Known unto God.' This long, grinding, war of attrition was not what Schlieffen had in mind at all. His plan, if it had worked as he intended it to, would literally have had the war over by the first Christmas.

But it was not merely the massive death toll which made the war so appalling: it was the ghastly discomfort of trench warfare. For four years men lived and died in stinking, often sodden, trenches, incessantly harassed by gunfire, snipers and gas, and infested with rats, lice, bugs and fleas. The only reason why more men did not die of disease was that they were killed by bullets, shells, or gas before disease could get a hold. Nothing in previous wars had prepared armies for horrors on this scale. There had, of course, been extremely unpleasant medieval sieges of towns and castles, and there had been some trench warfare in the Crimean War in 1855, but these had been limited in time and intensity. In the First World War there seemed to be no limit to what human beings on both sides were expected to endure.

As the months crawled on, all the belligerents began to feel that this situation was now the norm, and there was no end in sight in the foreseeable future. The armies were said to be 'locked together'. Just as nothing like it had preceded trench warfare in the First World War, so there has been nothing to match it since, even if we take into account the siege of Leningrad, the battle of Stalingrad, and the periods of trench warfare in the Korean War in 1951. None of those lasted as long, nor involved so many men.

Ironically, Schlieffen's thrustful plan had envisaged a war of rapid movement and decisive engagements. However, once it was checked, static warfare followed. Much the same occurred on the other fronts, although periodically the war looked like becoming one of rapid movement once more.

The inherent weakness of Schlieffen's concept was the underestimation of supply problems or, as they are now called, logistics. Huge armies on the march need enormous supplies of food, forage, and ammunition. 'Forage', for earlier armies, meant food for horses; today it represents the less bulky, but none the less vital, supply of petrol. (In the Second World War, the North-West Europe campaign of 1944–5 was slowed almost to the point of disaster by shortage of petrol – even with modern back-up resources.) The two German armies on the right wing of the German sweep in 1914 soon advanced faster and farther than their food supplies could follow. As these two armies alone numbered 600,000 men, it is obvious that even if they had plundered Belgium unmercifully they would still have faced dire shortages. (The total German forces launched into France numbered 1,500,000 men.) German regimental records reported that the troops had no bread for four days, and a day's food consisted of a piece of stale bread, a cup of soup, and a cup of coffee. From the fields and orchards through which they marched the Germans looted turnips and fruit, which they ate raw and often unripe. If they acquired potatoes, they had no facilities with them for cooking.

All this happened in spite of careful German planning. In the previous decade, Germany had increased the number of railway lines between central Germany and the western frontier. Liddell Hart quotes 550 trains crossing the Rhine bridges on 6 August, and on every one of the first fourteen days of the war a train crossed the Hohenzollern bridge at Cologne, *every ten minutes*.

But, of course, the moment the first shot is fired there descends over the entire front what has aptly been described as 'the fog of war'. Anything which can go wrong, probably does so. And warfare on this scale had never before been waged. In consequence, none of the senior officers had had experience of commanding such huge numbers in the field. Added to that was the fact that bold sweeping movements over hundreds of miles were alarmingly unorthodox to the conventionally trained German officers.

Although the sieges at Namur and Liège had gone extremely well for the Germans (to the dismay of the Allies), they had sent a shudder through the entire right wing of the German armies. Ammunition had been used up and needed to be replaced. Schedules had been disrupted. (The Germans had hoped that the Belgians would not offer resistance, but would remain neutral while allowing the passage of German troops through their territory.) But there was worse to come. The Belgians had managed to mobilise six infantry divisions and a cavalry division (a total of 117,000). They withdrew their field army to Antwerp. In that position it constituted a dangerous threat to the German flank. France had hastily mobilised 4,000,000 men and if the German knockout blow was not successful the French would not be easily defeated.

Britain's initial contribution was even smaller than Belgium's, totalling under 90,000 men in four infantry and one cavalry division. A division varied in size, but at this period usually signified 18,000 men, of whom about one-third would be support troops not actually involved in front-line fighting, although exposed to danger. Two or more divisions made a corps: two or more corps an army. These numbers dwindled later through attrition.

In addition, Britain retained two regular divisions in Britain for home defence against a possible German landing: there was also a territorial force of some seventeen divisions of which three were cavalry, but this had been raised on the understanding that it would not be employed overseas. The British Commander in Chief was Sir John French, and the British Expeditionary Force, as the Army in France was known, was grouped in two corps, one of which was commanded by Sir Douglas Haig and the other by Sir Horace Smith-Dorrien. The Commander of the French armies was General 'Papa' Joffre.

Joffre had been misled by his own Intelligence Staff into thinking that the best way to withstand a huge German invasion was to attack it. An advancing national army, which is made up of smaller component armies (some 300,000 strong) is particularly vulnerable where any two component armies are advancing side by side. A brisk attack, at the join, so to speak, should take both armies by surprise and cause considerable dislocation and loss of momentum, and at best, check the entire forward movement. However, in the event, the sheer size of the German invasion force made it very difficult to find a weak joint.

Nevertheless Joffre ordered the British force, which had landed and concentrated by 13 August, to move forward into Belgium. Meanwhile the French had made an attack on the German armies in the Lorraine area but had been checked and counter-attacked. From the point of view of the grand strategy of the Schlieffen Plan, the Germans should have fallen back on the Lorraine area in the face of the attack, thus drawing the French on into a trap which would close behind them. But the normally well-disciplined German army commanders were not obeying orders as they should have done.

The BEF advanced on the left to the Sambre and the Mons-Condé Canal. (Subsequently it was decided that they had gone too far.) On their right, the Fifth French Army also advanced towards the Sambre, but soon found that the weight of the German armies was too much for it: in consequence it fell back slightly and then stopped at Charleroi.

At the same time the BEF held the Germans at Mons (on 23/24 August). Both French and British armies fought well, particularly the British who were heavily outnumbered, and the delay they caused to the German army helped to disrupt the smooth working of the Schlieffen Plan even further. Quite rightly, Mons was recognised as an important victory by the British, although at first it was a lost battle, for it imposed a crucial delay on the Germans. A curious legend grew up about Mons, that angels had been seen fighting side by side with the British troops. The origin of this mysterious venture into human credulity has never been satisfactorily explained, but it was not the only fanciful story to raise morale at that time. The other was that the Russians had sent troops to France. They were reported to have landed at Glasgow and travelled in conditions of absolute secrecy through London during the hours of darkness. However, they had been observed by a porter (or porters) at King's Cross, who had seen the snow still on their boots and heard them talking in Russian. To anyone unfamiliar with the Scottish brogue this would, no doubt, be an easy conclusion to draw. The 'snow' was no doubt the white spats of a Scottish regiment hastening to join the BEF. It was rumoured that the story of the Russians, which was eagerly passed round, reached the ears of the Germans through Press reports and is said, without more evidence than hearsay, to have further undermined German confidence in the ability of the Schlieffen Plan to produce a quick victory. Wild rumours circulate spontaneously in wartime and are sometimes officially inspired, if thought good for morale or misleading to the enemy.

After delaying the Germans at Mons, the British Army went on a long fighting retreat. It acquired the nickname 'The Old Contemptibles', and held the title in great esteem. Again the Kaiser was credited with a remark he may or may not have made. It is alleged that on hearing that the British were sending an expeditionary force to France, he said, 'But they only have a contemptible little army,' (referring to its size, not its quality). Be that as it may, the army, though small, was well trained and highly efficient. Its great quality was steadiness under fire combined with excellent marksmanship. It was claimed that men fired fifteen rounds a minute from their Lee-Enfield .303in rifles and, as their fire never slackened, this gave the impression that it was coming from machine-guns. (Ten rounds a minute would be an excellent rate of fire: fifteen seems virtually impossible, as the Lee-Enfield magazines held only ten rounds.) The BEF were all regular soldiers, and no doubt some of them had seen action on the North-West Frontier of India or in the Boer War in Africa. Their performance inspired A.E. Housman to write his poem 'Epitaph on an Army of Mercenaries':

These in days when heaven was falling
The hour when earth's foundations fled
Followed their mercenary calling
And took their wages and are dead.
Their shoulders held the sky suspended
They stood, and earth's foundations stay
Which God abandoned, these defended
And saved the sum of things 'for pay'.

Housman, who was a lifelong Cambridge classical don, and not a soldier, was nevertheless obsessed with the pathos and heroism of soldiers dying for a cause they scarcely understood. However, the British Army was not truly a mercenary army. Mercenaries were (and are) soldiers who fight for whatever country employs them: they are not motivated by patriotism, although they will lay down their own lives without hesitation. The word 'soldier', incidentally, is derived from the old French word 'soude', meaning pay: in the Middle Ages before nationalism had established itself, soldiers hired themselves to the highest bidder, if they were not required for feudal service.

A fighting retreat is a difficult manoeuvre, but can be very effective in blunting the thrust of an attacking army and perhaps diverting it from its objectives: at best it will enable the losing side to bring up reinforcements and alter the tactical situation. Some of the regiments in I Corps marched 59 miles in 64 hours. Although at the end they were too tired to march further, they could, nevertheless, lie down and fire their rifles. Their main problem was to take with them their artillery, and not leave it behind for the enemy. One of the skills of this retreat was to appear to take up a position and then abandon it for a different one at the side or the rear. The advancing army then stormed into the abandoned position, only to be shelled in it by their own gunners, who were under the impression the British were still there.

On several occasions, notably at Landrecies, the Germans were on the point of encircling and cutting off sections of the retreating troops but were frustrated by a single company or regiment, making a desperate, self-sacrificing, stand.

In addition to the gruelling conditions of the long retreat in hot, exhausting, weather there were worries by both the French and British that the other was not performing to the agreed plan. Thus the French had been first to retreat but then the British overtook them. There were also arguments within the respective forces. Smith-Dorrien defied Sir John French by making a stand at Le Cateau (it was doubtful if he had any alternative as his troops were totally exhausted); and the French General Lanrezac made a counter-attack at Guise which the British thought was pointless in the circumstances, but in the event both these disrupted the German plan.

The Commander of the German First Army, General von Kluck, on the extreme right, had never been entirely convinced of the viability of a plan which required his troops to march on the outside of an enormous arc, while the troops on the inside were also moving forward, though more slowly. He became even more apprehensive when he realised that a gap was beginning to develop between his army and Second Army, under the command of General Prince von Bülow on his immediate left. Against orders, Kluck decided to close up. Furthermore, the British stand at Le Cateau and the French counter-attack at Guise gave both Kluck and Bülow the idea that there was now an opportunity to encircle both the BEF and the French army and destroy them. This seemed far better than for the two German armies to forge ahead, move to the right of Paris, and then come up behind the French army at a later stage. It was, however, fatal to German success as it failed to make the projected encirclement, but at the same time totally ruined the Schlieffen Plan.

Although the British and French armies continued to retreat, resistance was stiffening and Joffre, no mean tactician, was switching his best troops to the point where they looked like being needed. On the German side communications were poor, not only between the armies but also between the army commanders and their Commander in Chief, von Moltke. Von

Moltke, a mere shadow of his famous uncle, was capable of making mistakes on his own without being alarmed by inaccurate reports. He had already unwisely sent seven divisions of his best troops to guard against a sudden flank attack by Belgian troops from Antwerp, and had despatched another four to the eastern front to meet the Russian forces which were reported to be advancing towards Germany. He had also been told, and believed, that Russians were now reinforcing the troops in France (although he can hardly have believed they had snow on their boots) and he also feared that a British invasion force was about to attack Germany through Belgium while all the cream of the German armies were in France or Russia. In fact Churchill had sent a small force to Ostend and Zeebrugge to assist the Belgians in the inevitable siege of Antwerp, although it was unable to prevent its fall. Nowadays we hear that every breakdown or failure in business, education, or human relationship is due to a failure in communication, but there has rarely been such a disastrous failure in communication as occurred among the invading German armies of 1914. Although wireless, cars, motor bicycles and horsemen were available, and the Germans had a well-developed telegraph service, they failed to make proper use of any of these. It was subsequently learnt that when the German cavalry had come upon French telegraph services they had torn out the lines and smashed instruments, instead of leaving them to be used by their own forces.

However, in spite of all their blunders and setbacks the Germans were now getting unpleasantly close to Paris. Eventually some troops reached Meaux, which is a mere fourteen miles from the city. Fortunately, the hour brought forth the man. The saviour of Paris was its Military Governor, General Galliéni. An individual of unorthodox tactical genius, he sensed that as von Kluck's army moved south-east to close up with the other German armies advancing on Paris, its flank was dangerously exposed. A new French army – the Sixth – had just been raised to strengthen the defence of Paris, and Galliéni suggested to Joffre that it should join forces with the British and make a devastating attack on von Kluck's right flank; Joffre realised that desperate diseases require desperate remedies and agreed to try to persuade Sir John French to let the British take part. This was not easy for the British had just taken up positions after a 200-mile retreat, marching an average of fifteen miles a day without resting in between, and intermittently fighting off their pursuers.

The critical battle of the Marne then took place on 5 September. The Sixth Army tore into von Kluck's flank and the German general pulled back the van of his forces to meet it. Inevitably this opened up a gap between himself and von Bülow, which was soon 30 miles wide. Into the gap went the British army, though not as quickly as they should have done. However, their appearance sent a wave of dismay through the Germans, who realised only too well they were being attacked at the end of a long, vulnerable, line of communication. When the British force crossed the Marne, von Moltke ordered the German army to pull back and straighten its line. It was the conventional way to fight but it signified the final destruction of the brilliant, ruthless, attack which von Schlieffen had planned so long ago. It was not, of course, as easy as this description sounds and many men were killed as the Germans withdrew.

One of the more dramatic stories of the battle of the Marne concerns the taxi-drivers of Paris. On 7 September, when the battle still hung in the balance, a fresh division arrived in Paris, but at that stage in the fighting they were 40 miles from the critical area of the front. Galliéni therefore ordered the police to commandeer every taxi in Paris, fill them with soldiers and rush them to the front. Six hundred cabs were involved and each made several journeys. The villages through which they passed never forgot the spectacle.

From now on both armies raced to find a means of turning the other's flank. Too late the Germans tried to capture the Channel ports, such as Calais, which they could have taken easily a few weeks earlier. During 6–9 September the British pressed hard on von Kluck's retreating army. The soldiers of both sides were so exhausted by this time that only sheer will-power kept them going. It was probably worst for the Germans, for not only had they experienced days of insufficient food on long marches but they had the bitter realism that they were now being forced away from the objective which would have brought them decisive victory.

As the Germans fell back looking for a suitable place to stabilise their line and perhaps make a counter-attack round the British and French flanks, there began what came later to be known as 'The Race to the Sea'. In the early stage of their retreat the Germans had grouped a large force on the north-east of the Aisne, hoping to launch a further attack when this was reinforced. Here they were opposed by a French and British force. However, as there was an urgent and vital need to prevent the Germans seizing the Channel ports (which, as we saw, they could have done easily earlier in the campaign), the BEF moved in a wide sweep back to Abbeville, up to St Omer, and forward to Ypres. St Omer blocked the road to Boulogne, and Ypres equally blocked any attempt to reach Calais. Subsequently St Omer became the headquarters of the British Expeditionary Force, and Ypres the site of the most gruesome bloodbaths of the war. The line from Ypres to Nieuport on the coast was held by the Belgians and the rest of the line to Switzerland by a mixture of Allied troops. Many of the names along that line: Bethune, Lens, Arras, Bapaume, Verdun, St Quentin, would become infamous for nightmare scenes of suffering and death.

In extending their lines both sides had tried to include the best tactical features; in many cases these fell to the units which spotted their potential and reached them first. In general the line ran fairly straight but before reaching Ypres it turned sharply east and made a bow-shaped bulge out to Zonnebeke, before it turned back to Ploegsteert. From a tactical point of view this bow-shaped bulge was a mistake, for although it left Ypres in Allied hands, the fact that the Germans held the Passchendaele (now spelt Passendale) Ridge and most of the other features near it, meant they could shell Ypres at will but were themselves protected by the low, swampy ground in between. The line was not fully stabilised until 20 October, and by then both sides were digging in to prepare for what all agreed was going to be a long period of dour fighting. It soon became clear that 'digging in' was easier said than done, for in some sections the surface was rock-like chalk, in others marshy land where digging a trench did not make a defensive position but merely created a ditch full of water. However, when an enemy is firing at you, you stand in a trench whether it is a ditch filled with water or not. The most sodden area, as we shall see later, was the few miles between Ypres and the Passchendaele Ridge. Britain had entered the war to protect Belgian neutrality and, although it had failed to prevent the rest of the country being occupied, as long as Ypres remained in British hands it was a symbol of the eventual liberation of the country. Understandable, but the cost in lives was to be horrendous.

None of these positions was taken initially without fighting, in greater or lesser degree. However, the level of fighting at this stage was nothing to what would follow. There was, however, still an optimistic belief on both sides that a quick victory might be possible if the right steps were taken. A new general might find an unexpected weakness in the enemy lines or tactics. Von Moltke had been dismissed after the spectacular failure of the Schlieffen Plan, even though he had little faith in it himself. He was replaced by General Erich von Falkenhayn. On the French side another figure was coming to the fore, General Ferdinand Foch. General Douglas Haig, commanding 1st British Corps, had shown himself to be very steady in the long retreat. Sir John French, the Commander in Chief of the British Expeditionary Force, had never quite looked the part, but stayed in it for the time being. His flimsy reputation rested on a spirited cavalry charge in the Boer

War some fourteen years earlier. His private life was a tangle of debt and affairs with other men's wives. Like the other generals, he had never commanded such huge quantities of men before.

Meanwhile, even as the Schlieffen Plan was still faltering along in the west, a substantial threat to Germany was developing in the east. The Russians had mobilised more quickly than expected and two huge armies were advancing on Germany, the one in the south commanded by Samsonov, and the one in the north by Rennenkampf. These two were bitter enemies and had once had a fight in public on Moukden railway station. Communication between them was likely to be limited, a fact of which the Germans were aware. Communication at other levels within and between the Russian armies was equally poor owing to jealousies and incompetence, and what communication there was came over the wireless in clear, to the delight of the Germans. However, the first clash, at Gumbinnen on 20 August, produced a Russian victory and von Prittwitz, the German commander, contemplated falling back to the Vistula. When this disturbing news reached von Moltke, it alarmed him so much that he considered abandoning the Schlieffen Plan in order to transfer more troops to the Eastern front. However, before doing so he dismissed von Prittwitz and in his place appointed the 68-year-old General Paul von Hindenburg. As his Chief of Staff Hindenburg had Ludendorff, who had distinguished himself in the fighting in Belgium.

Fortunately for both their reputations, a young officer on von Prittwitz's staff, Max Hoffman by name, had already assessed the military situation and suggested to Ludendorff that as the Russian armies were apparently working independently it should be possible to tackle each in turn (although the Germans were numerically inferior to each), since they were too far apart to help each other, even if the wish were there.

On 29 August, the Germans fell upon Samsonov's army and destroyed it, capturing many excellent guns and taking 92,000 prisoners. This was the battle of Tannenberg which, though not actually fought at that place, was given the title to commemorate (and avenge) a defeat of the Teutonic Knights in 1410 by an army of Poles and Lithuanians. Samsonov tried to rally his troops but in doing so became lost in a forest and shot himself. Actually, although Tannenberg was a severe defeat for the Russians it was by no means conclusive and within days the Germans were encountering resistance from the remains of Samsonov's army.

It remained to deal with Rennenkampf. He proved a more wily opponent although in a series of battles among the Masurian lakes the Russians

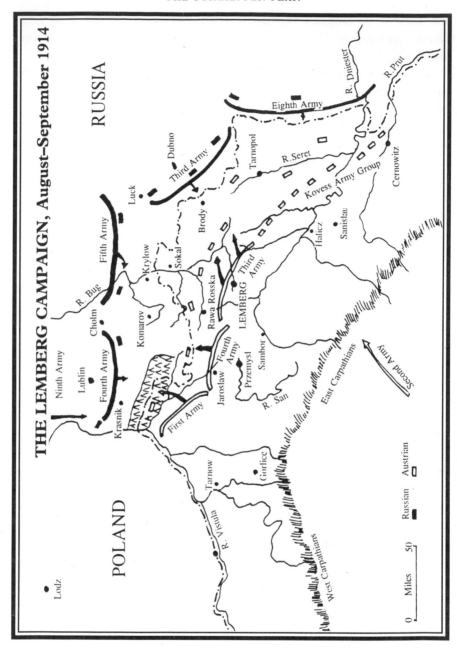

THE LEMBERG CAMPAIGN, August–September 1914

RUSSIA

POLAND

Lodz

Lublin

Ninth Army

Fourth Army

Krasnik

Cholm

R. Bug

Fifth Army

Komarov

Krylow

Sokal

Luck

Dubno

Third Army

Brody

Rawa Rosska

LEMBERG

Third Army

Eighth Army

Tarnopol

R. Seret

Kovess Army Group

Halicz

Stanislau

Cernowitz

R. Prut

R. Dniester

Fourth Army

Jaroslaw

Przemysl

Sambor

R. San

First Army

Tarnow

Gorlice

R. Vistula

West Carpathians

East Carpathians

Second Army

Miles

0   50

Russian

Austrian

34

lost many more men than the Germans. However, at the end of it all the Germans could consider the threat from the east had been blunted for the time being.

Tannenberg did much for Ludendorff's reputation, perhaps over-inflated it. Hoffman subsequently rose in rank to command the German forces on the Eastern Front.

The Russians were more successful in their attack on Austria. Their army invaded Galicia, reached Lemberg (the capital) and pressed on to control the remainder of the country. Austria, to her dismay, found herself fighting a war on two fronts, like her ally Germany. Having begun the war by attacking Serbia, she now found herself bound to continue on that front. Although not happy at allotting a large portion of her forces to fight Serbia, when every man might be needed to check the Russian invasion in Galicia, it was decided that the Serbs were too inexperienced and incompetent to offer much resistance and the troops would soon become available again for the Russian front. Austria had begun the Serbian campaign in mid-August. It was an unhappy venture. The Serbs, by no means as unsophisticated as the Austrians assumed, offered little resistance until the Austrian lines of communication were well extended, and then fell upon them. Much battered, the Austrians then withdrew to the frontier, intending to return when the greater danger from Russia had passed. There for the moment the matter rested. Unwise journalists in the West were delighted that little Serbia had successfully ejected the Austrian colossus, and assumed that this front would now remain static. The Serbs shared this view. But a rude awakening was coming.

So far, events in the European theatre seemed to have produced a drawn match. Thousands of lives had been lost, whole countries had been ravaged by invading armies (the Germans had been particularly brutal in France and Belgium, with the mistaken idea that terror tactics would cow the civilian population), and on all fronts there were reports of shortage of food, ammunition and equipment, but the end of the war, which at the beginning had seemed only several weeks away, had now receded into an uncertain future.

Meanwhile, both Britain and Germany looked forward to hearing reports of encouraging victories at sea. Many Germans, proud of the growing power of their navy, were eagerly looking forward to news of the first successful engagement. The British Admiralty was watchful to make sure they did not. Unfortunately for British naval pride, two German heavy cruisers (the *Goeben* and *Breslau*), which had been in the Mediterranean at the outbreak of war, slipped out through the Dardanelles and arrived at Constantinople on 10 August. As Turkey was still officially neutral, they should have been interned but the Turks, who had signed a secret alliance with Germany on 2 August, instead declared that they had been bought by them. As they continued to be manned by their German crews, the story can have deceived no one but its manufacturers. Two and a half months later (29–30 October), the Turkish fleet, led by the *Goeben*, bombarded Odessa, Sebastopol, and other Black Sea ports.

This was more than Russia was prepared to tolerate and she responded by declaring war on Turkey two days later (1 November) and France followed suit on 5 November. From the Allied point of view the sequence of events which had eventually propelled the Turks into the German camp was a diplomatic disaster. In the next four years Turkey would prove a stubborn opponent who would be responsible for some spectacular Allied reverses. From the German point of view, the shift of part of the war to the Middle East, where Britain had vital strategic interests, was an enormous advantage, for it tied down large numbers of British and Indian troops who would have been used to great effect on other fronts. Britain captured Basra on the Persian Gulf on 21 November, partly as a base for further operations and partly to protect British oil interests in Persia.

But the escape of the German cruisers in the Mediterranean was not the only event to make the British Admiralty thoughtful in 1914. Britain's navy exceeded that of Germany in every type of ship:

19	battleships	to	13
8	battlecruisers	to	5
63	cruisers	to	7
35	light cruisers	to	33
180	destroyers	to	163
44	submarines	to	38

In addition, France had capital ships as well as 80 destroyers and 75 submarines. Russia and Japan also had moderately strong navies. In the circumstances it was felt that Germany offered little threat, even though the British Empire had long, vulnerable sea lanes. In the event, although German submarines were never able to impede the traffic using the Dover Straits they caused havoc along the Atlantic sea routes.

In a straightforward, surface engagement the British experience seemed likely to be decisive. Thus, on 28 August Admiral Sir David Beatty took a fleet into German coastal waters (the Bight of Heligoland) and sank three German light cruisers, damaged others and took 1,000 prisoners. His own casualties were 35 killed. However, Germany retaliated three weeks later when three ancient British cruisers were torpedoed and sunk by a U boat (Unterseeboot = submarine) within an hour in coastal waters. It was a superb achievement by the German submarine, and the fact that the cruisers were old and slow and had stopped to pick up survivors did little to diminish the propaganda effect of it. A fortnight later a U boat sank the British cruiser *Hawke*, as it lay in a sheltered spot off the west coast of Scotland. A fortnight later, Britain lost a new battleship *Audacious* to a German mine. Meanwhile, a German cruiser, the *Emden*, was roaming around in the Indian Ocean, sinking Allied merchant shipping. She evaded attempts to capture her until she was sunk on 9 November by an Australian cruiser. In the Pacific the Germans had an East Asiatic squadron of fast cruisers under Admiral von Spee, which did considerable damage for four months. Off Coronel, Chile, on 1 November, the main portion of von Spee's fleet encountered a small British force commanded by Admiral Sir Christopher Cradock. Although the latter had two heavy cruisers (both of which were sunk), his command was no match for the Germans, who did not lose a single ship. However, the situation was reversed at the Falkland Islands on 8 December, when von Spee met a stronger British squadron commanded by Admiral Sturdee. The Germans quickly lost their four largest ships and the British had only 25 casualties.

This crushing defeat convinced the Germans that they must concentrate on U boats and mines and could not challenge British surface fleets, except perhaps in home waters. On pre-1914 maps in Britain, the North Sea was named the 'German Ocean'. They embarked on one morale-raising exercise of defying British sea power before the end of 1914. On 15 December, fifteen heavy cruisers set out across the North Sea under the command of Admiral Hipper. Undetected in the sea mist, they sailed down the north-east coast of Britain, successively bombarding Hartlepool, Whitby and Scarborough, killing 120 civilians and causing much damage. In spite of desperate attempts to engage them on their way back to port, the German raiders made good their escape. This encouraged Hipper to make another sortie on 15 January 1915, but this time he was less fortunate: the Royal Navy was better prepared and luckier with the weather. The ensuing Battle of the Dogger Bank is described in detail later.

Naval engagements were, however, only part of the war at sea. Britain planned to bring Germany to her knees by a naval blockade. Germany, for her part, decided to concentrate on trying to interfere with traffic of men, munitions and supplies travelling across the Straits of Dover, as well as supply ships from distant ports. Neutrals, such as America, bitterly resented the interference they were subjected to from both sides when searched for 'contraband'; that is, war materials. At this stage attacks on merchant shipping were conducted under the laws regulating warfare at sea: unrestricted submarine warfare would appear later.

Capturing German colonies, with one exception, proved quite easy. Togoland, on the west coast of Africa, was conquered by a joint Anglo-French operation in three weeks in August 1914; the Cameroons, which were invaded at three points as well as being attacked from the sea by another Anglo-French force, put up a stiffer fight, although the bulk of the German territory was captured in September. The last fragment of resistance, deep in the interior, held out till February 1916. September 1914 saw the opening of an attack on German South West Africa (now Namibia). This never looked like being easy in spite of the Allied advantage in numbers, and in the event the campaign lasted until July 1915. A major cause of the delay was a rebellion within the South African forces, led by certain South African officers who had fought against Britain in the Boer War fourteen years earlier and now saw this as an opportunity to take revenge for their defeat: however, it was suppressed by February 1915.

Tsingtao, a port in Shantung on Kiachow Bay, was captured by a joint Japanese and British force in September 1914, and then occupied until 1922 by Japan, who had thrown in her lot with the Allies on 15 August. The Japanese also occupied the Marianas, Carolines, and Marshalls, all isolated island groups in the Pacific. All would become the scene of fierce battles during the Second World War.

Western Samoa was surrendered to a New Zealand force supported by Allied warships in late August 1914. In September the Australians invaded New Britain, and went on to capture German New Guinea. The Germans had enlisted some local warriors and one of the naval party which Britain sent had the unusual experience of being wounded by a spear. Nauru followed on 6 November and the German part of the Solomon Islands in December. These remote territories became League of Nations Trust Territories in the post-war peace treaties.

All these comparatively bloodless successes were very comforting to the Allies, and helped build up morale in Britain. However, the situation in East Africa, which had looked equally easy in 1914, proved not to be so. Here the German commander was Paul von Lettow-Vorbeck, who proved to be one of the best generals Germany had produced. Assuming that the territory of German East Africa would surrender easily, a force had been sent from

India to land: it was repelled without difficulty. From then on the well-led German and African Askari force of some 24,000 occupied 150,000 British and Belgians sent against them, and was even taking the offensive into neighbouring countries in 1918. Fighting went on in this area until after the Armistice of 11 November in Europe: von Lettow-Vorbeck finally capitulated, unbeaten, on 25 November 1918. There was much criticism in Britain of this unimportant campaign which occupied many soldiers.

Although thousands of men had been killed on the various fronts in the four months of war in 1914, there was optimism on all sides that the conflict would end during the following year. Christmas Day 1914 saw a remarkable, never-to-be-repeated incident. Early that morning, British and German troops suddenly decided to crawl out of their trenches and exchange Christmas greetings, in the middle of No Man's Land. It was said that there were some attempts at a game of football. A few mementoes were exchanged, and some photographs were taken. By the end of the day both sides were slightly bored, and went back to their own trenches to celebrate Christmas in their own particular way as far as it was possible. The next day was back to normal: death and destruction.

When the Higher Commands of both sides heard of this fraternisation, they were infuriated and issued strict instructions that it should never happen again. Sadly, by the second winter of the war it would scarcely have been possible, so embittered had the soldiers become.

In spite of the mental adjustment to the fact that the war had not ended by Christmas, as had been hoped for and expected, enthusiasm for it by those who had not taken part in the fighting did not slacken. Volunteers continued to overwhelm the recruiting offices. The problem was not shortage of men, but of everything else: camps, weapons and instructors. Many of the people employed as instructors had learnt whatever they knew in the Boer War, in India, or from out-of-date manuals. Often training consisted of marching into the country, digging trenches, filling them in again, and marching back. Totally unsuitable people were commissioned and put in charge of young enthusiasts. The latter tolerated the discomforts and frustrations of their early days in the Army because they believed that once they were overseas military life would be well ordered and practical. If they were posted to regular battalions this became true until they were involved in the chaotic conditions of early trench warfare. Britain was different from the other combatants in having an all volunteer army: in other countries the armies which fought in 1914 were mainly a mixture of regulars and reservists. In all armies, before the grim realities of death and maiming were seen, there was a general sense of elation that this was a man's job, that it would impress one's wife or girl friend, that it would offer comradeship, possible glory, public esteem, the chance of easy sex, and, not least, a relief from the tedium of everyday existence. Most manual and clerical jobs were inherently boring.

Among the volunteers were the more thoughtful who had realised that there was a possibility that Germany might become powerful enough to conquer Britain, if not checked very soon. Warnings of this had come from three most unlikely sources in the decade preceding the war. Erskine Childers, an Irishman, had written *The Riddle of the Sands* , describing how easily England could be invaded and conquered in a surprise attack. H.H. Munro, who wrote under the pen name of 'Saki', was a brilliantly funny writer of short stories, but he struck a soberer note in *When William Came: the Story of London under the Hohenzollerns*, a warning against complacency. Munro was killed in the trenches in 1916. P.G. Wodehouse, not usually noted for Cassandra-like prophecies, had published *The Swoop, or How Clarence Saved England* in 1909 . This also concerns an invasion of England which was frustrated. Other, less literary and articulate people had been pondering the same possibilities and there was some relief in 1914 that we had not left it too late: the German menace had been unmasked by the invasion of Belgium and it was now time to settle the score.

Most of the young thought war was an exciting adventure, a form of crusade. Before they enlisted, many wrote poems which were published in local newspapers. Up till 1939 local newspapers often published poems of varying degrees of merit. Very few survived. The early poems which have survived are in shattering contrast to the later ones by Sassoon, Owen, Rosenberg and others who had experienced the horrors of trench warfare. Ironically, one of the most quoted of the earlier poems was by Laurence Binyon, an art historian, aged forty-five and over military age. It was, of course, romantic nonsense.

> *They went with songs to the battle, they were young*
> *Straight of limb, true of eye, steady and aglow*
> *They were staunch to the end against odds uncounted*
> *They fell with their faces to the foe.*

> *They shall grow not old, as we that are left grow old*
> *Age shall not weary them, nor the years condemn*
> *At the going down of the sun and in the morning*
> *We shall remember them.*

This sort of poem was answered by Siegfried Sassoon later:

You smug-faced crowds with kindling eye
Who watch the soldier lads go by
Slink home and pray you'll never know
The hell where youth and laughter go.

Julian Grenfell, who was later killed in the trenches, wrote:

The fighting man shall from the sun
Take warmth, and life from the glowing earth

And with the trees to newer birth
And find, when fighting shall be done
Great rest and fullness after dearth.

Rupert Brooke's poem 'the Soldier' conveys the attitude to war which many of his contemporaries felt in the early days:

If I should die, think only this of me:
That there's some corner of a foreign field
That is for ever England. There shall be
In that rich earth a richer dust concealed;
A dust whom England bore, shaped, made aware,
Gave, once, her flowers to love, her ways to roam,
A body of England's, breathing English air,
Washed by the rivers, blest by suns of home.

The same feelings are expressed in his poem 'The Dead':

Blow out, you bugles, over the rich Dead
There's none of them so lonely and poor of old,
But dying, has made a rarer gift than gold.

and again in 'Peace':

Now, God be thanked Who has matched us with His hour
And caught our youth, and wakened us from sleeping
With hand made sure, clear eye and sharpened power,

To turn, as swimmers into cleanness leaping,
Glad from a world grown old and cold and weary,
Leave the sick hearts that honour could not move,
And half-men, and their dirty songs and dreary,
And all the little emptiness of love!

And so on. Brooke had little to complain of in his pre-war life. Educated at Rugby and King's College, Cambridge, good-looking, athletic, with hosts of friends and plenty of money, he had travelled widely. On the outbreak of war he had considered joining up as a private but decided to wait for an opportunity of a commission. It came in September 1914, when Winston Churchill offered him one in the Royal Naval Division, which had been raised for amphibious operations. By this time Brooke's sonnets, which caught the mood of the moment, had made him famous. In October his unit sailed for Antwerp, where they took over some trenches from a Belgian regiment, outside the range of shellfire though they could hear it. Almost immediately they were told to withdraw and he saw the unromantic sight of thousands of refugees.

After leave at home, he was despatched to the Dardanelles (28 February 1915), but he never reached his destination. On 17 April he landed at Skyros, fit and well until the 20th, but then contracted blood-poisoning and died on the 23rd. One can only speculate on the sort of poems he would have written if he had survived to fight at Gallipoli, but one may be sure they would have borne little resemblance to his previous ones.

One of Brooke's friends, Herbert Asquith (the son of the Liberal Prime Minister), wrote a poem 'The Volunteer', which scaled fresh heights of unrealistic romance. It ran:

Here lies the clerk who half his life has spent
Toiling at ledgers in the city grey
Thinking that so his days would drift away
With no lance broken in life's tournament.
Yet ever twixt the books and his bright eyes
The gleaming eagles of the legions came
And horsemen, charging under phantom skies
Went thundering past beneath the oriflamme.

Undoubtedly many clerks did see war as a relief from office drudgery, but their fantasies were considerably less romantic than Asquith imagined.

Unfortunately, many well-educated young men, schoolmasters, lawyers, medical students, engineers, etc., were so infected with romantic patriotism that they enlisted as privates and welcomed the fact that they were rushed off to the front almost immediately to fill the gaps left by the casualties among the 'Old Contemptibles'. Many of them were soon killed in suicidal infantry attacks. A typical example was Kenneth Powell, an all-round athlete of international standard, whose proved leadership qualities would have been of inestimable value later. He was killed as a private soldier. Regiments such as the Inns of Court and the Artists Rifles were attractive units for they contained people who were already friends. In consequence scores of potential officers were killed in the early days of trench warfare, a process which led to acute shortage of qualified officers later in the war. This mistake was avoided in the Second World War, although that too experienced shortages of 'officer material' when early volunteers had been killed or become prisoners in France, North Africa, Greece and Singapore. In the opening stages of the First World War officers were easily distinguished by their uniform as they led their men in No Man's Land and were carefully selected as the best target for enemy fire.

Kitchener, who was on leave from his post as Governor of Egypt at the outbreak of war, was hastily appointed Secretary of State for War and took up office on 6 August. On first entering the War Office he was asked to give a specimen signature. He took up a pen and found it useless. He threw it away. 'What a War Office,' he said in disgust. 'Not a scrap of Army and not a pen that will write.'

Kitchener was a realist. He astonished his Cabinet colleagues by saying that the war would last at least three years and that it would be won by the *last* million trained men. As at the time Britain had a regular army of 125,000 men at home (most of whom became the BEF) and another 60,000 on important garrison duties overseas, these figures were almost impossible for most people to grasp. However, Kitchener knew that the Germans had already mobilised 1,500,000 men and were rapidly training and equipping more. Although the only ultimate answer to this problem would be conscription, Kitchener realised that until the need was blindingly obvious to the British government and British people, conscription would not be tolerated. As a first step, therefore, he proposed raising an additional army of 100,000 volunteers. These were 'the First Hundred Thousand'. To assist recruiting he agreed (reluctantly) that his face should appear on a poster with his finger pointing straight at the person who saw it. Underneath it bore the words, 'Your country needs YOU!'.

It certainly worked. As we saw earlier, recruits streamed in by the thousand. However, as Kitchener knew, 100,000 was not enough, and after two years conscription was brought in.

Once the initial euphoria died down in all countries it became clear that, as well as killing people, war brings in all sorts of unexpected hardships, long periods of separation, young widows, fatherless children, financial difficulties, hunger, shortages, and nervous strain. Women soon found they had to take an increasing share of responsibilities. Gradually, as there were no men to do tasks which formerly would have seemed impossible for what was then called 'the weaker sex', they were, by force of necessity, done by women. The trade unions viewed with distrust and hostility the invasion by women of formerly male preserves, but could not oppose it. Women soon were doing one of the most dangerous jobs in the war: working in munitions factories, exposed not merely to the chance of being killed by explosions but also to poisonous fumes and dangerous chemicals.

Much to their surprise, the 'Kitchener' volunteers were regarded, and treated, with disdain by the regular Army. Over the centuries the Army had become accustomed to being treated with contempt by civilians in peacetime but fawned upon in times of danger, a phenomenon well expressed by Kipling:

> It's Tommy this an' Tommy that,
>   an' "Chuck him out, the brute"
> But it's "Saviour of 'is country"
>   when the guns begin to shoot.

Now the boot was on the other foot.

This was particularly true of the lower ranks, but also among the officers. Robert Graves records in *Goodbye To All That* that when he joined the Royal Welch Fusiliers as a second lieutenant, he was ignored or snubbed in the Mess, and humiliated in front of the NCOs. Newly-joined officers were required to take part in saluting drill when they came out of the trenches: their instructors were NCOs (usually sergeants) who had clearly been briefed to treat junior officers unpleasantly though courteously. Graves, who came from the same social and educational background as the regular officers, swore he would outlive the lot. He did so: they were all dead within a year. Similarly unreasonable snobbery was encountered by the volunteers who, because they had been enlisted under the Kitchener scheme were referred to disdainfully as 'Kitcheners'. Their skills and experience may have been limited, but their courage was not. Many of the 'Kitcheners' died unflinching on the Somme in 1916. Later in the war everyone was so inextricably mixed that these ludicrous attitudes and jealousies almost disappeared, though not entirely.

In spite of their feudal attitudes, or perhaps because of them, many of the regular officers displayed remarkable indifference to death, danger, or even discomfort. Some commanding officers flatly refused to wear steel helmets, and would advance across No Man's Land carrying nothing more lethal than a walking-stick. Unfortunately a lot of stubborn, uncompromising adherence to tradition went with admirable courage. Cavalry officers refused, at first, to believe that a cavalry charge would not ride over machine guns and overwhelm the gunners: they learnt the lesson at the cost of their lives. There has been no shortage of hindsight criticism from those who were too young to experience the horrors of the First World War. Much of it has been lavished on British and French generals who were considered to be so steeped in traditional attitudes that they were incapable of original thought. Not surprisingly, the same criticisms have been levelled at all armies. Recruits in all countries are appalled by the apparently mindless repetitive training, the power given to sadistic instructors, the hopeless inferiority and unimportance of the individual. Armies first of all break down individuals into passive recipients of instruction by hardship, and petty restrictions. When soldiers are used to these conditions, they may perhaps obtain some responsibility and be promoted. If they survive the war, they become sentimental about the whole process and even speak of sadistic instructors with respect and affection. Only a very small proportion of instructors are actually sadistic, but the need to produce soldiers capable of enduring the rigours of battle demands a training schedule that is in itself sadistic. After all, no one is crueller than an enemy intent on killing you. Many soldiers who had joined in order to get away from the tedium of peacetime jobs were surprised to find that war consisted of long periods of boredom, often shared with companions one would never have chosen in peacetime, and shorter periods of acute terror. Of course, every serviceman or woman wonders how he or she would react when faced with the possibility of immediate death. No one, however outwardly brave, escapes an inner dread that perhaps it will all prove too much to bear. The Army, of course, is well aware of the existence of this feeling. In consequence, training is designed to remove instincts of self-preservation and replace them with automatic responses. Any wavering in the automatic response is countered by the people next in line, perhaps private soldiers, perhaps NCOs. As soon as the armies had settled down into the trenches, it became necessary to test the opposition and find out the quality and number of troops in the sector opposite one's own. This was partly done by patrols (working at night) and partly by local (or larger) attacks. In either there would be a distinct possibility of unpleasant deaths, sometimes because a man might be wounded and unintentionally left behind, perhaps impaled on a barbed wire entanglement, when his comrades had retreated. If he recovered consciousness he might perhaps be rescued the next night, but more probably would be unable to attract attention and would die a slow and agonising death. In order to enter into such potential situations without hesitation a high state of morale was needed and this had to be inculcated. If required to go 'over the top', that is move forward out of the trench in an attack across No Man's Land, a man would go because everyone else was going. If, however, his nerve failed and at the last minute he hung back, an officer or senior NCO behind would give him the alternative of being shot on the spot or taking his chance in the open. Once that situation was known, few even hesitated about going over the top, however much they dreaded it.

In 1914 recruits in all armies assumed that their own training system was uniquely the worst in the most stupid of all armies. It was not conceivable that other armies had not found a way to train soldiers better, more intelligently and more humanely. Few recruits had read any military history or novels such as *War and Peace* which might have indicated otherwise. Everybody knew what a martinet was, but who knew that it was originally the name of a French drill-master in the eighteenth century, or that the Roman army used to march and drill for hour after hour every day, as they believed that was the only way to win wars? As far back as 500 BC a Chinese soldier, Sun-tzu, had written a book entitled *The Art of War* in which he had said that large numbers of men are but lambs led to the slaughter unless properly trained. It was an indisputable truth. Unfortunately most of the soldiers in all armies of the First World War became as lambs led to the slaughter, even though properly trained.

Although Henri Barbusse's book *Under Fire* was published in France in 1916, it was virtually unknown in England for many years. When it was, every British soldier who read it recognised it for the simple, though terrible, truth. Erich Maria Remarque's book *All Quiet on the Western Front* did not appear till 1929, but when it did it was an immediate international success. Suddenly it was realised that life in the German army was exactly the same as it was in all others, the same injustices, hardships, inefficiencies, growing sense of hopelessness. Arnold Zweig's *The Case of Sergeant Grischa* provided a revealing insight into both the Russian and German armies when it appeared in 1927. Jaroslav Hasek, an Austro-Hungarian conscript, was captured on the Russian front but out of his experiences managed to write a brilliantly funny, satirical work entitled *The Good Soldier Schweik*. It was not completed before he died in 1923, but it is one of the most revealing books of the war.

Of the literature produced in the war we shall have more to say later. At this stage we are simply making the point that all armies during the First World War had many common factors. There were, of course, rays of light among the gloom. There were new experiences, new acquaintances (some of them becoming firm friends even if only for a short time), new places, and even humorous and enjoyable moments. Although soldiers would not have chosen the comrades they found themselves serving alongside, they found it interesting to be in squads which contained men from a wide variety of backgrounds, including perhaps a shady character, a smart-alec, a humorist, a born fixer, a musician (who might be anything from a mouth-organ player to a concert pianist), and a born actor. Cynically many soldiers learnt not to become too attached to their fellows, as the vagaries of army postings often split up friends.

Few soldiers had any doubts about whose side God was on in 1914. British troops knew in their hearts that they were the Christian soldiers they sang about in hymns on Church Parades; many prayed secretly for a safe return. The French hoped that 'Le bon Dieu' would look after them. The Germans also hoped God would look after them but also expected Him to take a suitably active rôle against England, a thought which they expressed in the words 'Gott strafe England'. 'Strafe' of course means 'punish', but was adopted by the British, as in 'a strafe', to mean 'destroy'.

Cynics said that God was on the side of the big battalions.

THE
WESTERN FRONT
The Trench Line
1914–18

CHAPTER 4

1914 – 1915

The later stages of the war in 1914 had carried some ominous portents for the future. By the end of October in the Ypres area ammunition was running so short that many guns were withdrawn from the line and those that remained were rationed to one shell every half hour. It was said that the inevitable humorist to be found in every unit used to call out to the German gunners, more liberally supplied than the British, 'Give over, Jerry, a bit. Our gun's broke.' Unfortunately, shortages were not only for the larger calibre guns, but also in the ammunition for rifles. Even among that which was available there was much that was faulty, and misfired. Even worse was the shortage of rifle oil, for after being clogged with mud, weapons often became unserviceable for lack of it.

The Belgians had evacuated Antwerp on 6 October and the Germans occupied it three days later. The Germans then concentrated their forces and moved towards Ypres. The Belgians had improved the defences of the area north of the town by flooding certain areas. However, the area immediately to the east of Ypres was virtually at sea level and over the centuries had been drained by an elaborate system of dykes and canals. Even in peacetime these could be overwhelmed by unduly heavy rain. The Belgians had warned the British that shelling the German positions in this area would destroy the complex drainage system and create a morass, but this information does not seem to have reached the appropriate quarter or, if it did, was ignored.

The Ypres battles began on 15 October when the Germans decided this was the moment to capture the city. The main thrust came from the direction of Menin, and caused the British to fall back to Gheluvelt. Another German thrust was countered at Langemarck, where the Germans lost fifteen hundred men. They were mostly students from one of the reserve divisions, which showed the British were not the only ones to allow their more talented young men to be killed in suicidal infantry attacks. The Germans established a large cemetery at Langemarck (which they held till 1916). It was a sombre sight, for the Germans buried their dead in a mass grave here, with the names at the side.

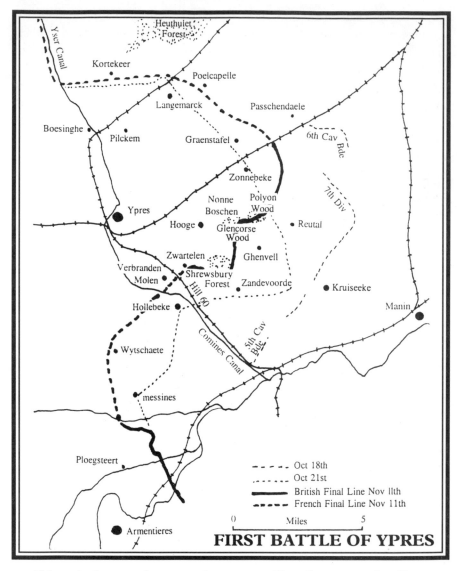

FIRST BATTLE OF YPRES

- – – – – Oct 18th
- · · · · · · Oct 21st
- ———— British Final Line Nov 11th
- ▬▬▬▬ French Final Line Nov 11th

0   Miles   5

Although the trench system here was still rudimentary, the Germans found the route to Ypres effectively blocked by dogged British infantry and artillery. Unfortunately for the Germans, the Kaiser had taken a special interest in the capture of Ypres and several times visited the troops in the area to encourage them to break through at all costs. Nothing, of course, is more productive of casualties than a battlefield which has acquired a symbolic importance much in excess of its strategic value. Later in the war, Verdun would become another such, and in the Second World War thousands would die at Stalingrad, more because it bore the name of the Russian dictator than for its military importance. Some harsh lessons were being learnt at Ypres. One was that it is unwise to have an important headquarters in a vulnerable position. Hooge château (which was completely obliterated in the following years) had been selected as the headquarters for both the 1st and 2nd British divisions. When it came under shellfire, both divisional commanders were wounded, one fatally, and many members of their staffs, who had essential information about the battle and resources, were killed.

After the war there was much criticism of generals being so far behind the lines that they did not know the conditions in which troops were fighting. In fact many staff officers often came close to the front line and were killed including 60 generals. However, the legend of generals being some 50 miles away from the actual fighting has persisted. Fiction is often much more memorable than stark fact.

The fighting around Gheluvelt produced one remarkable incident which if it had not happened would not have been thought possible. Owing to heavy losses, there was a gap in the British line which the Germans might penetrate and reach Ypres, once they realised the opportunity which lay in their grasp. The 2nd Battalion of the Worcestershire Regiment were rushed forward to close it. Led by Brigadier General Fitzclarence, they surged into Gheluvelt and retook it at the point of the bayonet. The Germans, astonished at this sudden vigorous counter attack and unaware it was a mere 800 men against a potential 10,000 fell back, broke off the action and counted their losses. The fighting continued later but the vital pressure was off Gheluvelt. Sadly, Fitzclarence was killed a few days later leading another desperate counter-attack.

This phase of the campaign acquired the name of the First Battle of Ypres, usually shortened to First Ypres. When the Germans decided to try no further for the time being, there had been 50,000 British casualties, 20,000 French, and 150,000 German. It is, of course usual for the attacking side, which is normally advancing towards prepared positions, to have the heavier losses and that is why for attack, a numerical superiority of at least three to one is advised. But the Germans had done much better than they knew, for they had destroyed many of the best and most experienced regiments of the British Army, who could only be replaced by volunteers and conscripts. The latter would not lack courage but that was no substitute for the skills, such as marksmanship, which could not be learned quickly and reach the same high standard.

As the winter set in, and that meant more rain, floods and snow, both sides dug in as best they could in the trenches. The Germans were in the fortunate possession of the higher, drier, ground, on which they built concrete blockhouses; the British, less well placed, worked frantically to improve their trenches and keep them clear of water by pumps but, even so, often had to stand for hours knee-deep in water. Along all sections of the front the usual accompaniments of trench warfare soon arrived. They were lice, fleas, bugs, rats, trench foot (a form of foot-rot which can be fatal and is always incapacitating), fevers, pneumonia, and all the ailments which inevitably accompany exposure, unburied bodies, rudimentary hygiene and perpetual damp. Both sides set up barbed-wire defences under cover of darkness; usually parties from each side crawled out on another night to cut through them in preparation for raids or a forthcoming attack.

Although the Western Front (France) has acquired the reputation of the worst area of the war, with considerable justification, there were others which were equally grim on a smaller scale. Mesopotamia (Iraq) was one of them; the Eastern Front another. The Western Front was some 350 miles long, the Eastern Front 1,150. Winter on the Western Front slowed down but never stopped hostilities; in the east it froze operations into immobility.

Casualties on the Eastern Front had been high on both sides, but the Russians had suffered the most. Overall it was estimated that there had been some 3,000,000 casualties by Christmas 1914, of which a disproportionate amount had been incurred by the Russians.

British and French strategy was mainly based on breaking through the German lines with massed infantry attacks and eventually reaching Berlin, if the Germans had not capitulated before that stage was reached. Although the French, with over 1,500,000 Germans in their country, were naturally anxious that their removal should be an early priority, they soon became so desperate with frustration that they were open-minded and even optimistic about other means of defeating Germany. They did not rule out the possibility that Germany could be brought to her knees by blockade, by an invasion via Belgium, or by attacking through what later became known as 'the soft underbelly of Europe', that is the Middle East. In the German camp there were two theories about the easiest and quickest way to find victory. One, advocated by Falkenhayn, was that it would be achieved in France, by artillery and infantry, after which Russia could be dealt with at leisure; the other, on which Hindenburg and Ludendorff were in harmony, believed that the key to victory was in Russia, after which the Allied forces in France and elsewhere could be dealt with at leisure. Certainly, the combined manpower of Germany and Austria, when no longer needed on the Eastern Front, might well be a decisive factor in the west. This view appealed to the Kaiser, who gave Hindenburg and Ludendorff priority, and four newly formed corps to support it.

The final German plan was that Russia should be defeated by the Austrians advancing in the south through Galicia, and the Germans in the north through Warsaw, Brest-Litovsk and Pinsk, thus creating a pincer movement. This advance was designed ultimately to create a line from Riga in the north to Czernowitz in the south. The Austrians made slow progress in the south, but Hindenburg was more successful in the north, though at a high cost. His offensive began with the first use of gas in the war, and it was chlorine, delivered by shellfire. The recipients were the inhabitants of Bulimov, a town between Lodz and Warsaw, but it had little effect owing to the intense cold which prevented it diffusing. The Germans were said to have fired the astonishing number of 18,000 shells. The Russians did not pass the information about this new weapon (gas) to their allies, an omission said to be explained by their failure to appreciate what it was. Later, in February, the Germans inflicted a crushing defeat on the Russians in what became known as the Winter Battle of Masuria, taking some 100,000 prisoners and inflicting a similar number of casualties. Fighting was now taking place in thick snow and the chief victor in this campaign was the renowned 'Russian Winter', which had defeated Napoleon and would contribute to the defeat of Hitler's army some three decades later. And, by March the Austrians were on the defensive, as the Russians pressed towards the Carpathians. Although the Austrians were capable soldiers, they were no match for the Russians. Falkenhayn, as Commander in Chief, decided that the Western Front was now sufficiently static to allow him to withdraw troops and use them in the east. It was a calculated gamble, for at any moment either the French or the British might launch an offensive to punch a hole through the German lines, but the potential prize in the east seemed to justify it.

The withdrawal of troops from the Western Front took place while Allied attention was taken up by the gas attack at Ypres in April 1915, which will be covered in more detail later.

This time the Germans concentrated on the southern sector although there was a small offensive in the north to add to Russian confusion. The Germans made rapid progress with the preparations, which included the transfer of heavy artillery. Their all round equipment was superb. They launched their attack on 2 May 1915, beginning with a relentless bombardment. In the First World War it was made abundantly clear when an attack was coming from the preliminary bombardment which was designed to 'soften up' the opposition. In later warfare, heavy bombing usually supplemented, or even took over, that rôle.

Unfortunately for the Russians, although they were dour fighters at close quarters, they were quite unprepared for the relentless force of the German offensive. By now the Russians had mobilised 6,000,000 men, but only had the arms and equipment for about half that number. In consequence soldiers were sent to the battlefield and held in reserve till the front line had overcome the enemy or been mostly killed themselves. Then the weaponless reserve picked up the rifles from the dead and prepared to use them. If the weapons they acquired had belonged to the enemy, it was unlikely that the Russians would know how they worked, and if they did, would only have had a limited amount of ammunition for them. Within two days of the opening of the first offensive in the south the Russian Third Army was torn to shreds, though once more the number of prisoners vastly exceeded those killed. Mackensen, commanding the victorious German Eleventh Army, was able to press forward 50 miles a week. Even so, the Russian threat had not been completely removed by these victories. There were still millions of potential Russian soldiers, still hundreds of miles of territory into which the Germans could be drawn and ambushed. Although Germany had removed the immediate danger of a Russian invasion, the war was still young, the Russians with all their faults had vast untapped resources, and Germany was still at war on two main fronts.

These battles between Russia and Germany, although on a massive scale, were too remote for most people in Britain to take into their concept of the war. Their immediate concern was France, where the trench lines were being extended, strengthened and deepened. Inevitably the British and French did not see the strategic picture in the same light. There was also a considerable divergence of opinion as to who should hold which section of the trenches. Eventually it was decided that the Belgians should hold the extreme northern sector from the coast to the Yser, the French should hold the sector south from the Yser including the Ypres salient, the British should hold the sector from Givenchy to La Bassée: and the French should hold the remainder. The British were not pleased to be allotted a sector so far from the coast, but that arrangement suited the French very well for they felt it ruled out any possibility of the British suddenly deciding to evacuate their troops for use elsewhere. It is interesting to recall that in the Second World War, when the Battle of France had been lost in 1940, and 338,000 soldiers were evacuated from Dunkirk, French feelings were scarcely mollified by the fact that 125,000 of them were French. Unfortunately – from the British point of view – most of the French who had been evacuated at considerable risk to the Royal Navy decided to return to France as civilians later, although it was occupied by the Germans. However, some stayed and joined the Free French forces.

Very naturally the French General Staff in 1915 were much concerned with the huge German salient which bulged out between Reims and Amiens, encompassing the town of Noyon which lay a mere 55 miles from Paris. When the French learnt, from prisoners and other intelligence sources, that in January 1915 there were eight fewer German divisions on the Western Front than there had been the previous November, owing to transfers of to the Eastern Front, and of those remaining most were only 80 percent of their full strength, it seemed to the French an opportune moment to eliminate this Noyon salient.

Salients penetrating the enemy lines are a mixed blessing. Although they offer an opportunity for further thrusts from their advanced position, they are easily shelled and they have two long vulnerable sides. If the enemy can cut deeply into the salient it may be possible for them to isolate all the forward troops in it.

The Noyon salient was dependent for its supply on a complex railway and road system. An advance eastwards into the Artois plateau would reach the centre of the German communications in the middle of the salient. An advance from Champagne northwards would be nearly as effective. Even better would be an advance from Verdun northwards, which could easily reach the Rhine. Joffre believed that steady pressure at any one of these would eventually produce the necessary break-through and then offer an opportunity to cut off the retreat of a large section of the German army.

The British could see good sense in the French plan but also favoured reaching the Passchendaele Ridge, east of Ypres, after which they visualised the cavalry racing across the open country beyond into Brussels and eventually Germany. Part of this force would then be able to recapture Antwerp and the remaining Channel ports. However, a less ambitious but desirable objective was the Aubers ridge, which extended over the twenty miles between La Bassée and Lille. A lesson which had been learnt quickly in this almost static war was that higher ground, however modest in elevation, was of enormous advantage: it was drier, easier to defend, and gave excellent opportunities for observation. Just south of La Bassée was Vimy Ridge, which dominated the whole of the Douai region.

In examining their prospects the French set small store on the British contribution. Although the dour defensive qualities of the British Army were

admired, its ability to launch a devastating attack and exploit a breakthrough was considered to be limited. The French were aware that in the
1914 battles Sir John French had stressed that when advancing no one division should get ahead of another without allowing those on the flanks to
catch up. This policy made sense in that it did not allow any division to
become trapped in an untenable salient, vulnerable to attack on both flanks,
but it did not appear to the French to be a tactic likely to eject the Germans
from France in the foreseeable future. Subsequently the wish of both armies
to demonstrate their fighting ability and impress their allies led to some
wasteful policies and misunderstandings. It has been said somewhat cynically that it is easier to deal with the enemy than with allies for with the
enemy you do at least know what he intends to do, whereas with an ally you
can never be sure. France and Britain had various mutual suspicions to overcome. France had a saying that England would always fight to the last
Frenchman and England felt that Gallic impetuosity would spell doom for
both sides. The French were very conscious of the fact that they were shoul-
dering the main burden of the fighting at this stage and felt that the British
should do more. It was, of course, vital that these suspicions and jealousies
should be eliminated from the Higher Command as soon as possible. In the
lower ranks the existence of rivalries and jealousies was less important.
French soldiers were envious of the higher pay received by British soldiers,
which made them attractive to the more venal types of women; the British
felt that France owed them something for being in France at all, and fighting to recover French territory.

Precisely the same arguments would be heard in the Second World War,
but this time the boot would be on the other foot. When the Americans
arrived in England in 1943 their uniforms were more elegant, their pay was
much greater, and they had access to luxury goods which had disappeared
from British shops years earlier (by 1943 the Second World War had already
lasted four years – as long as the whole of the first). To the more suscepti-
ble British girls, American soldiers were military versions of Hollywood film
stars, much to the fury of the British soldiery. Furthermore, American ser-
vicemen often expressed the view that they were saving England from the
Germans, but they had no intention of saving the British, or French, or
Dutch empires in the process. There was an English saying that the problem with Americans was that they were overpaid, oversexed, and over here;
to which Americans retorted that the Brits were underpaid, undersexed, and
under Eisenhower (the Commander in Chief, Allied Forces in Europe).
However, though Anglo-American friction was a feature of the Second

World War, it did not appear in the First, when American relationships with British and French were, for the most part, harmonious.

The French launched a major attack in the Champagne area on 15 February 1915; it gained some ground but at fearful cost. They had already launched an offensive in this area in late December and taken heavy casualties for small territorial gains. In the period since then the Germans had worked feverishly to improve their defences, and succeeded. In the month between 15 February and 15 March, the French captured 500 yards for a casualty list of 50,000. This did not inhibit them from launching another offensive against the St Mihiel salient in April, which failed with the loss of 64,000 men. This was the battle of the Woevre.

Meanwhile, although the Germans were generally on the defensive in the west, pending the successful outcome of their operations on the Eastern Front, they opened a diversionary offensive in the west on 22 April, which became known as the Second Battle of Ypres. It was not meant to be a major thrust which might capture the city, but was more in the nature of an experiment. It became infamous for the fact that it introduced genuinely poisonous gas to the Western Front, this time chlorine. Later the whole Ypres area would become saturated with gas of every variety, mainly mustard, although phosgene and others would soon appear. Troops were warned how to detect phosgene by their instructors. 'It smells like musty hay.' Many among the audience, having lived all their lives in towns, had never even smelt sweet hay, let alone the musty variety, which is relatively scarce. By the time they learnt to recognise the smell of phosgene, it was probably too late.

The Germans had been bombarding the Ypres area steadily throughout the third week in April and a number of shells had fallen on the town itself, causing many of the inhabitants to leave hastily: up till this point they thought they were relatively safe. In general the French and Belgians living near the front line tended to remain where they were, often cultivating their small farms under conditions of considerable danger. An interesting example of the French peasant's attitude to the war comes in a novel by R. H. Mottram, entitled *The Spanish Farm* (the name of the farm is a survival of the centuries past occupation of the area by Spanish troops). The book is an absorbing story as well as being informative.

Shelling continued on the 22nd, but was steady rather than intense. The area to the north-west of the town of Ypres was held by French troops from the 45th Reserve Division, who were mostly Algerians. Towards sunset, a yellowy-green mist appeared, not unlike that which creeps over damp fields as the winter approaches. This, however, was no benign mist. It was chlorine released from 5,700 cylinders. A desperate stream of French and Algerian soldiers were suddenly seen to be abandoning their trenches and rushing into the area behind. They were choking and coughing and pointing their fingers towards their throats. The French guns, which had been replying to the German bombardment, stopped and a few gun teams were seen to be trying to drag their guns to the rear. Suddenly there was a gap four miles long in the line protecting Ypres and, coincidentally, the line was four miles from Ypres itself at this point. The Germans could hardly believe their success. They advanced two miles and then stopped. They were not very confident in their own crude gasmasks, which were made of tow soaked in oxygen,* and they were afraid that if they moved too quickly they would catch up the drifting gas. They were also deterred by some very brave counter-attacks from Canadians in an adjoining sector. The Canadians had no gas masks either, but one of their soldiers, a chemist by profession, having sniffed the gas and guessed what it was, suggested covering their faces with handkerchiefs or bandages soaked with their own urine (the alkaline neutralising the acid). Once this was known, the idea spread rapidly. Helped by two Yorkshire territorial battalions, the Canadians actually pushed the Germans back.

The use of gas should not have come as a surprise. Captured prisoners had spoken of stacks of cylinders of gas in the German trenches. A deserter had warned about the imminent use of gas. Unfortunately the French corps commander flatly refused to believe the story. He thought it was a fantasy invented by his intelligence officers to impress him with their perspicacity.

This failure to act on vital information was not untypical. The channel by which information reaches the top is the intelligence officer (IO). Speaking the language of the enemy, he interrogates captured prisoners and studies captured maps or material. He also interviews soldiers who have returned from raids. Regrettably he is often a suspect figure himself. Usually he is a wartime soldier and therefore regarded as an amateur when speaking to a professional (i.e., a regular). Some intelligence officers are too naive or too lacking in experience to make a proper evaluation of their sources or the information they produce. If an IO makes a single statement which is later proved to be wrong, he is completely discredited. On a slightly more sinister note, his warnings may be believed, but because his information runs counter to a policy which the general is pursuing at the time, he is ignored.

---

* General Ferry, Commander of the French 11th Division, was told this by a German deserter, who produced one as proof.

One of the most bizarre examples of stupid bigotry comes from the Second World War when a German deserter (a Communist) told the Russians how and when the Germans were going to attack them in 1941. The man's unit had been briefed on its part in the attack. When the information was rushed to Stalin, he refused to believe it and ordered the man to be shot as being a subversive German spy. Before that could happen, the Germans launched their massive invasion. In spite of this, the Russians had time to carry out the sentence and execute the unfortunate German who had risked his life to warn them. Such is paranoia.

After the gas attack it was hoped that Joffre would divert French troops to the area and the ground lost would then be recovered in a counter-attack. It was not to be. Joffre was much more interested in his coming offensive near Arras and had no intention of weakening it by allowing troops to be sent to the Ypres area. Meanwhile the British trench line was pulled back to form a straighter, but still bulging, line, three miles from Ypres. Some lost ground was recovered in the process but at the cost of 60,000 casualties (twice those of the enemy). The French were not really interested in Belgium or the fact that the city of Ypres was now well within the range of German shellfire. This was folly on an extreme scale, for if the Germans broke through and captured Ypres they could slip in behind the entire Allied trench line as well as capturing the Channel ports. The British were, understandably, bitter.

The Allied offensive now switched further south, with the British cooperating with the French plan. This led to the murderous battles at Aubers Ridge and Festubert.

On 9 May a combined British and Indian force attacked the south-west end of the Aubers Ridge with the aim of assisting the French further south. For this battle the British had superior numbers, though still just under the recommended three to one. But the Germans had anticipated an attack here and built six-foot high defences, liberally entwined with wire. The initial British bombardment was limited to 40 minutes owing to the shell shortage, which was now becoming acute. In consequence, when the attack was launched the British force, which included many Indian units, was slaughtered wholesale in an assault which was a complete failure. In the adjoining sector the French advanced two miles and captured 2,000 prisoners and twelve guns. The Germans had then strengthened that sector by switching two divisions from the sector facing the British. The effect on Anglo-French relations may be imagined. There was, however, another point to be taken into consideration. The French had been able to begin their attack *with four hours of intensive bombardment.*

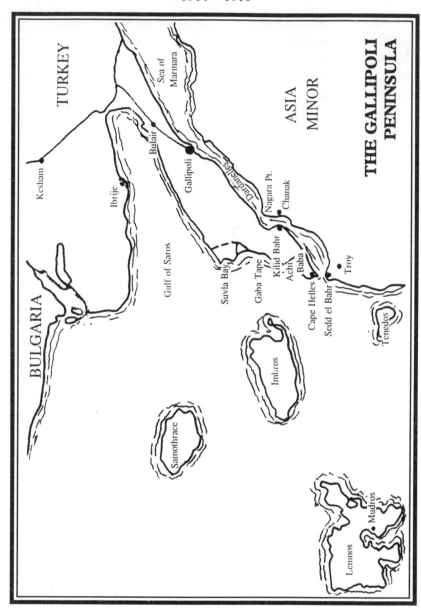

THE GALLIPOLI PENINSULA

TURKEY

Sea of Marmara

ASIA MINOR

Kesham

Bulair

Ibrije

Gallipoli

Dardanelles

Nagara Pt.

Chanak

Gulf of Saros

Kilid Bahr

Achi Baba

Suvla Bay

Gaba Tepe

Troy

Cape Helles

Sedd el Bahr

BULGARIA

Tenedos

Imbros

Samothrace

Lemnos

Mudros

Another factor was the clear warning of British intentions which had been given a month earlier. In order to facilitate the assault on Aubers Ridge the British had made an assault on the village of Neuve Chapelle, and captured it, taking 2,000 German prisoners. The cost had been high, for both sides had sustained 11,000 casualties. If the British had been able to follow up this attack they could probably have reached Aubers Ridge and captured it. But neither the reserves nor the necessary shells were available. The Germans, as we saw, heeded the warning and made no mistake with the defence on Aubers Ridge.

The shell shortage was the principal limiting factor on British tactics in 1915. British production was 22,000 a day, compared with the French 100,000 and Germany/Austria's production of 250,000. The reason for the low British production was obsolete factory equipment, some of it many years old, but it was also regrettably true that the work force in the factories steadily refused to increase its effort without substantial pay increases. The fact that their fellow citizens, sometimes even members of their own families, were dying in the trenches through lack of adequate guns and ammunition did not affect their attitude. Their view was that if the government wanted munitions, the government should pay top rates for them. If the soldiers in the trenches were short of ammunition, it was the fault of the government, not the munitions workers.

This attitude was found again in the Second World War when there were strikes in vital industries at the most crucial period of the war. Admittedly work in ammunition factories could be dangerous, though not to be compared with the danger of the trenches, but the manufacture of guns, aircraft or vehicles was no hardship at all. Soldiers thought that workers at home should be paid less for their safe and cushy jobs, and be conscripted too.

Shortages in France were made worse when a large proportion of the munitions which were manufactured was sent to the Dardanelles in 1915.

The Dardanelles campaign was a brilliant concept, but in the event turned into a classic example of muddle and miscalculation, ending in heavy casualties and ultimate disaster. The idea was originally Churchill's, for as early as December 1914 he had suggested that there might be easier ways of defeating Germany than by trying to force a way through the 1,500,000 German soldiers who were by then in France. A successful attack on the Dardanelles, which would free the straits for Allied shipping, would have enormous benefits. It would cripple Turkey, which had the potential to be a serious menace in the Middle East, as indeed she later proved to be. It would end the harassing of the Russian Black Sea ports and enable greatly needed supplies to reach Russia, it would influence countries which were wavering over which side they should join in the hope of sitting at the victors' table, and it would enable attacks to be launched on Austria, thus reducing her value as an ally to Germany. The prizes for success were thus immense.

Unfortunately, so were the hazards. The Dardanelles is the name given to a narrow passage between the Aegean and the Sea of Marmara, at the north-eastern end of which is Istanbul (Constantinople). Between the Sea of Marmara and the Black Sea is the Bosporus Strait. On the north-western side of the Sea of Marmara is the Gallipoli peninsula, also Turkish, on the northern side of which is the Gulf of Saros. The entrance to the Dardanelles was covered by a formidable range of guns, some very large, and between this and 'The Narrows', approximately half way up, there were minefields, all of which were illuminated by searchlights and protected by smaller guns in case anyone should try to find a way through in the darkness. At the entrance itself was an anti-submarine net. The most difficult part was undoubtedly The Narrows, where the strait is only 1,600 yards across and curves north; no ship stood a chance of getting through there unscathed unless the defences had been previously demolished. Nowadays, of course, the area would have been saturated with bombs, but these were the days before air armadas, and any demolition of defences must be provided by the navy. Germany had seconded to the Turks one of their more ingenious and thorough generals, Liman von Sanders, who gave them much valuable advice. He was to prove a formidable opponent to the Allies in the later campaign against the Turks.

The mistakes over the Dardanelles had begun early in the war. Incredible though it now seems, a mission from the Royal Navy was reorganising the Turkish navy up till the outbreak of the war in 1914, even though the Turkish army and government were establishing closer links with Germany. When war was declared against Germany, the Admiralty commandeered two dreadnoughts which were being built for Turkey in British shipyards. As we have seen, soon afterwards the Mediterranean fleet allowed two German cruisers to escape through the Dardanelles and take refuge in Turkey.

The second mistake was to send a combined Anglo-French fleet to bombard the shore forts of the Dardanelles on 3 November 1914. This inflicted heavy damage but was not followed up, and therefore served as a warning to the Turks of bigger assaults to come. Spurred on by von Sanders and his staff, the Turks rebuilt the forts, added other defences, and concentrated more troops in the area.

Churchill's hand was forced by the Russians, who appealed for help when they were being pushed back by a Turkish army attack in the Caucasus. He therefore decided to issue orders for an assault on the Dardanelles in February 1915 and, once again, this time on the 19th of that month, another Allied fleet bombarded the Turkish forts. Although Kitchener had flatly refused to release any troops from France, Churchill had been confident that the Royal Navy could handle this matter by themselves. He was right. The forts were once again blown to pieces by the Allied naval guns and a force of sailors and marines was landed. These defeated the opposition and blew up the remaining guns. Their success was so complete that if they had continued it is considered they could have reached Istanbul. Whether they would have been able to hold it against possible Turkish counter-attacks seems doubtful but in the event they were never put to the test.

Instead of taking this golden opportunity, a month was allowed to slip by before the inner forts were attacked. However, just when the forts were about to fall, several Allied ships ran into mines in the straits and were badly damaged. The Admiralty decided it would be wise to withdraw and await reinforcements of army troops before making the final assault on Istanbul. Two more months went by.

Disaster began when landings were made by British, Australian, New Zealand (these being together known as the Anzacs – Australian and New Zealand Army Corps), and French troops. The chosen spots were Kum Kale on the southern shore at the mouth of the straits, and on the northern shore at Cape Helles, and in what became known as Anzac Cove on the western side of the Gallipoli peninsula. Although the landings were made, the troops failed to penetrate inland and were pinned down on the beaches by a resolute Turkish defence. The troops showed outstanding courage but the casualty rates from enemy action and disease were appalling. Much could have been done to improve the situation if the leadership had been less elderly and more inspired. However, the root cause of the 1915 failure lay in the Admiralty's obstinate refusal to develop the computerised firing system invented by one Arthur Pollen before the war, embodied in what was known as the Argo clock. When ships are in motion, as the warships at the Dardanelles needed to be if they were not to be hit by shore batteries, their guns require immediate range adjustment if they are not to fire over, or fall short of, the target. The Navy had the firepower to knock out all the Turkish forts and shore guns if it could hit them but, using obsolete methods of range finding, it failed to do so and the minefields remained unswept under cover of the Turkish guns. The following year Jutland, a drawn battle, made British gunnery deficiencies

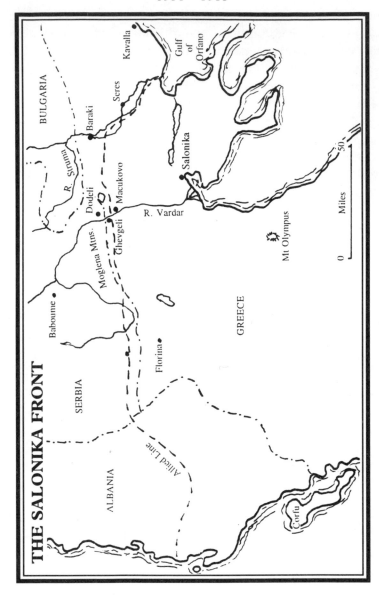

THE SALONIKA FRONT

even more glaringly obvious, but the Argo clock was not adopted by the Admiralty until 1926, eight years after the war had finished.

To make matters worse, German U boats arrived in the Dardanelles area during May 1915, thus making the task of supplying the Army with stores doubly difficult.

In an attempt to relieve the pressure on the other beaches, another landing was made on the north side of the Gallipoli peninsula at Suvla Bay. Fresh troops were used, but they were inexperienced and their commanders were incompetent. Even so, they fought their way ashore and half a company of Gurkhas managed to reach the crest of the ridge and look down on the other side onto the Dardanelles. Having done so, they were shelled by our own naval gunners who did not suspect that our own troops could have penetrated that far. In consequence, the Gurkhas had to fall back and the hard-won ridge was lost again. It was now all too clear that General Sir Ian Hamilton, the overall commander of the Expeditionary Force, was not the right man for this exacting post. His opponents, Liman von Sanders and Mustafa Kemal, later known as Ataturk, were obviously much better tacticians.

The war dragged on. This campaign which had been designed to take the pressure off the trench warfare in France had itself become a centre of trench warfare. If anything, it was worse than France. Ships were lost, and men were killed or died from diseases.

It would have been sensible to have called off the campaign and cut the Allied losses but, having come so close to success earlier, the Allied High Command convinced itself that with one final effort victory would be assured. Three more divisions (some 50,000 troops) were sent to Hamilton, but the Turks had also built up their forces and were as firmly entrenched as ever. Fresh landings were tried. But by now other matters in the Balkans were demanding urgent attention.

The Germans had decided that Serbia must now be removed from the war. While she was intact, Romania, with her oil supplies, would sit on the fence until one side or the other looked like winning; Bulgaria was in a similar position. Serbia was also a perpetual thorn in the side of Austria. As both those countries were now watching the Allied disaster in the Dardanelles, it seemed to the Germans that there could never be a better time to take them into partnership. In September German overtures received their reward: Bulgaria agreed to join the Central Powers, and in October she launched her army into Serbia. Meanwhile the Allies saw this German initiative in the Balkans as a threat to a more important country than Serbia: Greece. Greece had so far remained neutral, though favouring the Allies. The Allies decided that Greek neutrality could best be defended if an expeditionary force was landed at Salonika (now Thessaloniki). Under the command of a French general named Maurice Sarrail, it planned to link up with and help the Serbs. For this purpose, one French and two British divisions were moved from Gallipoli to Salonika. Unfortunately for the Serbs, this force arrived too late. The Bulgarian army was now sitting astride the rail route the Allies planned to use to relieve the Serbian Army. For the moment, all that the Salonika expeditionary force could do was to wire itself in and hope that its presence would deter the Germans from attacking Greece. For the next three years this enclave became what the Germans scathingly described as the biggest internment camp in Europe. However, in 1918 that particular joke fell flat when the Allied breakout helped to convince the Germans, already hard pressed on the Western Front, that the war was now lost.

The full force of the German, Austrian, Bulgarian attack had fallen on Serbia on 9 October. The Serbs were hopelessly outclassed in numbers and weapons, but they managed to take 23,000 Austrian prisoners and with them fall back to the coast. This retreat through the mountains ranks with the other epic retreats in history and shares the same characteristics, lack of food, weapons, organisation, and proper leadership. The survivors, about half the numbers of the original army, straggled to ports on the Adriatic, where they were picked up by French and Italian boats. Although then in the last stages of exhaustion and debilitation, many of them recovered after sympathetic care and nursing in Corfu. The Austrians completed their conquests in the area by overrunning Montenegro, after which it seemed that the Balkan situation had been 'settled' to the satisfaction of the Central Powers.

It was far from satisfactory for the Allies. They had lost everything except a toehold on Salonika from which they could gain little, but from which they dared not extract themselves in case that move should propel Greece into the arms of the enemy.

Meanwhile the Dardanelles campaign was progressing to its disastrous end. The reinforcements sent from Britain had been matched by the build-up of the Turkish army. Kitchener paid a brief visit in order to judge the situation on the spot with his own eyes. Hamilton had already been relieved of his post: his successor was General Charles Monro, but the battle was already lost. Since the outbreak of war Kitchener had held the Cabinet post of Secretary of State for War and although this was a civilian post, he clearly saw himself as a military commander. His prestige, built up over the years – in the Sudan in 1898, in the Boer War in 1900–2, as Commander in Chief in India, and as reformer of the British Army, meant that his opinions were incontestable. Now that he endorsed the view that the Allies should abandon the Dardanelles campaign, there was no point in delaying. The evacuation began in December 1915 and ended on 9 January 1916.

The Dardanelles 'sideshow' was one of the greatest disasters encountered by the British Army. Of the 489,000 Allied soldiers, just over half had been casualties, many from disease. Turkish numbers engaged, and consequent losses, were approximately the same. Churchill was considered largely to blame and left politics to take up soldiering in France, where he did very well as commanding officer of the 6th Royal Scots Fusiliers. Although his battalion was in a relatively quiet sector of the line, it was anything but restful when he was in command. However, when it was merged with another battalion in 1916, Churchill decided he would have more influence on the successful outcome of the war if he returned to politics. He therefore re-entered Parliament as a private member. His instinct was correct: in 1917 he became Minister of Munitions, a post outside the Cabinet but of great importance nevertheless.

However, while the campaign in the Dardanelles was heading for humiliating disaster, another Middle Eastern expedition of mixed fortunes was under way. This was the Mesopotamian (modern Iraq) campaign which had begun modestly with the occupation of Basra on the Persian Gulf by units of the Indian Army. The original intention in 1914 was the eminently sound one of guarding the oil wells: however, once that had been accomplished without difficulty it seemed sensible to press north with an army corps and overrun the remainder of the country. The Corps Commander was General Dixon, but the fighting would be mostly done by 6th Indian Division. After a counter-attack by 20,000 Turks had been defeated at Nasiriya (in April 1915), it did not seem that there would be much opposition before the force approached Baghdad. This view was strengthened when General Townshend reached Kut el Amara in September and defeated the defending Turkish force with comparative ease. Although Townshend was doubtful about pressing on towards Baghdad, his superiors urged him to do so. The result was the gruelling battle of Ctesiphon, after which his troops were so exhausted that he had no option but to retreat to Kut.

It was clear that the strength of the opposition had been badly underrated. Townshend, with 9,000 men, was besieged in Kut. Although periodic Turkish attempts to enter the town were repulsed during the next few months, Townshend's position became increasingly desperate. Attempts to relieve him, first under General Aylmer and then under General Maude, could not break through the besieging lines. Eventually in April 1916, at the end of his resources Townshend destroyed his guns, ammunition, and stores, and surrendered. He could have held out longer if he had not unwisely agreed to feed the civilian population as well as his own troops, and when this seemed no longer possible felt he had no alternative. Had he known that the civilian population had buried large stores of grain, which would have kept them alive without supplies from Townshend, he would not have sent desperate pleas for relief, and therefore caused premature, unsuccessful attempts to be made. If the relieving forces had waited long enough to build up substantial numbers, the tragedy of Kut would not have occurred.

Fortunately, in Kut there were only 9,000 troops, two thirds Indian, one third British. They were marched from Kut on long, exhausting journeys, treated with appalling brutality, and 5,000 were never heard of again.

In order to follow the misfortunes of those besieged in Kut it has been necessary to go forward into 1916. Most people at home were hardly aware of these events in the Middle East, although as the war continued there more troops would be sent and the campaign would be reported more fully. But, even by the end of the war, a large percentage of the population of Britain would remain completely ignorant of what had been happening in that area. It was difficult enough to follow events in France, let alone what campaigns were taking place in almost unknown areas, like Africa and the Middle East. (Even in the Second World War those who fought in Burma, the longest campaign in the entire war, found afterwards that the general public in Britain had remained completely unaware of the gruelling conditions of fighting on mountain and in jungle terrain, and this was after a revolution in communications.)

During 1915 the Allied High Command was having to come to terms with the fact that the Turks were going to be stubborn and difficult opponents. The lesson would not be fully appreciated until the end of the year, when the Dardanelles campaign ended in evacuation for no gain whatever. But much earlier, in February 1915, the Turks had shown their potential strength. 20,000 Turkish soldiers, carrying pontoons and guns, had crossed the arid 120 miles of the Sinai Desert, and created considerable alarm by doing so. They were repulsed, but there was every likelihood they would try again. The thought of losing control of the Suez Canal was so traumatic that the British High Command hastily diverted reinforcements to the area. Fortunately the Turks did not try again until eighteen months later and by then the British build-up was able not merely to counter the threat but also to launch a counter-attack. But that is a subject for a later stage in the book.

1915 was a year which set in train many events which were not settled until the end of the war. The campaign in France soon showed that there was no way to a quick and easy victory. The Germans steadily built up their strength in France to 2,000,000 men. The Allies had 1,000,000 men but they were trying to eject the Germans from prepared positions, and as mentioned, that needs at least a three to one superiority. Not least of the handicaps suffered by the soldiers fighting in France was that there was no coordinated supreme command. Sir John French, an amiable man but totally unsuitable for his vast task, was Commander in Chief of the BEF. The French were commanded by Joffre, who believed that victory could by won quickly by fierce attacks on the Germans. It was a delusion which would spell doom for many Frenchmen. Sir John French also believed in a vigorous attacking policy, even though he had insufficient munitions to back it. (As the winter of 1915 went by, it became absolutely clear that there would be no more morale-raising reports from the Eastern Front.) In hindsight it is easy to see the folly of massed infantry attack on prepared positions. But what, even in hindsight, was the alternative? The 2,000,000 Germans in France had every intention of staying there, and extending their area of occupation. There was no flank to be turned: there was no obvious means of breaking through. The fact that war requires the killing of people by every possible means, and therefore is horrific to civilised people, has created the delusion that there must be a better and easier means of achieving an objective than by wholesale slaughter. Experience, alas, shows that there is not. Because the Second World War had less obvious bloodbaths than the First, there has grown up the idea that it was relatively humane and painless. It is an illusion. Many more people were killed in the Second World War than the First, and huge numbers of them were civilians. Defeating the Germans and Japanese meant bombing their cities; equally Germany tried to defeat Britain by bombing and rocket attacks. Infantry played a full part in the Second World War too – in North Africa, Italy, North-West Europe, Burma and the Pacific islands, and most particularly in Russia. Even so, the casualties of the First World War have a particular horror because the path from being a civilian in Britain to becoming a front-line soldier in France, and a dead one at that, could be a matter of weeks or months. On both sides the Western Front resembled animals being driven into a crowded slaughterhouse. However, facts must be seen in proportion. The number of junior officers killed in the First World War (in which their expectation of life was roughly three weeks after arriving in France) was matched by the number of deaths among aircrew flying in Bomber Command between 1939 and 1945.

Although the 'home front', as it came to be known, was not as badly affected in the First World War as the Second, it did not remain completely unscathed. We have already seen the effect of the German bombardment of the North Sea ports. Far more menacing, however, were the Zeppelins. Today, Zeppelins appear almost comical with their vast size, unwarlike appearance and almost romantic history. But to the people of Britain in 1915 they were symbols of terror. What made them so particularly menacing was that there seemed to be no answer to them. In 1915, the future, in which there would presumably be more and more of them, was terrible to contemplate.

The original Zeppelin flight had been made in 1900 – on the German side of Lake Constance – it had lasted twenty minutes. The inventor, Fer-

dinand von Zeppelin, was a German army officer who had observed teth-
ered balloons used for observation in the American Civil War, and decided
they could be made more mobile. Later flights were a mixture of success and
failure; not least of his problems was persuading his compatriots that this
was a valuable instrument of war. The Zeppelins were lifted by hydrogen,
and when the motor fuel was used up at the end of a voyage, they were liable
to move skywards rather than come to earth and stay on it. Hydrogen did
not burn unless it was mixed with oxygen: it was therefore possible for an
artillery shell to pass right through a Zeppelin, destroying hydrogen gas cells
but not setting them alight. However, helium, which was non-flammable
even when mixed with oxygen, was soon substituted for hydrogen.

The first Zeppelin raid on England took place on 19 January 1915. One
of the three which set out had to turn back; the other two reached their
target, which was Yarmouth, and dropped a mixture of 110 pound bombs
and incendiaries. Four people were killed, sixteen injured, and some property was damaged; the effects were trivial but the portents were ominous.
Later raids killed more people and did extensive damage, particularly in
the north of England. British towns which were alerted that they were on
the path of approaching airships turned out their lights (the first black-
outs), but the Zeppelins usually located them by following roads and
rivers. When over the target the Zeppelin crews often dropped flares.
Britain responded by using searchlights and artillery fire, but most of the
time the Zeppelins flew above the range of either. A more effective
defence, a brainchild of Winston Churchill, then First Lord of the Admiralty, was to raid the Zeppelin bases and construction sites with ordinary
aircraft. However, this was insufficient to stop London being raided in
May 1915, and a really devastating blow being delivered on the capital in
the following September. By October 1915 there had been 22 raids on
Britain and although the casualties and damage were light by comparison
with the war theatres elsewhere, they were in the very heart of England and
there appeared to be no answer to them. With their proved success, Britain
realised that the future might be very much worse.

Apart from the effect that unstoppable raids would have on the national
morale, prompting criticisms that money and resources were being lavished
on distant fronts while nothing was being done to safeguard vital interests at
home, there was the possibility that in the not so distant future Zeppelins
could drop gas bombs − an appalling prospect. Although it was not apparent to the general public, considerable resources in the way of artillery and
searchlight crews were already being applied to counter the Zeppelin men-

ace and more would need to be diverted in the near future. It was not a happy thought in the light of the heavy losses sustained by ourselves and our allies in France, the threat of submarine warfare, the setbacks at Gallipoli and the gloomy news from the Eastern Front and the Balkans.

That the Germans were prepared to stop at nothing was shown when a German submarine torpedoed the British liner *Lusitania*. In fact, this was counter-productive, for among the 1,195 who went down with her were 128 Americans. Up till this point the USA had taken a detached view of the war, being prepared to sell to both sides, though irritated by the British assumption that they had a right to search neutral ships. However, the fact that Germany presumably had no compunction about killing neutral American citizens as well as innocent women and children was a final step to making America realise that this was a war against ruthless aggression in which she might sooner or later have to take part.

To the British, subject to their attacks, Zeppelins seemed invulnerable. However, for those manning them it was a very different picture. Zeppelins were particularly prone to mechanical breakdowns, to being driven off course or damaged by the vagaries of the weather. Sometimes, to avoid losing height, everything on board had been dropped out: there would clearly be a time when members of the crew would need to volunteer to follow — without parachutes. Landing a Zeppelin intact on British soil must be avoided at all costs, as this would betray vital secrets; damaged Zeppelins therefore flew out over the North Sea only too well aware that their chances of reaching home were slight.

Although there had been attacks on London, German policy was to avoid attacking cities unless they were centres of war production. This was because the German High Command realised that their cities were even more vulnerable than British cities and that the inevitable retaliation would hurt them more than they liked to contemplate.

The tide did not begin to turn till 1916. Nine Zeppelins raided the Midlands on one day and did considerable damage but one fell into the sea on the return trip, all the crew being drowned. 1 April saw another raid on London with three airships, but one was shot down by anti-aircraft fire.

However, there were still influential people in Germany who believed that the war might be won by Zeppelins alone. The year 1916 saw the launch of the super Zeppelins. They weighed 35 tons, were 650 feet long and 80 feet high, and could carry five tons of bombs. With all their bombs on board they could reach 13,000 feet, after release they could go much higher, putting them well out of reach of fighter aircraft. To deal with attacking aircraft at lower levels, they carried ten machine guns. At best they travelled at 65mph.

However, like many other war-winning weapons, the new Zeppelins failed to meet their builders' high expectations. In April 1916 five out of thirteen in a mass raid failed to battle their way through headwinds while trying to cross the North Sea: of those remaining, six failed to reach their specified targets, but had to bomb others of lesser importance. Worse was to come. In September a Zeppelin was shot down by a pilot in the Royal Flying Corps, William Leefe Robinson: he was awarded a VC.

Normally a VC requires three independent witnesses and must involve a 90–100% chance of death. Certainly, Robinson had a narrow escape when the burning airship nearly came down on top of him, but witnesses were unnecessary when the wreckage hit the ground.

Robinson himself was shot down soon afterwards over enemy territory and made a prisoner of war in Germany. He made numerous unsuccessful attempts to escape. Soon after his release in 1918 he contracted Spanish 'flu and died within a week.

Surprisingly, the shooting down of one Zeppelin was taken by the Germans to signify that the reign of the airship as an instrument of terror was over. The German army decided that the men and resources used on Zeppelins would be better spent on the troops in France, although it conceded that Zeppelins had a role to play in observation and supply. This was a severe blow to Peter Strasser, an ex-naval gunnery expert, who had been the driving force behind the Zeppelin project during the war, but he did not lose heart although everyone around him seemed to have done so. He was well aware that as long as Zeppelins could cruise in the skies above Britain, even if they dropped no bombs, they would have the effect of keeping British airmen and artillery in Britain instead of being sent to France, where they would be of great value to the Allied forces. The French were particularly critical of the number of men tied up in Britain to counter the Zeppelin threat. Had they known the full figure, they would probably have been even more irate. The British anti-aircraft defences alone employed 17,341 officers and men; in addition there were twelve squadrons of the Royal Flying Corps, employing 110 aircraft, 200 officers and 2000 men. The French did not need a specific anti-Zeppelin defence because, although Paris and other cities were occasionally bombed, the Zeppelins could only reach them by flying over the aircraft and artillery already deployed in France.

Strasser believed that the best way to silence his German critics was to build bigger and better aircraft and to achieve more impressive results. Soon he was able to display an even larger Zeppelin which would fly at 20,000 feet, although this meant that the crew had to use oxygen at that height and oxygen involved heavy containers which would take up badly needed bomb space. However, on 16 June 1917 one of the most advanced types of Zeppelin was shot down when it had ventured down to 13,000 feet in order to make the return trip. Above that height, cold, icing, and imperfect combustion of fuel, as well as frostbite and altitude sickness, leading to loss of consciousness, were hazards which should only be risked in extreme emergencies.

However, the Zeppelin was given a respite from an unexpected source. In 1917, the Germans, in desperation, had resorted to unrestricted submarine warfare. Zeppelins provided a useful source of observation, not merely to locate British convoys but also to note the position of destroyers and other Royal Navy anti-submarine craft. This use disappeared rapidly when a Zeppelin was shot down by a Sopwith Pup launched from a destroyer. The Zeppelin was taken completely by surprise for, cruising at 8,000 feet, it assumed it was well out of reach of enemy ground guns. Indeed it was, but not of those in aircraft.

However, Strasser did not lose faith. The main enemy of the Zeppelin now was the German Gotha bomber which, though less powerful and menacing than Zeppelins, was infinitely cheaper and more mobile.

On 19 October 1917, eleven Zeppelins, of which six were brand new models, all 644 feet long and 92 feet high and each carrying three tons of bombs, set off for Britain. With luck they would fly higher than any artillery fire or fighter could reach them. In their crews were brave and experienced men, some of whom had seen other Zeppelins shot down in previous raids. But only seven returned to Germany after a successful raid in which many important targets had been hit. Four were driven over France by bad weather and shot down by anti-aircraft fire. Unaware of their true position, they were cruising at 8,000 feet in the belief they were over Germany.

Strasser still did not lose heart, although he could well have done so. Five Zeppelins were destroyed when a hangar caught fire in January 1918. His response was to lead a successful raid in March, doing much damage in the Midlands and even reaching Liverpool. Flying at 20,000 feet they were above the range of the defences and were now much better protected against the altitude and weather. This raid coincided with the great German offensive in France and it now looked as if Germany was at last winning this gruelling war. Even when their armies were brought to a halt in France the following June, the situation still looked promising.

In August the biggest Zeppelin ever built took to the air with its crew knowing that it had the range to bomb the east coast of America. Strasser insisted on being on board. It was shot down near Yarmouth at 16,000 feet. Strasser died with it.

Most people have heard the word Zeppelin, even if they do not know it was named after its inventor, Graf von Zeppelin. Strasser, who perfected the design and thus caused the Allies infinite damage in diverted resources, damaged factories, disrupted production, and disturbed morale, is unknown except to a narrow range of specialists.

Terrifying and sinister though Zeppelins were to their unfortunate victims, there was something almost comical about these huge edifices carrying such a tiny load in proportion to their size. The courage and skill of those chosen to fly in them is reflected by the extraordinary adventure of a navigator whose gondola, suspended on long wires below the Zeppelin (so that he could observe targets from below clouds through which the Zeppelin might be passing) was cast off as it brushed the ground. The manoeuvre was done purposely in order to enable the Zeppelin to gain more height. The navigator's escape was not witnessed and subsequently he wandered through the British countryside for two months. He was captured by a coastal patrol eventually and was interned; he seems lucky not to have been shot as a spy.

CHAPTER 5

1915 – 1916

In following the developments in the Middle East, and then tracing the history of Zeppelins, we have moved some way ahead of the scene in France and the grim realities of prolonged trench warfare. The year 1915 was proving costly and frustrating for the Allies, with the failure of both French and British to push the German lines back or to make a breakthrough. Casualties were mounting steadily: by the end of the year they would total 2,000,000.

The British Army had never fully recovered from the magnificent effort of 1914 when the 'Old Contemptibles', the regular army, had withstood the full force of the German army, but lost the bulk of its trained men in the process. The first months of 1915 had seen the same regiments rebuilt with volunteers and territorials. They fought with great gallantry and determination, but in the process lost many of their senior officers and NCOs whose professionalism and knowledge were so badly needed.

Trench warfare was a new experience for both sides and both took some time to adapt to it. Although the front line trenches were now adequate for their purpose, the communication trenches were much less so. It is, perhaps, not surprising that a trench line nearly 400 miles long and several miles deep in an area where the existing maps were totally inadequate should have led to some bizarre situations in which artillerymen were quite likely to shell their own troops and commanding officers could never be quite certain where their own troops were in a fluctuating battle. Even if the Royal Flying Corps or observation balloons could locate enemy positions, they could not easily communicate their information to the infantry. Sometimes the reward for a sustained, courageous and successful infantry attack was to be left in an isolated position without food or water because communication had broken down, and no one else knew where the unit was.

In this war of attrition the Germans held certain advantages. Although the Schlieffen Plan had failed, they had still managed to occupy a huge portion of French territory, including many vital strategic points from which they could launch further offensives. All they had to do was to consolidate their defensive positions and let the Allies exhaust themselves in futile attacks. However, strategically they would have been wiser to retreat, shorten their lines and use the troops thus released to finish the war on the Eastern Front. By the time they realised that fact it was too late. And their efforts to make a breakthrough with their new terror weapon, gas, had been a failure.

Elsewhere the situation looked good for Germany. The Eastern Front was satisfactory and the Turks were proving extremely capable allies, far ahead of expectations. Not only were they fighting with skill and courage in the Dardanelles, they were also apparently well able to take care of Mesopotamia and Palestine, much to the embarrassment of the British. Submarine warfare was also proving highly successful.

On the other hand Italy, the long-standing member of the Triple Alliance, had defected to the Allies. On 23 May 1915 she had declared war on Austria and in August 1916 followed suit against Germany. She was to pay dearly for it. Her attempt to eliminate the Austrian army in Trentino and then invade the Austro-Hungarian plain led to the lengthy battle of the Isonzo (June to November, with breaks in between) which was a failure, resulting only in huge losses on both sides, possibly 160,000 each. It is always difficult to make an accurate count of casualties in large-scale war, for many of the wounded or missing may turn out to be killed or lost, while some of the missing may not be. The Germans did not record their losses methodically; the Russians took even less trouble.

At sea, honours were even between Austria and Italy. Italy had the heavier losses but the Austrians were limited to the Adriatic and were not particularly effective there.

Whether surface fleets would have a valid rôle was yet to be decided. They had certainly settled some important matters in the opening months of the war but whether there would be future battles between great navies remained to be seen. After the frenzy of the pre-war competition in capital ship building, the general public expected something spectacular, but the naval experts took a more cautious approach, the early battles in the southern hemisphere were not to be taken as a precedent. It was beginning to look as if naval warfare would be between submarines and destroyers, rather than battleship versus battleship. 1 January 1915 had sent a shiver down the back of the Admiralty when the *Formidable*, a battleship, was sunk by a submarine in the English Channel. However, later in the month (24th) there had been a surface action when a German squadron of battlecruisers, under the command of Admiral Hipper, met a British squadron under Admiral Beatty. The Germans, with four battlecruisers, were outclassed by Beatty's five.

Both squadrons had screening craft, consisting of light cruisers and destroyers, for it was the characteristic of large ships that they were vulnerable to submarines and torpedo-carrying craft, even though their own heavy armament could blast lesser ships out of the water if they could hit them. Knowing he was outnumbered, Hipper promptly decided to run back to Heligoland. Beatty's craft, which led the pursuit, was heavily damaged but two of the German battleships, *Blücher* and *Seydlitz*, were sunk. This was the Battle of the Dogger Bank.

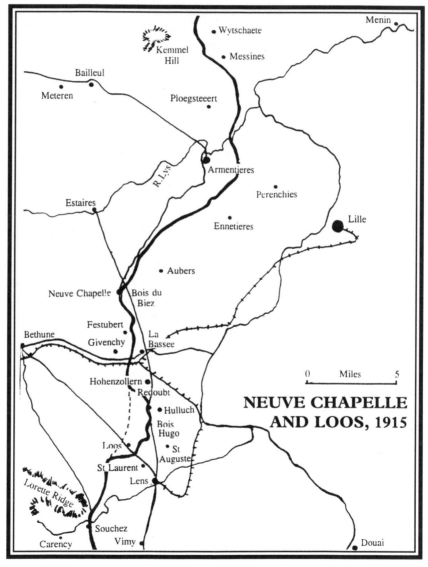

**NEUVE CHAPELLE
AND LOOS, 1915**

As mentioned earlier, the *Lusitania* was sunk in February 1915 but although this made Germany unpopular, it did not slow down the aggression or successes of the U boats. But submarine warfare was by no means one-sided: British submarines had many successes against German craft close to Germany.

Although previous attempts to batter a way through the German lines in France had been costly and unsuccessful, the Allied High Command decided on a joint Anglo-French offensive, to be launched in September while the weather might still allow for the exploitation of the anticipated gains. The attack was to be centred on Loos (pronounced 'Loss' by the French). The ensuing battle, although never ranked with the great struggles on the Somme or Passchendaele or Verdun, was nevertheless one of the most important in the war and one which could have shortened it by some three years if the Allied breakthrough had been successful, as it nearly was.

Loos is a mining village near Lens and in consequence was congested with dumps and pithead machinery. However, in order to reach it, attacking infantry would have to cross open ground and negotiate barbed wire, where they would be an easy target for enemy machine-gunners. Major General Richard Hilton, who at the time was a Forward Observation officer, subsequently wrote:

'A great deal of nonsense has been written about Loos. The real tragedy of that battle was its nearness to complete success. Most of us who reached the crest of Hill 70 and survived were firmly convinced we had broken through on that Sunday, 25th September, 1915. There seemed to be nothing ahead of us but an unoccupied and incomplete trench system. The only two things that prevented our advancing into the suburbs of Lens were, firstly the exhaustion of the Jocks (for they had undergone a bellyful of marching and fighting that day) and secondly the flanking fire of numerous German machine-guns which swept that bare hill from some factory buildings in Cité St Auguste [a suburb of Lens] to the south of us.

'All that we needed was more artillery ammunition to blast those clearly located machine-guns, and some fresh infantry to take over from the weary and depleted Jocks. But, alas, neither ammunition nor reinforcements were immediately available, and the great opportunity passed.'

Of course, even if there had been a breakthrough at Loos the opportunity could have been frittered away by an inadequate follow-up. But at that stage the war could still have been won by a strong thrust which could have developed into an Allied advance into Germany, or at least it could have created a situation of such peril to the German armies in France that they would have been pleased to make peace and withdraw before their position became too catastrophic.

The difference to the world if the war had ended in 1915 stuns imagination. Millions of valuable lives would have been saved; America would never have come into the war at all; Russia might never have had its revolution. The break-up of the Austro-Hungarian Empire and the Turkish empire would have been delayed and eventually, no doubt, taken a different form. By the time the Peacemakers began to draft their treaties in 1919 the world was totally different: natural aspirations had been encouraged so much that, after independence, parts of the former empires developed imperial ambitions of their own, and became repressive to their minority groups. Germany was sinking to the depths of the economic despair which produced the conditions for Hitler and his fascist supporters to seize power. There was, indeed, much at stake at Loos, although no one realised how much at the time.

The Loos battle was part of a wider offensive, with the French simultaneously driving towards Vimy Ridge, and, once more, at Champagne. In the event, the French push towards Vimy lasted a mere five days before Joffre cancelled it without informing his British colleagues of his intention. Champagne was on an altogether more ambitious scale. Casualties were in fact much heavier than at Loos, for the Germans lost 100,000 and the French half as many again. The gains by the French were negligible.

Although the British were almost successful at Loos, they were not originally in favour of an offensive in this area, preferring the Ypres sector. However, Joffre, now Commander in Chief of the French armies on the Western Front, and still living on his fame as the victor of Marne, managed to persuade the British High Command that this was the time and place for the decisive blow. In retrospect his optimism seems wildly unrealistic, for he named a cavalry objective *fifty miles east* of Loos once the German line had been broken.

Surprisingly, Joffre found a supporter in Kitchener, normally a man of extreme caution. But it is possible that Kitchener felt that some dramatic action must now be taken to take the pressure off the Russians and divert public attention from the disasters in the Dardanelles.

The tactics for nearly all infantry attacks throughout the war was a massive preliminary bombardment which was meant to intimidate the defenders and to cut all the wire which had been staked out to screen their positions. But the British were too short of shells and guns for that to be effective, even before experience showed that preliminary bombardments were rarely successful in cutting an adequate path through wire. With shell production as stated 22,000 a day, compared with 100,000 in France and 250,000 in Germany, it was only too obvious that this was not Britain's strong suit. Furthermore, the French had 117 guns per mile, the British 60. The British had in fact taken over the Loos sector from France the month before, with Joffre's assurance that it was ideal for infantry attack. This was not the way Haig and Rawlinson saw it, the latter commenting: 'My new front at Loos is as flat as the palm of my hand. Hardly any cover anywhere. Very difficult to attack. It will cost us dearly and we shall not get far.'

In fact, the approach to Loos is not quite flat for the village lies in a slight depression with long, gentle slopes coming from it, except in the east where there is a low hill which was named Hill 70. Approaching Hill 70 on the modern road, one hardly recognises it as a hill at all, but in the war the slight rise in the ground made it an important tactical point. Another notorious feature, Hill 60, in the Ypres area, was merely a heap made of the spoil from a railway cutting, and Passchendaele itself is merely a low ridge.

General Sir Douglas Haig was Commander in Chief of First Army, which would fight the battle of Loos, and he was by no means in favour of it. This was hardly surprising, for all the advantages lay with the Germans, who held the higher ground and had also had ample time to site their guns and wire the area, efficiently. However, Joffre was very keen to have a short, successful campaign before the winter set in and Kitchener, in addition to other reasons, felt it was necessary to demonstrate allied solidarity by supporting him. Sir John French, the Commander in Chief of the British Expeditionary Force, had memories of the way he had risen to fame by a successful cavalry dash in the Boer War and felt that a similar dash might be rewarded here. In the event, this battle would demonstrate Sir John French's deficiencies as a commander in chief.

Haig's objections to sending infantry into such well-defended positions were overcome by the decision to use gas as a preliminary to the attack. When the Germans had used gas at Ypres six months earlier, they had broken the convention of civilised behaviour in wartime, so now they should have a taste of their own medicine, it was reasoned. It may seem surprising that in war, the object of which is to kill so many of the enemy that they are forced to surrender that there should actually be a code of behaviour in doing so. In fact this 'code' had evolved over many centuries. In earlier wars, although civilians or prisoners had often been massacred in the most ruthless manner, knights had frequently been spared on account of the ransom they might command as prisoners. Medieval chivalry had elaborated upon this and drawn up a code of conduct by which members of the aristocracy should only be killed by their social equals. The development of the long-bow and crossbow, which kill from a distance without regard to the social status of their targets was therefore unpopular with the military aristocracy. However, over the years it had gradually become accepted that massacring the wounded or prisoners, the deliberate burning of towns, and the use of 'unfair' tactics, such as poisoning wells, should be outlawed by mutual agreement. However, if one combatant used an 'illegal' weapon, such as gas, the way was open for retaliation. Gas was used extensively by both sides in the later stages of the First World War but still regarded with distaste by the combatants, as being an 'unclean' weapon. (In the Second World War the major combatants all had stocks of gas but refrained from using it because the effects of retaliation were unpredictable.)

One of the reasons why local commanders are reluctant to use gas on the battlefield is that its effects may be unexpected: in fact that is what happened at Loos. Chlorine gas had been brought up to the front line in heavy cylinders. At ten minutes to six in the morning the taps were turned on and, using the prevailing wind, the gas was projected forward. Wind of the right speed and direction was vital or the gas would either hang around in the releasers' trenches or, worse still, drift backwards. At Loos it drifted forward on the right, but drifted backwards on the left. This was the disastrous culmination to the tremendous labour of carrying up 5,500 heavy gas cylinders, a task involving 8,000 men as porters. Where it drifted back it gassed many of the British troops, while those who were ahead of it were, in any case, mostly mown down by German machine-guns. The effects of gas were not limited to the human lungs or skin: it also rusted rifles and artillery breech blocks immediately, making them unusable.

The infantry which advanced towards the German lines carried a heavy burden of equipment. Riflemen carried two hundred rounds of rifle ammunition, three sandbags, and a basic food ration. Some would also be carrying picks, shovels, wire cutters and grenades. All had a primitive cloth gas mask with talc eye pieces which quickly misted up. Most of them were territorials who made up for in dash what they lacked in fighting experience. One unit, the 8th Battalion of the London Irish Regiment, kicked a Rugby football ahead of them as they went over the top. In the opening attack, several regiments were almost completely slaughtered. By astonishing courage and determination, some soldiers reached the German wire, only to find that it was too strong for their wirecutters to cut. (In theory, hardly any wire should have been left after the preliminary bombardment.) By the end of the first 24 hours there were 25,000 casualties.

Even so, there had been substantial gains. The Germans had been surprised first by the gas and then by the ferocity of the attack, which seemed to come forward however many men fell. This was the moment, when blood had been shed, and the German line had crumbled, that the reserves should have been brought into the attack. But this, sadly, was how Loos came to be branded 'failure'. The reserve consisted of XI Corps, a formation which had only been in France for a fortnight. Haig had wanted to have them brought up close to the front line and used to make the final breakthrough. French, and French was the Commander in Chief, felt they should be held well back until the results of the first day's fighting were known. French's view may have been guided less by humanitarian consideration than by the feeling that if inexperienced units made a breakthrough they would be so difficult to control that the Germans might see the opportunity of a counter-attack and the last state would be worse than the first. However, in fairness to French, it must be said that he was essentially a kindly man and he spent some time in the dressing station with the wounded. Whether a CinC should be in a hospital with the wounded when a major battle is raging around him is, of course, open to question.

Haig thought that French was totally mistaken in holding back the reserve division, which he felt was essential to the success of the attack.

At this time XI Corps consisted of two divisions, 21st and 24th, and a Guards Division. There were two other divisions in the Corps, 12th and 46th, but they would not come into the line till much later. The experiences of 21st and 24th Divisions were bizarre and horrifying. The commander of XI Corps was Lieutenant General R. C. B. Haking, an officer who had distinguished himself at the Staff College, Camberley but considerably less so in the battles earlier in the year, notably at Aubers Ridge where he had incurred heavy losses through recklessness. On the night before the Loos battle began, 21st and 24th Divisions were ordered to make their way forward. In order to hasten their progress Haking issued an order that they should not take their cookers with them. Instead they were told to take their packs and greatcoats and were given some extra bread and cheese and cold pea soup. Most of the time on their march it was raining and, as they had already been marching in the dark, and would continue to do so (on grounds of secrecy!), they were short of sleep and hungry and thirsty. Why they had been kept short of drinking water on the approach march has never been explained.

Chaos was inevitable. In rain and dark 40,000 men moved up to an area from which a stream of traffic was coming down. The latter consisted of ambulances, walking wounded, vehicles returning for supplies, and so on. The roads were narrow and confusing in the dark; at intervals they were crossed by railway lines which were being heavily used. But, in spite of the rain, the dark, the confusion, and the lack of accurate maps, most units managed to find their way to their allotted areas. There, cold, hungry and wet, they tried to hack trenches out of the rock-like chalk. Sometimes they were shelled by British guns because the gunners were unaware that the Germans had been driven out of these positions. Meanwhile the Germans had relieved many of their own front-line troops with fresh ones who had busied themselves all night fortifying their new positions, mostly with an entanglement of thick wire four feet high and twenty feet deep. It was a daunting situation but morale among these sorely tried Kitchener divisions was high and they went into the attack with astonishing courage and vigour. Inevitably, they were all scythed to a stop but before that happened they had gained ground. The cost in lives was appalling: the commanding officer of the Buffs was 61 years old; when he was killed twelve other officers died with him. (The youngest soldier on the Loos battlefield was fourteen: he survived the war.) Had these stout-hearted troops been available earlier, and been brought up sooner in less exhausting circumstances, their courage would not have been wasted.

At the moment they were being launched into the attack, Joffre called off the French offensive on Vimy Ridge on the grounds that the French artillery had failed to neutralise the German guns there. Even worse, for reasons which seem inexplicable, he gave strict instructions that no word of this cancellation must reach the ears of his British allies. Needless to say it did, though not till evening. They then realised that instead of having to resist a counter-attack by the Germans facing their own sector, they would also have to face reinforcements drawn from the Vimy sector, which the French were no longer threatening. They had already lost 8,000 men in what must have been one of the most remarkable feats of courage and endurance in military history.

It was becoming apparent that the fighting performance of British troops was better than anyone could have anticipated. Men with the minimum of training, and with poor equipment, were facing better-equipped, better-trained, German troops well-positioned in excellent defensive positions, and defeating them. The cost in lives was appalling, of course, but the Germans were becoming uneasily aware that they were confronting an army which would continue till victory was won or die in the process.

In spite of the 25,000 casualties in the first twenty-four hours, further attempts were made to press forward. But, as we saw, it was too late. The

Germans were particularly good at rushing up reserves and plugging gaps, if given the time. At Loos they had been given that time. During October they went on the offensive themselves and even recaptured lost ground. But it was obvious that there would now be stalemate in this sector. Haig thought it might be possible to launch another offensive, better planned, in early November, but the combination of heavy rain and accurate German shelling convinced him it would be useless. At the end of the battle of Loos the British casualty list was 60,000. It was, of course, small in relation to later battles and to the gains which might have been made. Gallipoli had cost 250,000 and ended in total failure; there were 300,000 men isolated in Salonika, also to no avail.

Among the criticisms of First World War generals was that they were too far removed from the front line to know what was happening in the places where the troops were dying; this was certainly not true at Loos, for three generals were actually killed in the battle. In a different sense it marked the end for Sir John French, for his handling of the battle was considered so inept that his continuation as CinC could not be tolerated. He was replaced by Haig the following December. Although French had not been a success in his exalted position, it should be remembered that he was over 60 when he took it over and he had always been hampered by shortage of artillery and ammunition. French tended to blame Kitchener and Haig for his dismissal, but in fact he would have been wiser to turn his eyes on to Joffre whose failure to press on with the Vimy attack, but treacherously let the British assume he was still doing so, made the position of the British much less tenable. French could have wondered why Joffre was so keen to fight this battle in the first place, if he was going to be so ineffective when it had hardly begun. Joffre, no doubt, saw it differently. Having decided that his own offensive was impossible, he decided not to tell his British allies as this would undoubtedly have discouraged them from pressing ahead, and perhaps breaking through.

Many of the survivors subsequently wrote vivid accounts of their traumatic experiences. C. J. T. Johnson recalled that:

'Bayonets were fixed at 6.30 a.m. [forty minutes after the release of the gas] and the first wave of the assaulting troops of the First Army scrambled out of their trenches in the fog of gas and smoke, barely able to distinguish a thing, loaded up with bombs, picks and shovels, extra ammunition, etc. Some had their gas masks down as gas was still hanging around in places. When the front was down and tucked into their tunics they could not see anything through their talc covered eyepieces and with the front rolled up the rain caused the chemicals in the flannel to seep out and make the eyes smart.

'As they scaled the parapet several appeared to slip back into the trench again, but on looking more closely it was seen that these men's masks had a rent in them and the grey flannel was turning red. The advancing men had now disappeared into the swirling mass of smoke and gas into which shells were now bursting, throwing up clods of earth and some of the men with it. The ground was strewn with dead and the movements of the wounded. Hands lifted among those still alive who were lying and crawling in the grasses, their tunics all torn. Some shouted for help and water.'

There was, of course, no stopping for the wounded, not even your brother or your best friend. Your job was to press on and win the battle. Stopping to help the wounded was a court-martial offence. The Germans could scarcely believe what they saw. A regimental diary ran:

'Ten columns in extended line in perfect alignment could clearly be distinguished, each one at more than a thousand men, and offering such a target as had never been seen before, or even thought possible. Never had the machine-gunners such straightforward work to do nor done it so effectively. They traversed to and fro along the enemy's ranks unceasingly.

'Our men stood on the fire steps, some even on the parapets and fired in glee into the mass of men advancing across the open ground. As the entire field of fire was covered with the enemy's infantry the effect was devastating and they could be seen falling literally in hundreds.'

Of course, if the gas had worked properly the German machine-gunners would have been dead or have fled from the scene. As it was, the lines of British infantry advanced over open ground much as their ancestors had done at Blenheim, Salamanca, the Alma and a dozen other battlefields. But though French and Haig had both been in the South African War of 1899–1902 and had learnt that well-concealed defences can inflict horrifying casualties on the attackers, the lesson appeared to have been forgotten. Meanwhile, the British infantry in this and other First World War battles reasoned that by their sacrifices and disregard for casualties they would eventually overwhelm the defence.

J. C. Moir wrote the following letter (now in the Imperial War Museum):

'My brother was lost at Loos: he was reported missing and no further information was ever received although we learnt he had survived the first terrible day, and was lost early the next morning when some advanced posts were given up.

'My mother in despair wrote to everyone she could find who might be able to give information – but to no avail.

'My brother was a student at Glasgow Technical College, and "joined up" when the appeal was made in September or October 1914. His platoon was composed entirely of University or Technical College students – privates all. Alas, few of them were ever to see Scotland again.

'Few people now understand the high motives and disregard for self-interest that activated these young lads at that terrible time.'

A typical letter home was the following:

'I suppose you've read in the papers by now that we've broken through the German lines and advanced nine miles along the whole British front. We have had some horrid long marches night and day but I've stuck it so far. Our C.O. told us that we intend driving the Germans back now and our efforts would either end the war or go a long way to do so. We were on the march yesterday when the news came through that the first and second line of German trenches had been taken, of course that cheered us up a lot. We are engaged in the biggest battle of the world now, and a day or two will see us in, but cheer up it will soon be over.'

The Germans, of course, had heavy losses too at Loos. Attitudes to the enemy had not yet hardened. German machine-gunners held their fire when watching the lightly wounded pick themselves up and struggle back to their own trenches: later in the war they would not do so. Prisoners on both sides were treated well, even with courtesy. Among those fighting at Loos was the Indian Corps, which had distinguished itself but had heavy losses in the earlier Spring battles. They distinguished themselves at Loos also, but had further losses there too.

In 1992 the grave of Rudyard Kipling's son was discovered at Loos. An officer in the Irish Guards, he had disappeared without trace in the battle. Kipling had searched the battlefield several times after the war, hoping to find the place where he had fallen, but never did. His grave, marked simply as 'An officer of the Irish Guards' was on the edge of the battlefield.

All soldiers carry two identity discs, each giving their name, regiment and religion. If they are killed and their bodies found and identified, they are given a very brief burial service according to their religion, if indeed there is time for any ceremony at all: usually their rifles are stuck in the ground to denote there is a body underneath. One identity disc stays with the body, the other, with any retrievable personal possessions the soldier may be carrying, are then sent home. Inevitably many are killed leaving no trace: thus their names appear in thousands on memorials such as that at Thiepval on the Somme or on the Menin Gate at Ypres.

As 1915 drew to a close there was a sober realisation that although men had died in millions the war was no nearer to ending. It seemed as if it would drag on interminably in a stalemate with Germany, Austria and Turkey reasonably satisfied with their performance and the Allies locked into positions from which the only way out was a war of attrition with massive casualties. There had, however, been positive gains. Italy had come in on the Allies' side by declaring war on Austria-Hungary, and the Americans were becoming steadily more incensed with Germany. The Royal Navy had improved its mine-sweeping technique with the introduction of paravane devices (which looked somewhat like torpedoes). There had been medical advances too that year: the dysentery bacillus had been identified and tetanus was being successfully combated with serum injections. The horrors of tetanus are largely forgotten now, but it was a dreaded disease until comparatively recent times. In July 1915 the Germans in South-West Africa had surrendered to Louis Botha, formerly an opponent in the South African War but now fighting on our side.

11 October, Edith Cavell, an English nurse, was shot by the Germans in Brussels. When the Germans had invaded the country, Nurse Cavell was the matron of the Berkendael Institute (a school for nurses), where she had been for seven years. Here she sheltered British, French and Belgian soldiers who had been trapped by the German occupation but who hoped to escape to neutral Holland. The Germans arrested her and, in spite of protests by the American and Spanish ministers, executed her. Had she been spying the execution might have been justified perhaps, but she had not, and was not even charged with it. Her last words were: 'Patriotism is not enough: I must have no hatred or bitterness for anyone.'

December saw various changes in the military and political hierarchy. Joffre was appointed Commander in Chief of the French forces, Haig replaced Sir John French as CinC in France and Flanders. Willie Robertson, who had risen by merit alone from trooper to general, became Chief of the Imperial General Staff. Churchill, as mentioned, resigned after Gallipoli and went to fight in France. Herbert Asquith, the Liberal Prime Minister, formed a coalition cabinet; in it David Lloyd George became Minister for Munitions. Although Lloyd George disagreed with Haig and Robertson that the most important area of the war was France and Belgium, this did not inhibit him from trying to supply them with the ammunition they required for their strategy. His energy in this new post was dynamic. He brought in assistance from the business world, overrode civil servants, and succeeded in persuading the Trade Unions that they must help the war effort whatever the cost.

At home, the growing casualty lists and sacrifices demanded by the war were producing a mood of gloom among the population which the theatres and music halls did their best to alleviate. One of the most popular wartime songs was written in 1915. It ran:

Pack up your troubles in your old kit bag
And smile, boys, smile.
While you've a Lucifer to light your fag
Smile boys, that's the style.
What's the use of worrying
It never was worth while.
So pack up your troubles in your old kit bag
And smile, smile, smile.

A lucifer was a synonym for a match, a fag was, of course, a cigarette, of which the cheapest version was the 'Woodbine'. The song was probably more popular with civilians and senior officers than the rank and file, who preferred something more cynical, or sentimental such as:

There's a long, long trail a-winding
Into the land of my dreams
Where the nightingales are singing
And a white moon beams...

Nightingales figured prominently in Second World War songs too.

Some methods of keeping cheerful were less innocuous. In order to attract workers into industry, some of it unpleasant, or dangerous – such as shell-making, high wages were being paid. Unfortunately much of this extra money was being spent on drink, leading to lower production and absenteeism. This was particularly noticeable in the shipyards, but they were by no means unique. The drink problem among men became so serious that a 'No Treating' law was introduced. It became an offence to offer another person a drink in a bar: the penalty was a fine of £100 or six months in prison (although it seems unlikely that the latter was ever carried out). To set a good example, King George V announced that he had given up drink for the duration and extended the prohibition to the Royal Household. It was reported that various MPs had followed his example: the announcement was treated with some scepticism. But at least 'No Treating' prevented factory and shipyard workers from spending their time buying rounds of drinks when they should have been making shells for their contemporaries in the trenches.

During 1915 the Government set up a 'Register of Women for War Service'. This was warmly welcomed by suffragettes, who felt it was another step towards women having the vote, and they pointed out that there were already 50,000 employed in this field, not merely in munitions factories but also in arduous outdoor jobs such as bus-driving and coal carrying. Many had come from domestic service, leading to wails of dismay from the better-off, who found that maids were becoming almost impossible to obtain, and far too independent when they were. Although factory employees worked a twelve hour day in a seven day week, they preferred this to over twelve hours a day as maids for half the money.

Taxation was rising rapidly. It hurt particularly when it hit tea and tobacco with a fifty percent increase. Up till 1915 postcards could be sent for a halfpenny: this now doubled. A more popular tax was that on war profits, aimed at 'the hard-faced men who were doing very well out of the war'.

And the Defence of the Realm Act (DORA) now provided one of those useful blanket pieces of legislation which could justify anything from suppressing a newspaper which was publishing information 'detrimental to the national safety', to withholding information about lack of Allied progress.

Rupert Brooke had died on 23 April 1915, on the way to the Dardanelles. Julian Grenfell had died of wounds in France, still preserving his idealism:

The thundering line of battle stands
And in the air death moans and sings
But Day shall clasp him with strong hands
And Night shall fold him in soft wings.

Their deaths marked the end of romantic poetry in this war. Their successors would write in a very different vein.

CHAPTER 6

Deadlock

The year 1916 began with the momentous but realistic decision in Britain that voluntary effort would not be enough to meet the demands of the army in France and that compulsory service must be introduced. The bill for conscription was passed on 6 January: although the majority was large, several ministers resigned in protest (among them the Home Secretary, Sir John Simon), seeing it as an encroachment on individual liberty. There would, of course, be exemptions for certain trades or professions, and conscientious objectors; however, the latter would have to answer some searching questions and would probably be directed to dangerous humanitarian work such as stretcher-bearing on the battlefield. It marked the end of the presentation of white feathers by young women to men whom they thought should be in the armed forces. Sometimes these had been given to soldiers on leave who had put on their civilian clothes as a change from uniform, or even to convalescent wounded. Women were not, of course, conscripted, but were now encouraged to take the place of men, notably in agriculture, and equal pay for equal jobs was introduced.

News from Berlin said that there were food riots in the city: certainly the blockade was having its effect on Germany, though not necessarily more than the warfare by U boats on Britain. Food rationing had been introduced in Germany the previous month.

Although the upper middle classes had cheerfully sent their sons off to the war, they were more reluctant to give up the standard of living to which they felt they were entitled. There had already been frequent advertisements asking the well off to dispense with a manservant (or two) so that he could join the Army: now there would be no need for that sort of appeal but instead they were asked to restrain their personal spending. As taxation had risen so much, and so many appeals had been made by the government for War Loan, and the import of spirits, cars, and pianos had been stopped, many families felt they were doing enough. However, the war had only been going for eighteen months: by the time it had been grinding along for four years, realism would have penetrated to every corner of British society.

April 1916 was a black month. On the 29th, Kut surrendered, but public interest was distracted by the 'Dublin Rising' which had begun four days earlier. Rebel forces had staged an uprising, in which British sentries had been shot at Dublin Castle, certain buildings had been set alight, and the Post Office in Sackville Street had been seized and made the headquarters of the newly-proclaimed 'Irish Republic'. British troops were sent to recover the building and the first days fighting saw eleven people killed and seventeen injured. The Easter Rising was partly organised by Sir Roger Casement, an Ulster Protestant who had entered British government service in the nineteenth century and become British Consul in Mozambique, Angola, the Congo Free State and Brazil. His report on atrocities carried out by white traders in Peru and Belgian rule in the Congo had become internationally famous and brought him a knighthood. However when in 1912 he showed sympathy with Catholic Irish nationalism, he began to alarm the British. In 1913 he went further and organised an anti-British force called the Irish National Volunteers, and in 1914, *after* the outbreak of war, he went to Berlin to try to enlist German officers to serve the Irish national cause. (At this time there was no independent Irish Republic, and until 1921 all Ireland was part of Great Britain.) Unfortunately for Casement's plans, the Germans thought that an expedition to Ireland held scant chance of success and refused to join or help, and his efforts to recruit from Irish prisoners of war in Germany was also a failure. In 1916 he decided that the planned revolt was doomed to failure and went back to Ireland in a German submarine to try to prevent it happening. He was soon discovered and was arrested on 29 April. He was convicted of treason and hanged on 29 June, in spite of the efforts of many powerful Englishmen to have the sentence set aside in view of his past services to the British Crown.

Meanwhile, of course, Irish regiments and Irishmen serving in English regiments were fighting with the utmost dedication with the British Army. Similarly thousands of Irishmen volunteered to fight in the Second World War, even though as citizens of Eire – the Irish Republic – they were not supposed to be doing so.

However, in the early months of 1916 Allied attention was mostly concentrated on Verdun. This strategically placed town had originally been a massive fortress but during 1914 and 1915 had been neglected by the French on the basis that if the Belgian forts had fallen to the German artillery so easily at the beginning of the war it was pointless relying on massive strongpoints: instead the area should be protected by mines and guns and bunkers, on the line of trench defences. Even when French intelligence learnt of heavy German troop concentrations near Verdun, they tended to regard them as a bluff to conceal an impending attack elsewhere on the front. Joffre, in fact, was so occupied with his own plans for a further offensive in the Champagne area that he was taken by surprise when the Germans launched a massive bombardment on Verdun on 21 February. The German Commander in Chief was now Falkenhayn and he believed that if the bombardment was heavy enough the German infantry would be able to walk right through the French lines. In fact, that was what the Germans did two years later, when the Allies thought they were winning the war comfortably.

The assault on Verdun was to become an epic in the chronicles of warfare. The Germans pounded the defence with heavy siege mortars and other powerful guns: they even introduced a new horror weapon, the flame-thrower, which would burn defending troops to death in their bunkers, and they hurled in infantry attack after infantry attack. But the French fought back. In eight days the Germans advanced four miles. Joffre then ordered that there would be no further retreats, tactical or otherwise. He rushed up reinforcements and appointed a general named Pétain to command the area. Ironically, this man who defended Verdun heroically during the First World War became the detested collaborator of the Second, and was imprisoned for treachery: he was lucky to escape execution, the fate handed out to some of his fellow collaborators. But in 1916 that was all far away in the unbelievable future.

Verdun was more than an ordinary battle, horrific though ordinary battles are. Pétain inspired his countrymen to fight back with an intensity which stunned the Germans. After the initial surprise the French organised their supplies to the vital sector and pounded the German positions day and night. In March the Germans launched another desperate attack, this time more to the west. But the French held. The ground and the forts were smashed to nauseating rubble, stinking with the bodies of men and horses which no one could bury. The battle which had begun in snow and rain continued through the brighter weather but it made no difference to this landscape of death and destruction.

In this battle of attrition the side which could best maintain its supplies was likely to be the ultimate winner. The Germans, of course, had the more extended lines of communication but had been preparing longer. They had built a good road system and fourteen railway lines. In stark contrast, the French had one narrow gauge railway, and one key road which appropriately became known as 'The Sacred Way' (La Voie Sacrée). It was 75 miles long and each week it carried 50,000 tons of munitions and 90,000 men forward. Traffic never stopped day or night – in spite of shelling, weather, and breakdowns. Any vehicle which was unable to continue for any reason was simply pushed off the road and abandoned. By June both sides realised that this battle had now reached a dimension which was beyond previous experience: both wished to stop but neither felt it could or should do so, having come so far. The situation was worse for the French for strategically this was a key point: on the other hand, there is a limit to human endurance. The

THE SOMME
and the retreating
German forces

0   Miles   5

Hindenburg Line

Croisilles

Bullecourt

Devastated

Area

Commecourt

Puisleux

Grevillers

Irles   Loupart   Bapaume
             Wood

Beaumont   Miraumont
Hamel
    Beaucourt   • Pys
        Grandcourt

Le Sars   Le Transloy

Theipval   Courcelette
            Martinpulch

    Pozitres

High Delville
Wood Wood   Morval

Boiselle   Bouleaux   Fregicourt
    Mametz   Bernafay   Wood
    Wood   Wood
                        Leuze
Albert   Wood   Rancourt

        • Mametz

Fricourt   Guillemont   • Maurepas

    Maricourt

R. Somme

•••• Line at July 1st
- - - Line at July 14th
— — Line at Sept. 18th
——— Line at Nov. 17th

French seemed to have reached that point when the Germans tried their new poison gas, phosgene, but they still held. The phrase, 'Ils ne passeront pas' began to be replaced by 'On les aura', as the French suspected that the Germans were at the end of their resources too. In July, Falkenhayn gave the order to cease attacking.

For Pétain enough was enough and he was content to hold the line and try to recover. However, holding the line was not enough for his two sub-commanders, Nivelle and Mangin, both of whom were anxious to build their own military reputations. Not content with retaining ground, they fought back to reoccupy former positions, eventually including the vital Fort Douaumont, lost at the very beginning of the battle: by 18 December they had succeeded, but at incalculable cost.

The casualty figures for the battle of Verdun are impossible to calculate accurately but seem to have been 350,000 Germans and 460,000 French. The French had not only lost most of their best troops but they had come to believe in Nivelle; in consequence he was given a command which he so completely mishandled that it virtually completed the destruction of the fighting will of France.

But long before the Battle of Verdun had ended an even more bloody battle had begun, this time on the Somme. When in the early months of 1916 it was clear that the Germans were aiming to break through at Verdun the British High Command realised that a diversion was necessary. This 'diversion' became the Battle of the Somme and it began on 1 July 1916, when the Battle of Verdun was still grinding along remorselessly.

However, it should be remembered that in between these major battles there was still fierce fighting at various points along the French lines. Although Falkenhayn had set his sights on capturing Verdun in 1916, he realised that it was necessary to keep up an offensive all along the line lest inactivity by the Germans should enable the British to make tactical gains which would be extremely unfavourable to the Germans. In February the Germans penetrated the British line at Boesinghe, but were driven out. In March they decided to capture a British observation point two miles south of Ypres, which British troops called 'The Bluff'. It was typical of many other 'high points' in the war, such as Hill 60 and Hill 70, both of which fig-ures represented their height in metres. Although insignificant in peacetime, in war they were key features, for whose capture gallons of blood were shed. 'The Bluff' was only thirty feet high and was composed of soil from the exca-vation of the Ypres–Comines canal. Situated just inside the British line it gave invaluable observation over the German positions opposite. In February, after mining, an artillery barrage and heavy infantry attack, the Germans captured the Bluff. In March, the British recaptured it in an attack which was marked by casualties running into thousands on both sides. The situation was therefore exactly as it had been two months earlier.

In April the Germans attacked Hulluch in the Loos area, using gas. They were making progress when the gas suddenly blew back over their own lines. As they ran backwards to escape the choking fumes, they were caught by a British artillery barrage which, if they had continued to come forward, would have missed them altogether. It was a repetition of what had happened to the British in the Battle of Loos the previous September. Gas, it was observed, did not only destroy men: it also destroyed vegetation down to the last blade of grass.

This traumatic experience did not prevent the Germans using gas again, even in the same month. This time it was at Wulverghem, and again it was a failure. However they were more successful in a surprise attack on the French when they captured the Pimple, a knoll on the northern end of Vimy Ridge. Vimy Ridge is nine miles long and extends from the valley of the Scarpe in front of Arras to the valley of the Souchez. On the other side of the Souchez valley is the notorious Notre Dame de Lorette ridge. The Germans held the whole length of the Vimy Ridge apart from the northern end which was shared with the French in close proximity.

Although the Somme was in one sense a diversion from the French agonies at Verdun, it was also a major battle in its own right by means of which Haig, now the British Commander in Chief, hoped to smash his way through the German line and then advance rapidly on the plain beyond. But even if victory on the Somme did nothing more than drive the Germans off the high plateau, it would be justified (in the eyes of the Allied High Command) for it would deprive the Germans of observation over a wide area and an excellent tactical position. The Battle of the Somme, like many other battles, is not accurately named, as it would more properly be called the Battle of the Ancre, which bisects the battlefield. However, it has passed into history as the Battle of the Somme, and a name synonymous with slaughter.

The actual battlefield lies between Gommecourt in the north and Maricourt in the south. The river Somme flows east–west south of Maricourt and turns sharply south at Péronne. South-east of Péronne lies St Quentin. The river Ancre runs roughly east-west across the battlefield. On the north of the Ancre lie the villages of Beaumont Hamel and Serre; on the southern side is Thiepval where, with other monuments, there is the 'Memorial to the Missing', a huge arch, designed by Sir Edwin Lutyens. On its panels of stone are recorded the names of 73,412 Allied soldiers whose bodies were never found. Although the Somme plateau is only 130 metres high, it contains many small villages and hillocks, all of which would be fought for in relentless bloody battles. High Wood, Delville Wood and Ginchy, referred to later, lie south-south-west of Thiepval.

The Somme area had been relatively quiet since it had been occupied by the Germans in 1914. Up till July 1915, according to Liddell Hart, it was possible for British battalions to drill undisturbed, in full view of the Germans. A few months later any attempt to do so would produce an artillery barrage. The Germans noted more sinister preparations than infantry drilling in the early months of 1916. They saw the British establishing ammunition dumps and engaging in engineering works, such as digging trenches, burying cables and making various other preparations which suggested an imminent offensive.

Although the huge losses on the Somme have always been blamed on Haig, it should be remembered that originally he had no wish to attack there, preferring the area further north. However Joffre was strongly in favour of the British mounting an offensive on the Somme, seeing it as a useful link with his own plans: he differed from Haig in his concept of the type of battle, thinking it should be a steady war of attrition. Haig and his subordinate commanders thought the idea of a piecemeal advance was misguided, and instead favoured a huge artillery barrage and then an all-out infantry assault. Such a tactic was, of course, standard practice in the First World War, and again in the Second. On occasion, in order to effect surprise, the infantry would attack without the artillery (or airpower) preparing the way, but it was a high-risk proceeding.

The British would bear the brunt of the attack on the Somme, for the French agonies at Verdun meant that they had few troops to spare. Originally the French had agreed to attack on a front of 25 miles, using sixteen divisions, but as Verdun ground on, the French front on the Somme was reduced to eight miles, and their contribution in divisions to eight. Although Haig did not realise it at the time, this foreshadowed the future. Having won the battle of the Somme at enormous cost, he would find himself having to shoulder more and more burdens as the effect of the very high French losses, culminating in Nivelle's folly, reduced French effectiveness and the will to fight.

Haig made one mistake before the battle which proved very costly indeed. When he suggested to his subordinate commanders that, after the preliminary bombardment and before the infantry attacks began, small parties should be sent to make sure the wire had been satisfactorily cut, he accepted their assurances that this was unnecessary. Pilots of the Royal Flying Corps, who had flown over the battlefield, agreed that the devastation of the bombardment had been so great that the German defences were in ruins. Sadly this was not so. The Germans had spent their period of occupation prudently: they had established sophisticated deep dugouts in the chalk and wired, not just one defensive line but a whole series of lines, one behind the other. Meanwhile, aware that gas can be an awkward weapon to use, Haig's divisional and brigade commanders had decided against it: in fact they told Haig that it was not even necessary to use smoke to cover the advance; they said it might be counter-productive and prevent units finding and reaching their allotted objectives.

Much of the blame for the Somme disaster can be laid at Joffre's door, for he had said he was not ready to attack on 29 June, as originally planned, and requested a postponement of two days: he also had zero hour put back from before dawn till 7.30am, when the battlefield would be light. This postponement meant that the British troops, who had moved into the forward position on the 29th, spent 48 hours exposed to torrential rain, while being also deafened by gunfire. The rain stopped on 1 July and was replaced by brilliant sunshine and broiling heat. When the attack began, the infantry went forward in waves, the men shoulder to shoulder, at a slow walk. They could not move much faster, for each man was carrying 66lbs mostly ammunition, and the ground over which they advanced had been torn up by the preliminary bombardment. Soon they had another obstacle, the bodies of those who had been advancing in front of them.

The Germans, as at Loos, could scarcely believe their eyes. They emerged from their deep dugouts unharmed, set up their machine-guns and traversed the slowly advancing lines of infantry. Observers further back saw the soldiers fall in lines, as if in some gymnastic exercise, but this was no exercise, for most of them were dead.

At the worst, the lines of the two armies were 800 yards apart: at best, they were 50 but that was enough for the German machine-gunners, who began scything the soldiers down as soon as they left the trenches. Those soldiers who, miraculously, reached the German wire, found it mostly uncut.

Before the attack it had seemed reasonable to assume that the troops would need all the equipment they were carrying when they settled down to consolidate their newly-captured position. In the event they were so vulnerable to the German machine-guns as they advanced in the open, that whether they moved fast or slowly would make little difference to the result.

But it was not all failure. 13 Corps reached Montauban, which was its allotted objective. Mametz was also captured. The 36th (Ulster) Division, which had been allotted Grandcourt, north of Thiepval, reached it and waited for reinforcements so that it could carry on and turn in behind German positions which could easily have been taken at that moment; they fell after massive bloodshed much later. Unfortunately for the 36th's heroic efforts, the promised reinforcements never reached them for they had been diverted to secure a less important objective, which they failed to do.

The casualties on the first day of the Somme were horrific. The corrected figure was 57,470, of which 19,290 had been killed. 35,493 were wounded: many of these would die of their injuries later. 2,000 men were listed as missing, which probably meant that they had been blown to pieces, none of which could be identified. The remains, if found, would be hastily buried. Although in the war cemeteries there are thousands of graves bearing the names of the soldier beneath, this is only part of the picture: in France one in four soldiers killed was unidentified, and in Belgium the number became one in three.

After the shock of the initial bloodbath the British and French Higher Command had to decide what to do next, if anything. In the event it was decided that as so much blood had been spilt on the first day, the Germans must be at the limit of their resources too and the attack should be continued. Joffre certainly thought the attack should persist, and tried to order Haig to press on in the areas where the failures had been so costly: he was very pleased with the performance of his own troops who had done well in the less strongly-held areas in the south. Haig had no intention of taking orders from the French, even though he personally was on good terms with Joffre, but he decided that further attacks by Fourth Army, under General Rawlinson, might be profitable. This time, however, the tactics were varied. Instead of advancing in broad daylight, Rawlinson sent his troops forward in a night advance followed by a single bombardment and a dawn attack. This, of course, was the tactic which should have been used on the first day, but which had been rejected on the basis that the troops involved were too inexperienced to fight in this way, in that it is all too easy to press on to the wrong objective and even fire on one's own side by mistake. This time, however, it was a success. Nevertheless it did not dislodge the Germans from their key positions on the plateau, but only brought the armies closer together in what resulted in murderous close-quarter fighting.

A typical battle was that for Delville Wood. This was captured by 7th Division on 14 July but soon afterwards was retaken by the Germans in a massive counter-attack. It would remain in German hands till 15 September but in the meantime thousands of lives would be lost in trying to recover it. On 15 July, knowing that the Germans were now back in this useful strategic area, the South African Brigade attacked, in torrential rain, and kept on for five days. By the end of that time the wood, or what was left of it after shellfire, was still in German hands, but the South African Brigade, which had begun the battle with 3,153 soldiers, now numbered only 780. The Anzacs (Australian and New Zealand Corps) had even more devastating losses at Pozières, gaining a mile for a cost of 23,000 casualties. Nevertheless the Allied line was moving gradually forward. The Germans, who might have been expected to have lower casualties than the Allies, in fact had suffered worse. This was because the German battalion commanders insisted that every time ground was lost an immediate counter-attack must be made to recover it. From the beginning of the war they had rigorously adhered to Falkenhayn's order that all ground which had been lost must immediately be retaken, and that any officer who gave up an inch of ground, even for tactical reasons, was to be court-martialled at once. If the British tactics had been suicidal, this was worse. The Battle of the Somme has been described by British military historians as 'the death of an army', thinking in terms of the army which Kitchener had built up from volunteers. In fact it was the death of two armies, for the German army suffered so heavily that German historians considered that their casualty figures on the Somme had made defeat virtually inevitable: the loss in trained and experienced manpower was devastating, but the damage to morale, they considered, was even greater. However, the latter point seems debatable. The German army stood up to the Ypres battles the following year and showed no lack of morale when it launched the Spring offensive of 1918.

Although the Somme battle had been designed for a swift victory by an assault with overwhelming power, and not a battle of attrition, it soon developed into the latter. Nevertheless there was no lack of imaginative planning (within the limits of possibility) on the Allied side. Haig envisaged a breakthrough between Le Sars and Morval while the French came up in a pincer movement on the right. The British would then be able to turn north and get in behind key German positions. The great assault would be launched on 15 September. Although this was three and a half months after the opening day of the Somme battle, it would still leave time for gains to be consolidated before the winter, perhaps even for the war to be won. There was enormous optimism in Allied HQ about a new special weapon. It was a well-kept secret, for it took the Germans by complete surprise; it was the tank.

In fact it should not have taken anyone by surprise, for armoured fighting vehicles had a long ancestry, dating back to the war chariots of 3,000 BC. These appeared in many ancient sculptures and friezes and appear to have been covered with plates of armour. They were usually drawn by semi-wild horses or asses, which must have made their handling somewhat unpredictable, but they had the same function as a modern tank: surprise leading to a breakthrough and consequent disruption of the enemy's dispositions and morale. The French army had produced a steam-powered tank in 1770 and an armoured car in 1902; in 1903 the Germans had also produced an armoured car. Although tracks had been invented in the eighteenth century, they were considered inferior to wheels and were not developed. In the years immediately before the First World War the French, British and German general staffs had all turned down proposals for tracked vehicles. In 1912 the British War Office had received detailed plans for a tank but had filed them away and forgotten them. It was said that, before they vanished into obscurity someone had written across the front page 'This man is mad'. They might have stayed in a filing cupboard for ever if the inventor, noting that tanks had developed along the lines he had suggested, had not applied to the Royal Commission on Awards to Inventors in 1919. Although he was able to point out that years of experiments and costly mistakes would have been saved if his original plan had been adopted, the Commission decided that this did not justify an award.

A modern reader might ask why there should have been this hostility to a modern version of a weapon which had proved so useful in the past. That same reader might see parallels in other weapons which were invented then neglected for centuries for apparently inexplicable reasons. Rockets have a lineage stretching back to medieval times, but came as a surprise when launched by the Germans in 1944. 'Greek fire' and its mysterious components created devastation in the Middle Ages, long before it reappeared in flame-throwers in the present century. The answer lies in the fact that by mutual agreement the war-leaders in various countries outlawed certain types of weapon (just like the non-proliferation treaty on nuclear arms today). Their reason for doing so was their respect for the horse with all its panoply of armour, cavalry charges, and chivalry. The first example of the attempt to suppress a weapon which threatened the horse's domination of the battlefield was the banning of the crossbow by the Lateran Council at Rome in 1140. It was described as a weapon too devastating to be used by people of Christian nations, but the real reason was that it was too indiscriminating: it could kill a king or a knight as easily as a peasant-soldier, and in medieval warfare that ruled out possibilities of ransom. Banning the crossbow did not stop its use but, hundreds of years later, the scorn directed at early forms of tank undoubtedly crippled their development.

The power of the horse over men's emotions was also clearly demonstrated by the fact that most of the First World War generals had risen to their high positions via cavalry regiments. In 1914 some regimental commanders were still forcibly stating that a cavalry charge could soon ride down machine-gunners. The lessons of the Boer War of 1899–1902 were wilfully neglected.

Although Haig was a 'cavalry general' and an international polo player, he welcomed the tank and was bitterly disappointed when it failed to produce the results expected of it. This had not prevented him from being criticised for misusing what tanks he had but criticism was ill founded, as we shall see later.

By 1915 when the fighting in France had settled down into trench warfare it was clear that something was needed to break the deadlock. Surprisingly, in 1915 the only organisation likely to possess the knowledge to build tanks was the Royal Naval Air Service, which used them to protect the squadron based on Dunkirk. Fortunately, the First Lord of the Admiralty was Winston Churchill, under whose aegis the RNAS flourished, and he gave the development of the tank every encouragement. The first 'real tank' was built by William Foster and Co in their Lincoln factory. The staff there were told that anyone who enquired what they were doing was to be told 'manufacturing water tanks' and the name stayed. By December 1915 a second prototype had been built and tested. Two months later, the British Army ordered 100. The December prototype is now on display in the tank museum at Bovington, among many later and modern tanks.

The French, who had been conducting similar experiments, also produced a version of a tank at the same time. It was less sophisticated than the British version, but the French government was satisfied and ordered 400.

Haig had hoped that the tanks would be ready to take part in the opening offensive on 1 July 1916, but they were not. Had there been even only a few dozen available, the fearful carnage of that first day might have been avoided, for it is unlikely that the German machine-gunners would have stayed at their posts when these lumbering and apparently invincible monsters came lurching towards them.

By September 1916, 150 British tanks had been manufactured. 60 were taken to France but, as became all too well-known later, tanks are very likely to break down, and only 49 were available for 15 September. Even that figure was reduced by the time they reached their battle positions and only 32 were available for the critical occasion.

When the attack was launched, nine tanks did well, nine were too slow to keep pace with the infantry they were supposed to be supporting, nine broke down mechanically, and five became bogged down on the battlefield.

Nevertheless, they were a success and the overall effect was dramatic. If the number had been greater, there seems little doubt that the long-wished-for breakthrough would have been achieved.

There are two further 'ifs' about the Battle of the Somme. If the initial bombardment, or platoons sallying out at night with wirecutters, had made gaps in the wire, cavalry would have been invaluable on the Somme. They could have 'gone over the top' the moment the bombardment stopped and reached the gaps in the wire before the German machine-gunners were properly in position. In the event, the latter had plenty of time to organise themselves for the slaughter of the slow-moving infantry.

As we shall see, cavalry would still play a considerable part in the First World War, and horses and mules would be vital means of transport in all armies in both world wars. But we must now return to the Somme.

Through September, October, and November the battle ground on. Tanks continued to be used and at Thiepval the appearance of three so disconcerted the Germans that this blood-soaked village finally fell to the British on 28 September. Like many positions on the Somme, it was particularly difficult to capture because the defences underground were nearly as formidable as those above. Some of the underground refuges had been dug by the Germans themselves but others were the galleries from chalk mining over the centuries. The attacking British troops were quite unaware of the strength of the German defences when they rushed enthusiastically forward on the first day of the battle. Encumbered though they were, some managed to break into a run; here again a football (this time by the East Surreys) was kicked ahead. The last two German defences to fall were Beaumont Hamel and Beaucourt on 13 November.

Haig wished to break off the battle (i.e., cease attacking) in September and reserve some of his troops for use in other areas but Joffre was insistent that this would be folly as complete success was so close; he was well aware that the drain on the Germans on the Somme had reduced their effort at Verdun, and this had enabled the French to recover ground in that area.

Haig, usually portrayed as a ruthless automaton but in reality a man of compassion and artistic sensibility driven by a powerful sense of duty, described the Somme battlefield in the final stages.

'The ground, sodden with rain and broken everywhere with innumerable shell-holes, can only be described as a morass, almost bottomless in places: between the lines and for many thousands of yards behind them it is almost – and in some localities, quite – impassable. The supply of food and ammunition is carried out with the greatest difficulty and immense labour, and the men are so worn out by this and by the maintenance and construction of trenches that frequent reliefs, carried out under exhausting conditions, are unavoidable.

'In the front trenches there had been no opportunity to provide adequate cover against either fire or weather. Between the front and reserve positions on the reverse slopes of the Bazentin Ridge – Ginchy, Guillemont, Longueval, the Bazentins, Pozières – stretched a sea of mud more than two miles in extent, and the valley of the Ancre was a veritable slough of despond. Movement across these wastes was by way of duckboard tracks which, exposed as they were to hostile shellfire and the disintegrating action of the mud and rain, could only be maintained by arduous and unending labour. Stretcher bearers, with never less than four men to a stretcher, made the journey down from regimental aid posts through mud which no wheeled carrier could negotiate.'

Frostbite, trench foot, nephritis and dysentery all took their toll and, inevitably, every man in the trenches had minor irritation from insects, such as flies, bugs, lice and fleas.

But there was worse to come at Passchendaele the following year.

In the four and a half month battle of the Somme the Allied lines had moved forward approximately five miles: the front was only fourteen miles long but, of course, it included vital strategic parts. The British, who had held three quarters of the front, had suffered some 420,000 casualties, the French lost 205,000. There may have been a few thousand more who were simply 'missing'. The German casualty figures were 680,000, but even this may be too low as the Germans were less conscientious about keeping a record of their casualties, citing 'a shortage of clerks', and in addition did not usually include the less seriously wounded. With the advantage of their carefully prepared positions on natural defences, the German casualties should have been a fraction of those of the Allies, but the policy, referred to earlier, of always trying to retake lost ground, had cost them dearly. After the Somme, this suicidal order was rescinded. A member of the German General Staff, Captain von Hentig, subsequently wrote:

'The Somme was the muddy grave of the German field army and of its faith in the ability of the German leaders. The German Field Command, which entered the war with enormous superiority, was defeated by the superior techniques of its opponents. It had fallen behind them in the application of destructive forces and was compelled to throw division after division without protection against them into the cauldron of the battle of annihilation.'

The British Tommy would have been surprised to know that. It appeared differently to him as he lived and died in sodden, stinking trenches.

The Somme saw the end of the idealism which had fired many volunteers. We have noted the wasteful recruitment of medical students, engineers, chemists, and other educated and highly intelligent men into infantry battalions in which they were subsequently slaughtered wholesale. But idealism was by no means confined to one section of society. All over the country men had joined up because their friends, in clubs or teams or localities, had joined up too, hoping to stay together. Although normally in the Army such plans go astray very quickly, in the First World War men did tend to stay in the same units, at least in the early stages. However, on the Somme this fact had a devastating effect on certain regiments which had acquired nicknames like the 'Bradford Pals', the 'Manchester Pals' or the 'Liverpool Pals'. There were several others. 'Pal' is a word which has fallen into disuse: the word 'chum', which succeeded in the Second World War, was less emotive. You always knew your pal would stand by you whatever happened: you might not be so sure of your chum. 'The 'Liverpool Pals' were the 17th, 18th, 19th and 20th battalions of the King's (Liverpool) Regiment and had been mostly recruited by Lord Derby. The fact that they were 'the Pals' made them extremely keen and competitive. They would not only show the Germans what Liverpool lads could do, they would also show other British regiments: they were cheerful even though they found some of the training irksome. Private Steele was a runner (messenger):

'The colonel called me over and said "Go and see what's happened." So I went along the trench and I got up on top and the first thing I saw was all the dead fellows just lying there, higgledy-piggledy all over the place, some two, three and four high – one mass of dead men as far as you could see, right and left. The first one I came across was a Captain, Captain Brockbank, he'd been hit twice. One of the fellows told me that he'd been hit but got up and then been hit again in the throat. Further on I found Lieutenant Withy and Lieutenant Herdman, he'd had his head blown off by a German bomb.' The Colonel was killed soon afterwards.

The Somme, as we now know, marked the midway part of the war but at the time it seemed the culmination of everyone's efforts and therefore a time to arrange a peace. It was premature, for so far the fighting had settled nothing. The Germans were still firmly established in France and their allies, the Turks, had produced a great victory in Gallipoli. On the Eastern Front the Russians had won an important campaign, but then been held. The Germans therefore thought it would be a good time to negotiate a peace which would leave them substantial gains. Although martial ardour was still rampant in the Higher Command, there were also Germans, such as Bethmann-Hollweg, the Imperial Chancellor, who thought that although Germany could still win the war, the methods they would have to employ, such as unrestrained submarine warfare, were not acceptable. The arrogant peace proposal, presented to neutral states and the Vatican on 16 December, showed little sign that Germany had relinquished her ambitions. Her demands were:

1. All her colonies, except those in the Pacific should be returned to her.
2. She should receive the Congo Free State from Belgium.
3. She should retain the Briey–Longwy basin, which, linked with Luxembourg, should become a state of the German empire.
4. She should be granted either direct influence over Belgium, or the possession of Liège.
5. Courland (Latvia) and Lithuania should become part of the German empire and German influence should be extended in the Balkans.

Although Bethmann-Hollweg had doubts about the long-term effects of German military policies, he realised he had to tread carefully or his own position might be compromised. He had trusted in Falkenhayn's ability to produce victory but when Verdun had proved an expensive disaster, and the Somme showed that German morale was beginning to falter, it became clear that Falkenhayn should be replaced by someone with new ideas. That view was opposed by Falkenhayn's supporters, who countered by claiming that the recent German defeats were not the fault of the military but of the inadequate civilian back-up, which had failed to increase production to the necessary levels. The advantage of the last two years during the period of Allied 'shell-famine' had now disappeared and the Allied munitions factories had caught up, but that could scarcely be blamed on the German factories. But as the Germans came under increasing pressure, there grew up a feeling that the military should run the national economy. A scapegoat was sought in the civilian as well as in the military field, though the latter produced the first victim. Falkenhayn was dismissed on 29 August 1916, when both the battles of the Somme and Verdun were still grinding on. He was replaced by Hindenburg. Hindenburg was already 69; he had retired from the German army in 1911 as a general but had been recalled in 1914: he would become a major force in German military life and politics right up till his death in 1934 at the age of 87.

Hindenburg was of Prussian Junker (aristocratic) stock and although not particularly gifted intellectually, had impressive looks and always appeared totally in command of any situation in which he found himself. The general public admired him because he seemed a soldier to his finger-tips; he had first seen action in the Austro-Prussian war of 1866, when he was still a cadet (aged eleven). Like certain others of his type, he was often given the credit for the activities of his more talented subordinates. Earlier in this book we saw him as a Commander in Chief on the Eastern Front in 1914 when the Russian armies advanced towards Germany. His subordinate Ludendorff had sized up the situation (using information supplied by one of *his* subordinates), but Hindenburg had received nearly all the credit for the subsequent victory.

Hindenburg had no inhibitions about how Germany should win the war when he became Commander in Chief of the German Land Forces. He was still accompanied by Ludendorff and both believed in the concept of 'total war'. In 1916 that meant allowing submarines to sink any ship remotely suspected of carrying cargoes for the Allies. Naturally Bethmann-Hollweg's more moderate approach to winning the war seemed to Hindenburg to be unrealistic and obstructive, so the Imperial Chancellor was gradually eased out, finally departing in July 1917; he was replaced by a man of considerably lesser stature, Georg Michaelis. Although Bethmann-Hollweg bears some responsibility for encouraging the Austrians to take what action they thought appropriate against Serbia in July 1914, he was not a war-monger, and had a liberal view of politics. But he was a realist and, while he had developed considerable doubts about the ability of the Germans to win the war if the army could not achieve some spectacular military victories in the immediate future, he was also only too well aware that, if the German navy pursued the policy of unrestricted submarine warfare, America would soon join the Allies and thus make the defeat of Germany certain.

This realisation of the resources and numbers that America would be able to throw into the scales against Germany undoubtedly caused Bethmann-Hollweg to encourage Woodrow Wilson, the American President, to put forward his own peace proposition. He was well aware that Wilson was a high-minded idealist who would nevertheless welcome the prestige which he would gain if he brought the war to an end. For several months Wilson had been trying to ascertain what conditions the belligerents would accept for a cease-fire, but did not find their replies encouraging; therefore on 22

January 1917 he informed the US Senate that peace could only be achieved if the belligerents agreed to accept it without victory. Furthermore, he declared, peace must be organised by a League of Nations. Among the general requirements for a peace, said Wilson, were the acceptance that no country should dominate another, or the land or sea, and that there should be a limitation on armaments. A week after he had made this speech the German ambassador in Washington delivered a note saying that Germany intended to pursue the policy of unrestricted submarine warfare because the United States was not taking a sufficiently strong approach to making a peace treaty. No doubt the Hindenburg-Ludendorff team thought that this would cause Wilson to redouble his efforts to make the Allies accept the German peace terms of the previous December. In the event it had the reverse effect. The United States was particularly sensitive to the threat of unrestricted submarine warfare as large numbers of American ships, loaded with valuable trade goods, preferred to wait in American ports rather than venture out and be plunged to the bottom of the Atlantic.

The German High Command believed that unrestricted submarine warfare would bring victory within six months, probably by starving Britain into surrender. It was unlikely that this would have happened, and in any case, the convoy system, reluctantly adopted by the Admiralty, soon greatly reduced the effectiveness of the U boats. But the Germans were aware that before that victory the US might intervene in the war. Timing was therefore of the greatest importance. Although the entry of America was not likely to have an immediate effect on anything but the morale of the belligerents in the short term, the eventual effect would be decisive.

Faced with the possibility that America was on the point of joining the Allies and wishing to make that intervention less effective if it happened, the German Foreign Secretary, Arthur Zimmerman, sent a telegram on 16 January 1917 to Mexico proposing that she should enter into an alliance with Germany for which she would be amply rewarded after Germany's subsequent victory. The telegram also suggested that Japan should be brought into the war on the side of Germany (by the promise of territory). The Mexicans' reward was to be Texas, New Mexico and Arizona, all of which had formerly been part of Mexico. However, the telegram was intercepted and decoded by British Intelligence and was published by Woodrow Wilson on 1 March 1917. (Five weeks later the USA declared war on Germany.) Subsequently there were claims that the telegram was a fake designed by perfidious British Intelligence to lure the USA into the war: however, investigations showed that the telegram was genuine. Zimmerman was well known for his telegrams.

Falkenhayn's star was now descending rapidly. He was sent first to fight against Romania, then to help Turkey. When he failed to prevent the Allies capturing Jerusalem, he was replaced by General Otto Liman von Sanders, one of the most successful German generals. Falkenhayn ended the war commanding an army in Lithuania. He died in 1922.

Although the horrors of Verdun and the Somme inevitably focused attention on France in 1916, the war was of course proceeding in other theatres too. A month before the Battle of the Somme the largest naval battle of the war took place at Jutland. There had been lesser clashes at sea previously, as we have noted, and the submarine menace was obviously growing, but the public knew that one day the monster ships of the British and German navies would lumber into the middle of some remote area and pound each other until it was clear to all which was the winner. In the event the battle failed to produce that vital statistic.

The Commander of the German High Seas Fleet was Admiral Scheer, a tough old sea-dog who liked the prospect of a hard fight. His Vice Admiral Franz von Hipper commanded the Scouting Forces: he was probably a quicker thinker than Scheer but was also looking forward to a decisive battle. Opposing them were Admiral Sir John Jellicoe commanding the British Grand Fleet and Vice Admiral Sir David Beatty, commander of the First Battle Cruiser Squadron. Beatty was the more colourful figure: he wore his cap at a jaunty angle and was the right man to grasp a swift opportunity. Jellicoe was more cautious, made so by the fact that he was, as Winston Churchill deftly put it, 'the man who could lose the war in an afternoon'. In consequence it was the Germans who took the initiative on 31 May 1916. They had no empire to defend: they could afford to take risks. Even if their battleships were all sunk they could still rely on their submarines to devastate the shipping which was bringing essential cargoes to Britain. Germany had more to gain and less to lose than Britain when this long-awaited clash of the juggernauts eventually occurred.

Scheer decided that if he sent out his cruisers in the direction of the Skagerrak (the strait between Norway and Denmark) the move would bring out Beatty's cruisers which could then be drawn towards the huge guns of the German High Seas Fleet. It was not a challenge which Beatty was likely to ignore.

Overall the British had the advantage of superior numbers and weight. They had 28 battleships, nine battlecruisers, eight armoured cruisers, 36 light cruisers, and 78 destroyers. The Germans had 22 battleships, five battlecruisers, eleven light cruisers and 61 destroyers. But if the German Scouting Forces could destroy Beatty's cruisers by luring them to their doom under the guns of the High Seas Fleet, the Germans would have the overall supremacy.

The battle began at 3.48pm when the battlecruisers came in sight of each other just off the Skagerrak. As planned, Hipper immediately reversed and was delighted to find that Beatty promptly gave chase.

Naval warfare was, of course, much more complicated than it seemed to the outsider. Battleships, with their huge guns, could demolish smaller opponents, whom their guns probably outranged and certainly outclassed in power. On the other hand, finding targets at a range of some twenty miles requires great skill and experience. Furthermore, although battleships could destroy smaller surface craft with ease, they were themselves vulnerable to torpedoes, usually but not invariably fired by submarines. Battleships themselves needed a protective screen of destroyers whose speed and manoeuvrability were adapted to coping with U boats. (There were, as well, other ships specially equipped to lure submarines to their doom; they were known as 'Q' ships). Successful naval warfare therefore required the mind of a chess-player. One impetuous move could mean irretrievable disaster.

Beatty fell into the trap which the Germans had set and encountered disaster earlier than might have been anticipated. The opening shots were fired when the two cruiser squadrons were still eight miles apart. Beatty had four fast battleships under his command but they were not as fast as the cruisers and were well behind when the action began. Disconcertingly the German gunners proved superior to the British, and *Tiger* and *Lion* (Beatty's flagships) were both crippled. *Indefatigable* was then sunk with loss of all but two hands: *Queen Mary* went down at the same time: only nine men out of a crew of 1275 survived. *Princess Royal* was hit but not sunk. By now, Beatty's battleships had caught up and one of them sank the *Von der Tann*. But the Germans had had the best of the fight. Beatty then uttered his classic remark to his Flag-Captain: 'Chatfield, there seems to be something wrong with our bloody ships today.' He followed it with an order to close up on the Germans.

There was indeed something wrong, as there had been at Gallipoli: it was the fact that the gunners were not using Pollen's Argo clock. However, the loss of Beatty's two ships was not entirely owing to poor shooting by the British Navy but also to a design fault in the ammunition hoists, which made them particularly vulnerable when hit.

Beatty's squadron set the *Seydlitz* on fire and damaged *Lutzow* and *Derfflinger*. The main fleets clashed as dusk was beginning to fall. Scheer saw the trap into which he was now running but, as he turned to escape it, succeeded in sinking another British ship, this time the somewhat inappropriately named *Invincible*.

Beatty was subsequently criticised for being too impetuous; Jellicoe for being too cautious. The battle, too complex to be described in detail in the space available here, continued through the night. Scheer's battlecruisers were continually battered by Beatty but only one was sunk: the remainder managed to limp home. When dawn broke there was not a German ship in sight and Jellicoe reluctantly returned to harbour (Scapa and Rosyth), claiming victory. Certainly he was in possession of the field (or sea), but in the action the British had lost three battlecruisers, three armoured cruisers and eight destroyers, with a total of 6097 men killed or drowned. The Germans had lost one battlecruiser, one battleship, four light cruisers and five destroyers: 2545 German sailors had been killed or drowned.

He who fights and runs away
Returns to fight another day.

This is not necessarily true and was certainly not true of the Germans at Jutland.

Scheer did begin to venture out again on 19 August, but on hearing that the British Grand Fleet was nearby returned promptly to harbour. Although the Germans claimed victory at Jutland, they decided not to send out their High Seas Fleet for a second full-scale encounter: they felt that luck had been on their side at Jutland, and that a second naval battle, after the British had realised their tactical mistakes in the first, would prove disastrous.

Jellicoe had not lost the war in an afternoon, as he might have done, and the British blockade of Germany still remained firmly in place. On the other hand, Germany reasoned that even though she could not win the mastery of the seas with surface craft, she could do so with submarines. This became clear to the Admiralty too and the following November Jellicoe relinquished command of the British High Seas Fleet to Beatty and instead took the post of First Sea Lord with the brief to combat the submarine menace. There was certainly plenty to worry about. During 1916, sinkings of shipping with cargoes destined for the Allies averaged 190,000 tons a *month*. In 1915 they had been half that amount. If the trend was not checked, and reversed, the Allies would be in desperate straits. The measure which would prove effective against the submarine menace was the convoy system, but the Admiralty was unwilling to try it before the situation left them no alternative.

An unexpected effect of the Jutland battle was the death of Kitchener. At the end of May Kitchener had set out to Russia on HMS *Hampshire*, on a mission to bolster Russian morale and help keep them in the war. On 5 June the *Hampshire* struck a mine off the Orkneys and sank: the mine was one of a number which had been laid by a German submarine on the probable path of the British Fleet when it went out to confront the German High Seas Fleet: the battle had been over for nearly a week when it claimed its victim.

A heavy gale was blowing when the *Hampshire* went down and this prevented any boats being launched: most of them were smashed to pieces in the davits and the cruiser sank in ten minutes. Over 150 men clambered aboard the three rafts, but most dropped off through cold and exposure and only fourteen reached the sheer cliffs of Marwick Head, a mile and a half away: two died after landing. One survivor had seen Kitchener walking on the deck and talking calmly just before the ship went down: he was obviously resigned to his fate.

Although Kitchener's importance had lessened since he had launched the early recruiting appeals and the Kitchener Armies and he was now 66, he still had enormous prestige, particularly abroad. His reputation had been the reason for the invitation to Russia, for the Czar felt that his presence would do much to invigorate all sectors of the community there. (In the Second World War Churchill acquired a similar reputation: although criticised by his colleagues he was venerated by the general public and was an awesome figure to friends and foes abroad. Cartoonists and propagandists sometimes defeat their own purposes by depicting enemy leaders as ruthless, unstoppable savages.) For a long time the British public refused to believe that Kitchener was dead: he represented England in a way no other wartime leader had done, and parents had named their children after him. The fact that his body never appeared among those washed ashore gave rise to the belief that he was on a secret mission from which he would return suddenly with the formula for swift victory. By mid-1916, with the French being battered at Verdun, and in July the appalling news of the casualties at the Somme, not to mention the disappointment that the German navy had not been sunk, all combined to make a need for some miraculous saviour urgent.

Germany also had need of a saviour, particularly now that her early advantages seemed to have ebbed away. Ludendorff realised that whatever the propagandists said, he had lost the battle of the Somme and Verdun and in consequence the Allies were not likely to give him any respite. He knew only too well that the drain on manpower could not go on for ever: Germany had no colonies overseas from which fit, determined, volunteers would arrive in battalions. Even worse was the danger that America, with its apparently unlimited manpower, would soon be tilting the scales against him.

So far we have said little about the air war, apart from the Zeppelins. The Royal Flying Corps had been established in 1912 with a military and a naval wing. Inevitably the two were rivals because the War Office and the Admiralty were jealous of each other and eventually, in 1914, the Naval Wing became the Royal Naval Air Service. Enlisting in either required not merely courage and optimism but also private means, for candidates had to learn to fly at their own expense. Not surprisingly there were arguments about the best colour for their uniforms, leading eventually to the compromise of light, rather than navy, blue, and the general appearance of a cavalry officer's uniform with breeches, riding boots, and patch pocket. The cut of the uniform had to be smart, but practical enough for a pilot who required considerable flexibility in his clothing.

Germany had also established an air force in 1913, the Fliegertruppe. The German navy followed suit the same year. Both made extensive use of Taube aircraft which had originated in Austria. 'Taube' means 'dove', a singularly inappropriate title in the circumstances.

However, the French were the leaders in world aviation. They had been the first to recognise the achievements of the Wright brothers, whose feats had been belittled in the USA, and Louis Blériot had been the first pilot to fly the English Channel. The French domination of the aircraft manufacturing industry is clearly shown by the terms which remain with us today: aileron and fuselage. In all countries the air forces had to contend with prejudice. Aeroplanes were noisy and unpredictable and these characteristics seemed to extend to the people connected with them, who seemed indifferent to military and naval traditions. In the early part of the war the rival air forces felt they had more in common with each other than with their own blimpish seniors and would often wave to or otherwise acknowledge each other. This attitude could not, and did not last, but even in the murderous combats which took place later there were often elements of chivalry which harked back almost to medieval warfare.

At the beginning of the war, none of the belligerents visualised the potential of aircraft, which were at first only seen as a better version of observation balloons. Germany, which had the strongest all-round air force, was more concerned with Zeppelins, although, as we saw, these too had problems before being fully accepted. From static observation it was a short step to tactical and then strategic reconnaissance, as aircraft grew more powerful. From this it was another short step to arming aircraft (with machine-guns) for defence against each other. Later, machine-guns would be used for harassing troops or trains, but in the early days such ground-hugging ventures were liable to end in disaster. The French were the first in the field with bombers (and a Frenchman made the first intentional parachute descent), but the British were the first to produce a specially designed fighter, the Vickers FB5.

Unfortunately for the Allies a great opportunity was missed when a young Dutch designer named Anthony Fokker was rebuffed when he wished to put his inventive skills at the disposal of Britain in the pre-war years. He found a more cordial reception in Germany and in 1912 set up a small factory near Berlin. During the war he produced over 40 different types of aircraft for Germany, all of which gave Allied airmen great problems. Initially the problem with using machine-guns in aeroplanes had been where to mount them so that their bullets did not cut pieces out of the propellers or unbalance the aircraft with their weight: Fokker produced a gearing system which enabled the synchronised guns to fire through the propeller. He was only 22 when he set up his factory: he emigrated to the USA after the war and became naturalised. He died in 1939 at the age of 49: one wonders what contributions his fertile mind might have made to the Second World War had he lived longer.

Soon, air forces of every country were producing their aces. They were a different breed from most war heroes, for they fought their battles high in the sky in flimsy contraptions and if they failed were clearly seen to do so. On the ground they lived on remote airfields away from their fellow combatants. Most of them spent too long in the air and had too little recreation, but all were fatalistic, scornful of attempts to impose discipline on them, and only too glad to be away from the trenches which they often flew over. They soon ignored the regulations for uniform and wore scarves, sweaters and specially designed flying boots. They drank too much, not merely to relieve the strain but because they knew that their superiors in rank disapproved.

Oswald Boelcke was the first German 'ace', and many think the greatest German fighter pilot. In his two years in the German air force he shot down 40 Allied aircraft and also produced the standard rules of combat which proved of inestimable value to pilots in both world wars. The son of a teacher, he had been considered a somewhat ineffective young man. He was 25 when he was killed in 1916. The better known Max Immelmann became a pilot in March 1915 and was killed in June 1916, shot down near Lens. In his time he had shot down some fifteen Allied aircraft and had also invented the famous 'Immelmann turn': flying a Fokker 'E' type armed with a forward-firing machine-gun, he would climb, turn and roll if attacked, and by this manoeuvre would come in behind the aircraft which, seconds before, had been attacking him.

British aces included Lanoe Hawker, VC, DSO, who bombed a Zeppelin on the ground near Ghent, from a height of 200 feet. For this he received the DSO. Soon afterwards he shot down three German aircraft in one day, although all were better armed than his own aircraft. He was shot down by von Richthofen in November 1916: he was 25.

Albert Ball VC was only 20 when he was killed. He had joined the army at the age of eighteen, managed to transfer to the RFC in January 1916, and flew a Bristol 'Scout' single-seater aircraft with such enormous daring and success that he became a legendary figure, much to his embarrassment. He was killed in May 1917; by that time he had shot down 44 German aircraft.

Georges Guynemer was born in 1894, in Paris. His attempts to join the French air force in 1914 were rejected: he was thought to be a very poor physical specimen. Undeterred, he contrived to be accepted as a student mechanic, and from that, by means of parental influence, trained as a pilot. He flew a Spad, and shot down 54 enemy aircraft before being killed in 1917. His body was never found.

Although possessing a French name, Raoul Lufbery was actually an American, the son of French immigrants. He enlisted in the Escadrille Americaine, a form of airborne Foreign Legion consisting of American volunteers. When the Escadrille formed in 1916 America was still neutral and as the Germans objected to the word 'American' being used by a French squadron it was therefore dropped and 'Lafayette' substituted. Lufbery was the first American to win a British Military Cross. He was killed in May 1918.

William Bishop, born in 1894, had come to Britain in the Canadian army but soon transferred to the Royal Flying Corps. Like many other aces, he flew a French aircraft, the Nieuport. It had a maximum speed of 110mph, could reach 17,000 feet and carried either a Lewis or a Vickers gun. Bishop achieved remarkable feats of daring in which he not only shot down 72 enemy aircraft but also machine-gunned many ground installations. He survived the war and died in 1956.

Machine-gunning or bombing troops or aircraft on the ground soon acquired the name, strafing. It is not unusual for one side to adopt a word used by the other and misuse it. As we have seen, 'strafe' actually means 'punish' and in the early days of the war the invocation 'Gott strafe England' was often heard, though it was not clear what offence (apart from opposing Germany) England was to be punished for.

The Russian air ace, Ivan Smirnov, had begun his military life in the Russian infantry but transferred to the air force in 1915, at the age of 20. He flew French aircraft and in spite of the inevitable problems of flying foreign aircraft in from Russia, where maintenance and the provision of spares was far from satisfactory, Smirnov shot down twelve German aeroplanes. When the Bolsheviks seized power in Russia, Smirnov learnt (from a friendly source) that all the Air Force officers were going to be shot by the revolutionaries, so he hastily removed himself to England.

There were, of course, other fliers who merited the description 'air aces' but probably the most famous of all was Manfred von Richthofen, 'the Red Baron'. He shot down 80 Allied aircraft before he was killed in 1918. Von Richthofen, who was 22 when the war began and an officer in a Lancer regiment, transferred to the air force in 1915. To his disappointment he was engaged in bombing and harassing ground troops for the early part of his career but in 1916, when he was 'adopted' by Boelcke for fighter work, his record soon became spectacular. He created an elite unit, which became known as 'the Richthofen circus'. Highly intelligent, and a first-class organiser, von Richthofen found his position as a national idol somewhat irksome and tried to avoid publicity: however, his achievements, his occasional narrow escapes, and his aura of youthful, immortal glamour meant that he was as stimulating to German morale as he was depressing to that of the enemy. Hundreds of Allied pilots aspired to shoot down the Red Baron, but all knew that their chances were slender. Not every hero looked the part, but von Richthofen did. When the German armies were being slowly pushed back on the Somme and at Passchendaele, the German public, already tightening its belt as the blockade strangled the country's economy, looked on him as a symbol of hope for final victory. His death was ascribed to Captain Arthur Brown, of the Canadian Air Arm, although there was a possibility that others (anti-aircraft gunners) might have had a hand in it. His fame and skill were later used by the Nazi propaganda machine, although his character suggests that that would not have been to his liking.

Of course, the air aces were only a small part, although an important one, of the air war. Germany managed to bomb Paris 24 times, dropping 700 bombs and killing 266 civilians during the war: some of the bombs came from Zeppelins. London fared much worse, a combination of aircraft and Zeppelins killed 800 civilians in London alone in the last two years of the war. However, raids like this, although damaging to morale, were not likely to dislocate the war effort and in 1917 Britain allotted a portion of the air force to bomb strategic targets, such as munitions factories and marshalling yards for that very purpose. Berlin, of course, was well out of range but Cologne, Düsseldorf, Coblenz and Stuttgart were not.

The growth of air power had been spectacular. There was never any lack of volunteers for, although the life of a fighter pilot might be brief it was statistically longer than that of the junior infantry officer, which he would otherwise have been. Britain's Air Force grew from the original handful to 2,600 aircraft: the French to 3, 857. The Germans, whose production fell in the last stages of the war, never managed more than 2,800 and the Austrians only mustered 600. Of course, quantity was not everything and the quality of the German Air Force was very high. The Italians only managed 800 but the Americans, although late starters, soon numbered 6,000. However, the unpreparedness of the Americans for the war they entered in 1917 meant that in the Air Force, as in many other forms of armament, they relied on foreign suppliers: only 1,200 of their aircraft were built in the USA.

In the last year of the war the skies, particularly over the trenches, were buzzing with aircraft, particularly so before a large offensive. In Britain on 1 April 1918 the airmen shook off their army and navy shackles and became the Royal Air Force: it was the brain child of Major General Sir Hugh Trenchard. The Navy continued to retain the Royal Naval Air Service, which would soon be using converted battleships as aircraft carriers. Later the Army would develop its own Army Air Co-operation Service. Sadly there were jealousies between the services which detracted from efficiency, and cost lives.

In the USA, Brigadier General William (Billy) Mitchell was the driving force behind the establishment of the US Army Air Force.

Most of the aerial combats took place over the British sector, mainly because in the latter stages of the war that was where the majority of the ground fighting took place. The publicity given to individual air aces tended to obscure the fact that most air operations employed considerable numbers (one of the air aces, a Canadian named William Barker, once found himself wounded and confronting 60 Fokkers, four of whom he managed to shoot down). Air combat was much more than haphazard encounters between talented amateurs: it was a matter of carefully-planned tactics, study of the vulnerability of the enemy's machines, and the development of an instinct which made pilots aware of impending danger even before they had sighted an opponent.

The final figures for the air war were sobering rather than glamorous. The Germans had had 5,853 killed, 7,302 wounded, and nearly 3,000 missing, most of the latter probably prisoners. The British lost a combined total of 6,166 killed, 7,245 wounded and 3,212 missing. Although apparently precise, these figures may have in fact varied by a few hundred either way. Accurate figures for other air forces are not known. But air power had not merely demonstrated it had come to stay: it had proved itself very effective, even decisive, in this war.

By 1916, which was when this chapter began, the war had spread not merely to many countries but was also being fought on the ground, under the ground by mining, on the sea and under the sea by submarines, in the factories and on the land by women, and in the air, above the trenches and behind the lines, by aeroplanes and Zeppelins.

The undercover war has been so glamorised in fiction that certain facts have been obscured. It was often sordid and boring, and to be successful needed the assistance of some extremely unpleasant people. It often involved treachery, cruelty and bribery. Its more obvious objectives were discovering the enemy's plans and therefore causing, or preventing, the sinking of ships or launching of attacks. Spying was practised by respectable people in neutral countries. Fear of an 'enemy in the midst' produced hysterical reaction against alleged spies, caused the shooting of many innocent people, and even extended to waves of anti-semitism. Constantine Fitzgibbon, an Anglophile American who served with the Irish Guards at the beginning of the Second World War, noted that 'more British warship tonnage was blown up in harbour, usually British harbours, by German saboteurs, than was sunk at Jutland.' A different type of spy listened to radio transmissions, or telephone conversations. On 5 August 1914 a British cable ship cut the German transatlantic cable. Subsequently Germany had to use other transatlantic cables, all of which were easily tapped by the British or French.

Valuable information was sometimes gleaned from eavesdropping on the conversations of prisoners of war who talked to each other endlessly and often indiscreetly, out of pure boredom: even more valuable information came from deserters. However, as we saw, senior commanders were often inclined to be sceptical about the information given them by intelligence officers, and when the Germans took the French by surprise by using gas at Ypres in 1915, the French had had ample warning from deserters and ignored it. Belligerents were not above torturing prisoners or deserters if they thought they were holding back vital information; it was sometimes self-defeating as the unfortunate victim often 'confessed' what he knew his interrogator wanted to hear in order to obtain respite from pain or hunger.

All the services used codes, and the capture of an enemy code book could be vital. But few deceptions were as audacious and successful as the German who managed to get himself a job in the British Post Office and from there to move on to the Censorship Department. Any useful information he obtained from the letters he censored was passed on, usually to an address in a neutral country, in an envelope franked 'Passed by the Censor'. Fortunately for the Allies, ordinary letters are unlikely to contain secret information of vital importance.

The most famous, though not necessarily the most important, spy was Mata Hari, a Dutch woman married to a Dutch man with the surprising name of McLeod (from a remote Scottish ancestor). As he was a drunkard who beat her, she left him and went to Paris where she became an actress and part-time call-girl. She was recruited into the German secret service, by whom she was handsomely paid, but she was discovered and shot by the French in 1917. In spite of later attempts to belittle her talent, she was a good actress and a brave woman.

Both sides gave considerable thought to indirect methods of undermining the enemy's morale. Newspapers in neutral countries were sedulously courted, even bribed, to print 'news' items about one's own forces or the enemy's. If the former, it would probably be a completely false announcement of an impending attack, or one's strength, or wartime production; if about the enemy, it might reflect adversely on his position, internal problems, or the sexual proclivities of its leaders. The more perverted the latter might be made out to be, the better the propaganda value. Reports of extravagant and luxurious living combined with corruption in high places were thought to undermine the morale of troops in the field, who were living in conditions of deprivation and degradation.

Outstanding in the British Intelligence service was Admiral Reginald 'Blinker' Hall (he had a slight facial tick). Intelligence work ran in his blood for his father had been the first Director of Naval Intelligence. Blinker succeeded to his chair in 1914. One of his first acts was to appoint a Cambridge Professor of Mechanical Engineering to assemble a staff of codebreakers. Their work was done in Room 40 of the Admiralty and gave vital information about German shipping and other movements. As the war progressed, the Germans changed their codes with increasing frequency, finally doing it daily. The expertise of Room 40 soon extended to other service matters, and eventually included diplomatic ciphers. The Zimmerman Telegram, referred to earlier, which helped to bring America into the war, was in a code which Room 40 decrypted.

Hall's team, which continued to operate as 'Room 40', and eventually included eminent civilians lightly disguised as officers of the Royal Naval Volunteer Reserve, and even *women*, was not to the liking of the more conservative members of the Admiralty or Foreign Office but managed to live alongside their colleagues in reasonable harmony because Hall gave them good, easily acceptable, disciplinary advice. Overseas were more of Hall's agents, such as the writers, Somerset Maugham, Compton Mackenzie and A. E. W. Mason: some of them used their wartime experiences after the war in their works of fiction and got into trouble for doing so. Hall also maintained a close relationship with Sir Basil Thomson, of Scotland Yard, who ran the 'Special Branch' for counter espionage, and Military Intelligence (MI5 for counter espionage and MI6, the 'Secret Service', for intelligence gathering).

The German counterpart was Department IIIb of the Army High Command, whose head was Colonel Walther Nicolai. This had four principal divisions: Section 1 gathered general intelligence, Section 2 was counter espionage, Section 3 was deception, and Section 4 was sabotage. General Intelligence was passed direct to the relevant department (army, navy, or air force), which knew how to evaluate it. In the German service there was no special organisation for pursuing economic warfare, although the importance of submarines in this field was appreciated.

French Intelligence was in two main groups: the Deuxième Bureau which gathered general intelligence, and the Cinquième Bureau which was specifically concerned with espionage.

Russia had had a secret service for centuries but most of the time it had been looking for enemies inside the state, rather than outside. The enormous size of Russia, and the number of potential unruly groups within it, seemed to the Russian leaders to call for a police state. During the First World War the Russian secret police were known as the Okhrana. Later they became the NKVD, then the MVD and finally the KGB.

Throughout the war all intelligence organisations worked with varying degrees of success to obtain information about their enemies (and sometimes about their allies), to catch spies, to sabotage, to distribute propaganda and to obtain political influence in neutral countries. The loss of Turkey to Germany was partly blamed on British intelligence but it does not seem that much credit was given to the intelligence services when Italy decided to join the Allies. Workers in intelligence become accustomed to having their failures denounced while their triumphs are unrecorded. Even after retirement they probably have to live in obscurity.

CHAPTER 7

1916 – 1917

O ne of the more irritating aspects of warfare, particularly to those who find themselves fighting, is the use of the expression 'sideshow'. The implication of the word is that victories or defeats in certain areas could not make any difference to the final outcome of hostilities. In consequence, soldiers who fought in the Middle East, Italy, or the African colonies were left with the impression that nobody cared much about the conditions in which they were fighting, or even the result. They believed, rightly, that a 'sideshow' was considered by the public, to be easier, or less dangerous and less uncomfortable than the Western Front or even Eastern Europe. In fact, it was very rare for this to be so. Many of the 'sideshows' mirrored or were even worse than the fighting in France. We have noted the siege of Kut and the appalling fate of those who were taken prisoner there. The Mesopotamian theatre continued to be one of the most uncomfortable of the war, although it never again quite matched the horrors of Gallipoli.

In the closing months or 1915, a new and forceful figure had come to the fore in Mesopotamia, General Sir Stanley Maude. He built up his forces until, in December, he felt ready to launch an attack which the Turks would not be able to withstand. He knew very well what he was up against, for he had commanded a division in the third attempt to relieve Kut. Although he had not been successful, he had demonstrated that he was the best man to be Commander in Chief, which he soon became. After Kut had fallen in April 1916, Maude had spent the following months building up the strength and morale of his army. By December he was ready and on the 13th he launched an attack along each side of the river Tigris. A key objective was Sannaiyat, a strongly-held Turkish position just north of Kut. As long as the Turks held Sannaiyat, British gunboats could not proceed further up the river and harass any Turkish troops falling back along its banks. On 17 February Maude's I Corps attacked Sannaiyat: on 22 February they captured it. As the Turks withdrew, Maude's II Corps, which had been making its way up the south bank (Kut was on the north), crossed the river and played havoc with the retreating Turkish troops.

Maude paused to reorganise his forces and supplies and then pressed on towards Baghdad. When the Turks appeared to be making a stand on the north bank, he transferred a substantial force to the south bank so that it threatened their rear. He captured Baghdad on 11 March 1917 and continued the advance to the north and east. Sideshow or not, it was a remarkable achievement. It was a gruelling campaign, notable for discomfort caused partly by the dogged resistance of the Turks but more so by the climate. Soldiers lived in tents or trenches and in the hot season the temperature was 120° Fahrenheit. There was dust everywhere, and soldiers were tormented by every variety of insect from flies to lice. The comforts which make life slightly more bearable under these conditions, fresh vegetables and fruit, and a varied diet, were totally absent owing to the problems of transport. The medical services learnt many lessons in this campaign, and made sure that whatever could be done to keep down disease and attendant ills was done. Hygiene and commonsense precautions such as not eating certain types of food was not merely insisted on by word, but was enforced by military law.

Certain afflictions, such as sunburn or venereal diseases, were treated as self-inflicted wounds. An important lesson learnt in the field was that though conditions for surgery were far from satisfactory, speed in removing contaminated flesh was often of life-saving importance.

Baghdad was a valuable prize: it consolidated the British hold on Mesopotamia and by doing so ended German hopes of a surprise push through to the Gulf. Maude now had his eye on further prizes, notably Mosul in the north-west. At this time Mosul was famous as a commercial centre: its oilfields had not yet been developed. In Biblical times the Assyrian city of Nineveh had stood on this site; later, as Mosul, the town became famous for finely woven cloth, and gave its name to 'muslin'. But Maude was not destined to reach Mosul. After making preparations for another step in his successful campaign, and having captured Tekrit, he died of cholera on 18 November. Coincidentally, a German general had died in the very same house in Baghdad eighteen months earlier. Cholera is a water-borne infection whose causes were not understood in 1916; it is a terrifying disease, for a man may be laughing and talking one day, only to be dead, totally dehydrated, a few hours later. The speed at which cholera strikes its victims, and also spreads, has created the impression that it is different from ordinary diseases. If a person is lucky enough to survive an attack, recovery may be surprisingly rapid. Similarly a cholera epidemic may ravage an area, then suddenly cease. Its causes and control are now better understood, but its sudden, unpredictable deadliness made its potential victims take an almost fatalistic view of it.

In military history records the conquest of Mesopotamia looks relatively untroubled, apart from the setback at Kut in April 1916. Edmund Candler, an official witness of the campaign, published an account of it in 1918 which told a very different story. Candler considered that after British forces were firmly established in the south, and therefore able to protect the Anglo-Persian oilfields, there was no need to continue the campaign northwards, and in fact it was folly to do so. But politicians in the House of Commons considered that if we pressed on towards Baghdad in 1915 this would 'secure the neutrality of the Arabs and generally maintain the authority of our Flag in the East' (Asquith, 3 November, 1915). That vague ambition led to the despatch of a totally inadequate force to Kut and subsequent disaster.

Candler noted that every place the army camped in had its own peculiar plague: 'dysentery, fever, skin diseases, jaundice, boils and eruptions of every kind.

'The heat of the desert in trenches and tents is staggering. One feels as if one were standing at the edge of a huge fire in a high wind, licked by gusts of flame.

'The flies were unbelievable. You could not eat without swallowing flies. You waved your spoon in the air to shake them off; you put your biscuits and bully beef in your pocket and surreptitiously conveyed them in closed fist to your mouth, but you swallowed flies all the same. They settled in clouds on everything. When you wrote you could not see the end of your pen: one in twenty would bite.'

At night flies were replaced by mosquitoes. 'In one camp I struck a species which could bite through cord riding breeches.

'The sand fly is another and more insidious plague. A net with a mesh fine enough to exclude him is suffocating and he will keep one awake at night with a host of thin acid playing on one's face. He is also the transmitter of a microbe which will lay you by the heels for three days with a virulent fever.'

And, of course, sand. 'You eat sand, breathe sand, lie on sand, have sand in your ears and eyes and clothes.

'Thanks to a saving sense of humour and his native resilience of spirit, the British soldier is unbowed by these climatic buffetings. He keeps his end up through all the plagues of Mesopotamia.

'"When it's 'ot, it's _____ 'ot and when it's cold, it's _____ cold, and there's no _____ in between." The British soldier has only two adjectives.

Supply the blanks and you have a succinct definition of the meteorological conditions of Mesopotamia from the popular point of view.'

But it did not quench his fighting spirit: 'The action at Sannaiyat was a singularly bloody and desperate affair. Three of the raiding parties were drawn from 28th Brigade, the Leicesters, the 53rd Sikhs and 56th Rifles: the fourth was drawn from the Sappers. All the officers (seven) were lost, killed or missing, and a large proportion of the rank and file.'

And, 'We assaulted on a 600 yards front. Here there was some desperate hand-to-hand fighting with bayonets and bombs. The Gurkhas carried the redoubt on the mound .... saw red and translated their vision into fact: two hundred Turkish dead were found within a radius of 300 yards that morning.

'There was a thick fog, very favourable to a surprise, and the Turks, who had been lying up in the scrub suddenly loomed out of the mist like a foot-ball crowd. The Manchesters were pinned into a trench from which it was difficult to use their rifles, their Lewis guns jammed with dirt, but the small party hung on, cut off from all support and fought to a finish with bomb and bayonet, until they were practically exterminated; the Turkish dead found on the spot the next morning outnumbered ours.

'The Turk was an enemy against whom few of us felt any bitterness of spirit.' They admired Turkish courage and tenacity. However, the Arabs, who would eventually inherit the country, were heartily disliked. Some were fighting on the side of the Turks but even more were simply pillaging for themselves. 'The more the forward areas became congested with our troops the more he raided and looted at night, cutting the wire between the block-houses, evading our bomb traps and getting off with our rifles, horses and ammunition, generally untouched.'

In the rear area, the desert Arabs were even more of a sinister nuisance. They would fire at vehicles for no apparent reason and were such expert thieves that nothing was safe, even though it was carefully guarded.

In view of the fact that Iraq (as Mesopotamia is now called) is a centre of considerable interest to the western world in the 1990s, we need to look into its political as well as military situation in the First World War. Although Baghdad had been under Turkish rule for nearly four hundred years, it had earlier traditions of being an independent state centuries before that. (It is, of course, an alleged site of the Garden of Eden.) The British aim was that after the Germans and Turks had been expelled, Mesopotamia should become an independent state under British supervision. This indeed is what happened: it later became a British mandate under League of Nations supervision. Although a League of Nations was in Woodrow Wilson's mind as early as 1916, it was not clearly established in anyone else's.

However, looking slightly ahead, British rule was firmly established in 1918, with the understanding that the country must be modernised at British expense and should be granted independence when it was ready for it. (It became independent in 1933.) Unfortunately for British hopes of a smooth period of development in the post-war period, the Iraqis misunderstood the word mandate, which in Arabic means 'domination', and rose in rebellion, murdering British political officers in large numbers.

But in 1916, although the campaign in Iraq was progressing satisfactorily, the ejection of the Turks from their imperial territories was proving slow and complicated. Gallipoli had shown the world, and perhaps the Turks themselves, how doggedly they could fight. Although in the nineteenth century the Turkish Empire had been described by the Russian Czar as 'a very sick man', its political ineptitude was not mirrored in their army. Two months before the British Expeditionary Force had landed in the Dardanelles, the Turks had surprised the British in Egypt by making an attack on the Suez Canal. Although this attack had been repulsed, it had set alarm bells ringing, for it had shown that the Sinai desert was not the insurmountable barrier it had been thought to be. In August 1916, aware that Maude was preparing his next campaign in Mesopotamia, the Turks in Palestine had launched another attack against the canal. This time they sent an expedition of 1,800 under a senior commander, but they overlooked the fact that, after the evacuation of the Dardanelles large numbers of troops had passed through Egypt, allowing a sizeable number to be diverted to the defence of the canal. In consequence, the Turkish force was defeated at Romani and 4,000 Turks were taken prisoner. The British High Command in Egypt decided that now was the time to go on the offensive and prepare the campaign to wrest possession of Palestine from the Turks.

Not surprisingly, the British public, stunned by the Battle of the Somme this year, were in no position to appreciate the efforts made in a remote series of 'sideshows', whose place names were even less familiar than those in France.

Meanwhile, another star was rising on the Middle Eastern scene. This was T. E. Lawrence, who soon acquired the title of 'Lawrence of Arabia'.

Lawrence had all the qualifications to be a charismatic figure. He was the illegitimate son of Sir Thomas Chapman and the governess of his daughters. Having left his wife, Chapman had four more children by the governess, Sara Maden, with whom he lived in what was to all intents and purposes a happy, though unofficial, marriage. T.E., who was brilliant academically, graduated from Jesus College, Oxford, became a Fellow of Magdalen College and travelled and studied extensively in the Middle East. On the outbreak of war his knowledge of the Middle East brought him into the War Office to work as a civilian employee in the Map Department and by December 1914 he had become a lieutenant in Cairo. Here he specialised in intelligence, interrogating prisoners and making maps. He noted the disastrous Dardanelles campaign and formed the opinion that the Turks might be defeated by more subtle methods than bombardment and bayonet charges. In his view, the Arabs were ready to revolt against the Turks, but needed money, supplies, and organisation. Not surprisingly, his originality, combined with considerable self-esteem, contrived to upset a lot of his colleagues. Since those days, the Lawrence legend has been distorted in works of fiction.

It is appropriate, therefore, to put the record straight with a comment by Admiral J. H. Godfrey, who became Director of Intelligence in the Admiralty in the Second World War.

'A great deal of rubbish has been written about Lawrence, who was almost an exact contemporary of mine, having been born in August 1888. Now the films have taken him up, glamorising him and trying to create a character utterly different from the man I knew in 1916. Ninety percent of him was practical, logical, hard-working and amazingly knowledgeable about Middle East archaeology, topography and Arabic roots. He loathed publicity, like a great many other people, and when it was thrust upon him he developed his own sort of protective covering. It so happens that soldiers at GHQ did not at first appreciate his ideas and unconventional behaviour, and towards them he adopted a puckishly disdainful manner which they naturally found hard to bear. The general staff attitude at Cairo irritated him and he liked having a dig at them. He cared nothing for uniforms, and at that time GHQ was very booted, spurred and red tabbed, and remote from the fighting soldier. All the people in the topographical world in Egypt and in the geodetic survey admired him tremendously and it was a pity he had a chip on his shoulder about the military Staff officers who swarmed at the Continental Hotel and did not try to understand this badly-dressed little man who cared nothing for clothes and rank and annoyed them by his unconscious mannerisms and indifference to appearance. For example, he would go about wearing only one red tab, or a lieutenant colonel's pips on one shoulder, with his coat unbuttoned and no tie, until both were very sensibly abolished.'

Lawrence's contempt for his fellow staff officers reflected his disgust at the ineptitude of the planning policies which had led to the disasters at Gallipoli and Kut. He considered that Britain would defeat the Turks more easily if instead of engaging in long expeditions and bloody campaigns, she linked up with the Arab independence movement which was now emerging.

Turkey, otherwise known as the Ottoman Empire, had reached the height of its power and prestige in the sixteenth century when it had controlled the Balkans, Hungary, the Middle East and North Africa as far as Algeria, but by the twentieth century had shrunk considerably. Nevertheless, in 1914 it still ruled vast territories. Although conquering Turkish possessions in Mesopotamia and Palestine tied down a number of British and Dominion troops, it also opened up considerable opportunities for bribing allies with pieces of Turkish territory in other areas. In 1915 Russia was promised Constantinople (Istanbul) and the Straits, and Italy the Dodecanese (with possibly more to come). The Anglo-French Sykes-Picot agreement of 3 January 1916 divided the post-war spheres of influence of those two countries: France was to control Syria and the territories eastwards up to Mosul: this was confirmed by a Mandate in the 1919 Peace Treaties, and at the end of the Mandate in 1946, although independent, Syria still remained under French influence. Britain was to administer and develop Mesopotamia as a Mandate until it became independent Iraq in 1933. Palestine was to be administered by an international regime, although, of course, it later became a British Mandate which ended when the republic of Israel was created in 1948. Britain made promises of local independence to various Arab leaders, and these were implemented in the creation of the post-war states of Iraq, Transjordan, and the Hejaz (later to be Saudi Arabia). Large sums of money were paid to Arab leaders during the war to assist them to make life difficult for their Turkish overlords. At the time they were not aware of the plans the Allies had for retaining spheres of influence in the former Turkish territory: however, when the Bolsheviks seized power in Russia in 1917 and published their secret treaties as examples of the perfidy of capitalism, the disclosure caused fury and disgust among the Arabs, who had thought they were to be the immediate rather than ultimate heirs. After the war these arrangements were all criticised, as being cynically expedient, but few of the critics took into account the fact that they were planned during a life and death struggle in which the aim was survival and in which certain injustices were bound to occur.

The most controversial of the agreements, which was made on 2 November 1917, promised the Jews a National Home in Palestine. In 1894 a movement called Zionism had been created with a view to settling Jews in Palestine, an Arab country though loosely under Turkish rule. Zionism had prospered and had settled 100,000 Jews in Palestine where the Arabs at first made no objection. However, during the war Dr Chaim Weizmann, head of the Zionist movement, was an industrial chemist who, while working for the Admiralty, had perfected a method of making alcohol from wood. This remedied a grave deficiency in the manufacture of explosives, which, owing to the vast quantities required on the Western Front, were becoming dangerously short. Lloyd George was so grateful to Weizmann that he asked him what reward he would like – a British title perhaps. Weizmann declined titles or money but requested a National Home for the Jewish people in Palestine. Lloyd George agreed readily, unaware perhaps that there were 12,000,000 Jews worldwide, and that the Arabs, who had lived in the country for some two thousand years, saw it as their own in spite of Turkish domination. His promise was formulated in the Balfour Declaration of 2 November 1917. The Arabs resented this British interference in what they thought should be their own country and attempted to make life as unpleasant as possible for everyone else in it. When Palestine became Israel in 1948, it was immediately attacked by the surrounding Arab countries but defeated them heavily. In the 1990s, the resentment felt by the Arabs at having a Jewish state planted in their midst still lingers on.

With hindsight it is obvious that whatever arrangements were made for the future of the former Turkish Empire, Britain and France would try to retain a large influence in this nodal point of world communications, let alone its vast oil reserves. All this was in the distant future when Lawrence, who sympathised with Arab aspirations for independence, applied his talents to organising them into guerrilla fighters to harass the Turks. His principal weapon was sabotage and he trained his troops to blow up railway lines and bridges, but he also attacked Turkish soldiers and was attacked by them in turn. A fruitful place to begin was the Hejaz, the territory which runs along the eastern shores of the Red Sea. A railway line ran from Aleppo in Syria down to Medina, which is about 200 miles north of Mecca.

Lawrence's best work was done between 1917 and 1918. Beginning with the capture of Aqaba, he travelled widely through the Arab lands, was wounded, captured, escaped and fought again. He was awarded the DSO, but refused to accept it as he felt that the Arabs with whom he fought had been betrayed in the Peace agreements. He told his story in *Seven Pillars of Wisdom* (abridged as *Revolt in the Desert*), subsequently served in the RAF and the Tank Corps under assumed names, in the lowest possible ranks. He was killed in a motor-cycle accident in 1935. A talented, enigmatic, complex man.

Right: By honouring this treaty made in 1839, Britain entered the First World War in 1914.

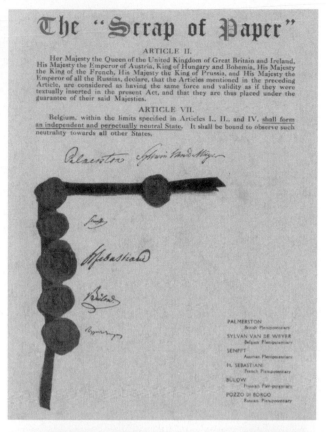

The "Scrap of Paper"

ARTICLE II.

Her Majesty the Queen of the United Kingdom of Great Britain and Ireland, His Majesty the Emperor of Austria, King of Hungary and Bohemia, His Majesty the King of the French, His Majesty the King of Prussia, and His Majesty the Emperor of all the Russias, declare, that the Articles mentioned in the preceding Article, are considered as having the same force and validity as if they were textually inserted in the present Act, and that they are thus placed under the guarantee of their said Majesties.

ARTICLE VII.

Belgium, within the limits specified in Articles I., II., and IV., shall form an independent and perpetually neutral State. It shall be bound to observe such neutrality towards all other States.

PALMERSTON
British Plenipotentiary

SYLVAN VAN DE WEYER
Belgian Plenipotentiary

SENFFT
Austrian Plenipotentiary

H. SEBASTIANI
French Plenipotentiary

BÜLOW
Prussian Plenipotentiary

POZZO DI BORGO
Russian Plenipotentiary

Right: T. von Bethmann-Hollweg, the German Chancellor.

Above: Winston Churchill in 1915.

Above right: Vice Admiral Sir F. C. D. Sturdee, who destroyed the German fleet at the Falkland Islands in 1914.

Below: Facing, left to right, Field Marshal von Hindenburg, Kaiser Wilhelm II, General Ludendorff.

Right: Facing, left to right, at XIV Corps Headquarters, Meaux, 12 September 1916, are Albert Thomas, French Minister of Munitions; Field Marshal Sir Douglas Haig; Marshal Joseph Joffre; and Lloyd George. The latter seems unimpressed by Haig's arguments.

Below: Crown Prince Rupprecht of Bavaria.

Below right: General von Kluck.

Above left: General Galliéni – an unorthodox genius.

Above: General von Mackensen.

Left: General Foch.

Right: Admiral Earl Beatty.

Right: Admiral Sir John Jellicoe.

Left: The Cloth Hall, Ypres, in 1914.

Lower left: Ruins of the Cloth Hall as seen from St Martin's Cathedral in 1918.

Above: German dreadnoughts of the air. The 'Zeppelins' were an important factor in the principle of 'frightfulness'. Their evolution and development was marked by a long series of disasters which practically ruined the inventor, Count Zeppelin, and their further improvement as a practical war machine was largely due to private enterprise and capital subscribed by private means.

Right: Lieutenant William Leefe Robinson, VC, the successful destroyer of a Zeppelin at Cuffley, Hertfordshire, on 3 September 1916. Robinson was shot down over German lines the following year and imprisoned. Released in 1918 he died soon after of influenza.

Left: The King's African Rifles crossing the Ruwu River, German East Africa.

Right: A Mark IV tank on 12 October 1917 at St Julien. The track has been blown off by gunfire.

Left: Facing, left to right, are General Sir Herbert Plumer, Lieutenant General the Honourable Herbert Lawrence and Field Marshal Sir Douglas Haig. Taken at GHQ BEF, 1918.

Right: Wounded. Beaumont Hamel, 1916.

Above: The village of Passchendaele, November 1917. The church was on the hillock in the centre background.

Below: Manhandling a 9.2in howitzer at Pilckem, 1917.

Right: A typical Bairnsfather cartoon. Bairnsfather had fought in the trenches in 1914 and 1915 and had been wounded in action. Born in India and educated at the same school as Rudyard Kipling, he became official cartoonist to the British Army in the First World War and to the US Army in Europe in the Second.

The New Submarine Danger

"They'll be torpedoin' us if we stick 'ere much longer, Bill"

Above: Major General E. H. Allenby.

Right: Field Marshal Alfred Kraus, 1917, architect of the Caporetto victory.

Below: 'C3'. The outer side of the Zeebrugge mole.

Above: M. Kerensky
saluting his troops.

Right: Lord Fiohor.

Left: John Norton Griffiths with his 2.5 ton Rolls Royce. He was the mastermind of the Messines tunnelling.

Left: Zillebeke, 1914.

Left: Zillebeke after the battle. The mound is all that remains of the church.

Right: General Sir Hubert Gough, Commander of the Fifth Army.

Right: Haig riding at the head of the Peace Procession in 1919.

Left: Cemetery at Sanctuary Wood. Thousands of headstones in war cemeteries bore the simple inscription, 'Known unto God'.

Left: Passchendaele 1986 – the battlefield in whose mud thousands disappeared without trace and where the casualties were approximately 250,000 on each side in four months.

Left: Tyne Cot Memorial today, the largest war cemetery in the Commonwealth.

Below: View from Tyne Cot showing the countryside over which troops advanced. German bunkers in the cemetery, 1984.

In tracing the exploits of Lawrence we have moved away from the other major campaign in this area, which was preparing to conquer Palestine. It began in the latter months of 1916 when the Egyptian Expeditionary Force prepared a line of communications across the Sinai desert by building a railway and a water pipe-line. The Turks, in view of the pressure they were being subjected to elsewhere, retired from the Sinai and took up strong defensive positions at Gaza and Beersheba. The Commander in Chief Egypt, Sir Archibald Murray, had no intention of creating a second Kut-type disaster and approached his problem cautiously. The troops in the Sinai desert, commanded by Sir Charles Dobell, consisted of three Territorial Divisions, the ANZAC Mounted Division, the Imperial Mounted Division and the Camel Corps. These contained excellent soldiers but most of their equipment, and some of their commanders, were obsolete, if not archaic.

Before embarking on the Palestine campaign we must now pick up the threads on the other 'sideshows', note the political and leadership changes, and return to the European battles.

East Africa was an annoying theatre because no progress had been made in capturing German's last remaining colony. Colonel von Lettow-Vorbeck was proving a military genius who had begun with a mere 5,000 men under arms, of which only a few hundred were European, but as the war progressed built this up to 4,000 Europeans and 20,000 extremely warlike Africans (known as Askaris). Von Lettow-Vorbeck's principal handicap was shortage of arms and military supplies. Nevertheless he had almost contemptuously repelled an attempted British landing, at Tanga in 1915, causing 800 casualties. Although the British were blockading the coast, ships got through in 1915 and 1916 (though the first was sunk, its cargo was salvaged). Defeating the Germans meant not only beating their troops but also overrunning the terrain in which they were holding out: much of this was thick bush.

The South African government, confident after its successes against the Germans in South-West Africa, now decided to settle the East African problem once and for all. General Smuts, who had shown himself a master of guerrilla tactics during the Boer War (fighting *against* Britain) was made Commander in Chief of a force consisting of two cavalry brigades, two infantry brigades and an artillery brigade, which was now despatched to assist the mixed British, African and Indian force already engaged in trying to subdue von Lettow-Vorbeck. Its first engagement, which occurred on 12 February, was not successful and the infantry brigade was sharply repulsed by its German-led opponents and was lucky not to be annihilated. However-er, the mounted troops did better and during the summer of 1916 the force made steady progress. Dar-es-Salaam was occupied on 4 September and von Lettow-Vorbeck narrowly escaped capture soon afterwards.

It was said of the Boer War that 'the doctor killed more than the butch-er', meaning that diseases killed more of the combatants than bullets did. East Africa looked like repeating the same scenario. However, as Africans appeared to be able to survive and fight in that climate much better than Europeans, the British decided to raise more African regiments. The King's African Rifles was already in existence and new battalions were raised and added to its strength. They were joined by a brigade from the West African Frontier Force. Although von Lettow-Vorbeck was pushed down to the far south of the country, he had still not been forced to surrender and experi-ence suggested that any slackening of the Allied effort against him would soon see him breaking out and rampaging through the country again. Mean-while Smuts was called to London in January 1917 in order to become a member of the Imperial War Cabinet. His appointment was taken over by General Hoskins, but four months later Hoskins was succeeded by General van Deventer. Here, for the moment, we must leave the African scene.

One other event needs to be chronicled before we return to the European scene. In January 1916, the Russians, deciding that the Turks were still fully occupied with Gallipoli, launched an attack on the Caucasus front. Direct-ed by General Yudenich, they advanced 50 miles into Turkey, captured Erzurum and Trebizond and settled down at Erzincan to consolidate their gains.

Another Russian force, of divisional strength, invaded Persia, captured Hamadam and Karino but were held at Khanikin (Khaneh Khuodi).

In December of 1916 Joffre was succeeded as Commander in Chief of the French army by General Robert Nivelle. As we saw earlier, Nivelle had shown an aggressive spirit in the closing stages of the Verdun battle, and was held in high esteem, though by no one more highly than himself. France needed a charismatic figure who would bring success: their armies had never fully recovered their confidence from the fearful losses they had suffered during 1915 in their unsuccessful offensive. After those, Verdun had seemed the last straw. Nevertheless, it was realised that if the situation was bad for France it must be worse for her opponents who had, after all, been defeat-ed at both Verdun and the Somme. In spite of the dismal history of failed initiatives, Nivelle sincerely believed that now was the time to win the war with a single, decisive blow. By this time the German superiority in guns had been matched and surpassed. But the essence of his thinking was that this masterstroke must be controlled by one man – himself.

Nivelle was very convincing. He visited London in January 1917 and talked with Lloyd George, who had replaced Asquith as Prime Minister a month earlier. Nivelle had an English mother and was bilingual. He got on well with Lloyd George who was deeply disturbed at the steady drain on British manpower. A successful thrust, on a large scale, claimed Nivelle, would be less costly in the long term for it would bring the war to an end reasonably soon. Lloyd George, of course, had his own ideas about strategy and still believed that a thrust up from Salonika would also be a war-winning move. However, his proposal to reinforce Salonika was opposed by Haig and Nivelle. Haig had no stomach for further adventures outside France. Romania had been persuaded to come in on the Allied side the previous August, but had soon been overwhelmed by the Germans, and an expedition from Salonika had been unable to save her.

Although Haig thought that Nivelle looked like being an effective Commander in Chief (though not as friendly a one as Joffre), he had doubts about Lloyd George. Their backgrounds were so completely different that it was almost inevitable that they should hold different viewpoints. Haig was a professional soldier with a public school and university background who had never been short of money: Lloyd George was a fiery Welshman who had made his own way via politics and tended to distrust and dislike wealthy patrician types, such as Haig. Haig thought Lloyd George was unstable: Lloyd George thought that Haig was stable in that he had a rock-like determination to go his own way even if it meant the extermination of the entire youth of Britain in trench warfare.

Lloyd George felt a strong kinship with the young men who were dying in their thousands in the trenches for he came from the same background as the average soldier. His father had died when he was a year old, leaving his mother virtually destitute and the family moved back to Wales where they were brought up by her brother, who was a shoemaker. This uncle, who was also a Baptist minister, managed to start young David on a career as a solicitor. Throughout his life Lloyd George thought that everywhere, but particularly in Wales and Ireland, the poor were oppressed by the rich. He became an extremely successful Minister of Munitions, and eventually forced the Admiralty to adopt the convoy system to counter submarines, but he felt that the war could not be won with Haig as Commander in Chief. King George V, who disliked Lloyd George, had contrived to make Haig's position more secure by instigating his promotion to Field Marshal in December 1916.

Lloyd George had then decided that, although he could not get rid of Haig, he could put shackles on him by ensuring that he had to defer to Nivelle.

One of Haig's staunchest friends and allies was Sir William Robertson, who had come from a background as poor as that of Lloyd George but had risen from it, not by politics but in the Army. Robertson's story would be incredible if it were not true. He had enlisted as a private soldier in a cavalry regiment (the 16th Lancers), just before his eighteenth birthday. Fortunately he was highly intelligent and rose through the ranks of his elite regiment by sheer intellectual merit. He became fluent in six languages, although he had never mastered his own, and dropped aitches or inserted them wrongly. Robertson detested and distrusted Lloyd George, and his views were confirmed when he heard that the Frenchman, Nivelle, was going to be able to give orders to Haig. Although Lloyd George was proved sadly wrong in his view of Nivelle, it did not stop him trying to undermine Haig and Robertson (who was Chief of the Imperial General Staff), and later in 1917 he deliberately kept Haig short of troops. Nevertheless Lloyd George was a great man who made an enormous contribution to winning the war and improving the lot of his fellow citizens. His scandalous private behaviour, his dishonesty and ruthlessness were too much for many of his contemporaries to bear, but it is interesting to recall that in 1940 Churchill offered him a post in the War Cabinet, which he declined. He died in 1945.

In the Spring of 1917 all the optimism and idealism which had characterised the opening of the war had now dispersed. The Germans hoped that by defeating the Russians they could release more of their own troops to use in the west against France and Britain. They hoped that the submarine campaign would starve Britain into surrender. Meanwhile, Britain and France hoped that the blockade was sapping the German will to fight and that one big 'push' (a favourite word in this war) would break through the German lines in France. But Nivelle knew exactly how the war could be won – by concentrated firepower. What he did not know was that the Germans were abandoning the targets onto which that firepower was to be concentrated and were building a much more formidable line further back.

Haig had never believed that the easiest way through the German lines was in the centre (preferring the north), but had little option but to defer to Nivelle's strategy. Apart from the political considerations, there were strong practical reasons why he should do so. He had 61 divisions at his disposal: Nivelle had 115. He had 1,157 large guns, including howitzers: Nivelle had 4,970. Haig was relieved that the French were now prepared to shoulder the major burden instead of leaving it to him, as had happened in the Battle of the Somme.

Nivelle's strategy visualised the French occupying the centre stage while the British attacked north of the Somme, as well as in the south in the sector which had previously been occupied by the French Sixth Army. Haig was not happy to see the British forces divided in order for the French to be able to concentrate theirs. He noted that the main French attacks were to be made in the Champagne area, where they had previously been unsuccessful, but Nivelle had no doubts about the correctness of his own approach. Surprisingly he seems to have been unaware of the fact that the Germans were methodically destroying the terrain they had been occupying for the last three years: farms were burnt, orchards destroyed, roads mined, even wells poisoned.

Haig accepted the need for him to attack the Arras sector and thus draw in German reserves so that they would not be available to the enemy to plug gaps when Nivelle made his expected breakthrough, but he disliked this difficult secondary role. Sensing Haig's reluctance to attack in an area in which he saw little hope of success, Nivelle reassured him that if for any reason the French attack was not a resounding success, Nivelle's army would then give full support to the attack through Belgium which Haig always favoured. Haig was not unmindful of the fact that success in Belgium would liberate the Channel ports, notably Zeebrugge and Ostend, which were thought to be the main U boat bases. The Admiralty, while delaying the introduction of the convoy system, was firmly, but wrongly, convinced that the nerve centre of the U boat menace was along the Belgian coastline.

The Army, of course, felt tremendous gratitude and respect for the Royal Navy which was ferrying millions of soldiers back and forth across the Channel in spite of periodic German attempts to interfere with this traffic. The Channel was protected by the Dover Patrol, a miscellany of escort craft whose task was to protect the transport which conveyed Allied troops and stores to and from France. By 1917 nearly a million wounded men had been evacuated, and every day between 12 and 15,000 men were transported across the Channel: at the end of the war 10,000,000 men had passed through Dover and even more through Folkestone. All this was through waters littered with wrecks and mines and vulnerable to attacks by enemy destroyers, submarines or aircraft.

For their onerous task one might have expected the Dover Patrol would consist of a fleet of fast modern warships. On the contrary, it was made up of one obsolete battleship, a few cruisers, a cross-channel steamer which had been converted into a floating sea-plane base, and a motley collection of trawlers, drifters, armed yachts and motor launches: it was based on Dover and Dunkirk. After initial attempts to test its strength, the Germans decided that the best they could hope for was an occasional hit and run raid.

Not least of the achievements of the Dover Patrol was maintaining an illuminated route, protected by minefields and surface craft, from England to France. The illuminations were the product of the fertile brain of Wing Commander Brock, whose family were manufacturers of fireworks. Brock, who had the unique distinction of being a wing commander in the Air Force, lieutenant commander in the Navy, and lieutenant colonel in the Army simultaneously, was a prolific inventor. Before the Channel was illuminated, German submarines used to travel on the surface at night at top speed. This enabled them to skim over nets, which inevitably drooped; provided they did not encounter any mines or patrol craft they could reach the Atlantic much more rapidly than if they had to take the longer route round Scotland. Once the Channel was lit up, these night-time adventures became impossible. However, the fact that there was no concealing darkness meant that British craft using the Channel were extremely vulnerable to air attack.

The Admiralty never discarded its belief that Zeebrugge and Ostend were packed with U boats until the end of the war when it was disclosed that their resources had been greatly exaggerated. Nevertheless, that discovery was eighteen months away when Haig was considering British strategy and it seemed to him that he had a duty to the Admiralty to lighten its burden as soon as possible by occupying the Belgian coast. The French, who had internal lines of communication, were not interested in Britain's problem of transporting troops to and fro across the Channel.

A considerable thorn in Haig's flesh was Major General Sir Henry Wilson, who was the liaison officer between the British and French staffs. Wilson was Director of Military Operations in the War Office at the beginning of the war and was a close friend of the French General Ferdinand Foch. He believed that British military policy should be guided by French needs and was suspected, quite correctly by Haig, of working to achieve this. Although his support of Nivelle turned out to be extremely unwise, he was not deflected from favouring French strategic ideas. In 1918 he worked closely with Lloyd George to engineer the appointment of Foch as Supreme Commander, Allied Forces in France. After the war, he infuriated southern Irishmen by his views on Ireland's best policy, and was assassinated on his doorstep in London by two members of the IRA on 22 June 1922.

Haig's position in 1917, with both the British Prime Minister and the official liaison officer hostile to him, was not easy. By 1917 he was already seen as the Commander in Chief who had presided over the appalling Battle of the Somme. Later critics nicknamed him 'Butcher Haig', but did not appear to notice that the generals on both sides were equally devoid of ideas in this war of attrition. There were, of course, no tactical options in this static warfare: when millions of men are firmly entrenched within an area some ten miles wide and 400 hundred miles long, with the sea at one end and the mountains of a neutral country at the other, the only possible way of making a breakthrough is by weight of firepower and numbers. Inevitably hundreds of thousands of men will be killed.

Ludendorff had no scruples about sacrificing thousands of Germans in infantry attacks, but at this stage realised that he must conserve manpower as much as possible. He had lost 680,000 on the Somme and another 280,000 at Verdun: that rate of losses could not go on. Fortunately for Ludendorff, Germany was now winning the war on the Eastern Front and soon huge reinforcements would be available from that area. Although he realised that any form of retreat would be damaging to morale, he considered that the end would justify the means. He set about building what was officially termed the Siegfried Stellung, but which British soldiers called the Hindenburg Line. It ran from Arras through Cambrai and St Quentin to Soissons. Originally the German line here had bulged forward encompassing the Somme (already lost) but now was 35 miles to the rear of Bapaume and Peronne. The Siegfried Stellung was built by prisoners taken on the Russian front. It was formidable by any standards.

German strategists appear to have a faith in walls which is not justified by experience. In the Second World War they made short work of the famous French Maginot Line, but then proceeded to build the Siegfried Line to protect the western frontier of Germany. It did not do so. Their 'West Wall' along the northern coast of France was also formidable, but was breached in a day in 1944.

As Lloyd George was keen to arouse Haig's enthusiasm for Nivelle's opinion, he made a great effort to ensure that Haig's own offensive also enjoyed some success, and for the Arras offensive ensured that Haig had three armies at his disposal and a three to one superiority in heavy guns and howitzers. He also had 60 tanks and four cavalry divisions to exploit any breakthrough.

Haig's Arras battle began on 9 April, in sleet and snow, and was very successful initially. Vimy Ridge was captured by the Canadians in First Army: this area had been the graveyard of many previous attempts by the French. Eleven thousand prisoners and many guns were captured along the front and there were substantial gains overall, but after five miles the offensive came to a halt on the outskirts of the Hindenburg line. This is where the Arras battle should have stopped, for it had served its purpose as a diversion. Unfortunately Haig felt that he was under an obligation to Nivelle to continue and did so on 23 April. This time progress was slight.

Meanwhile Nivelle's offensive, which had begun on 16 April, had proved an almost complete disaster. The earlier stages had been disrupted by the German 'scorched earth' preparations, and the 'booby-traps' had taken their toll. When the main forces clashed, the French lost 96,125 against the Germans' 83,000. The battle which Nivelle had predicted would be over in two days was still grinding along on the ninth.

For the sorely-tried French army this bloodbath was the last straw. High hopes had been dashed and all confidence in Nivelle and his officers disappeared. Then the unthinkable happened. Along the entire front the French army refused to continue the battle: in some sectors there was actual mutiny instead of passive disobedience, and all along the line men began to desert. Huge gaps were left as men streamed to the rear. The French Higher Command dared not acknowledge the existence of the mutiny and Nivelle was not dismissed, although Pétain, the hero of Verdun, was appointed Chief of the French General Staff, with a view of restoring French morale. Even Haig did not know the truth until the beginning of May. Fortunately for the Allies, the Germans did not know either, or they would simply have walked through the gaps and reached Paris.

When Haig learnt the appalling truth he had to behave as if it had not happened. He was busy enough with his own hard-slogging Arras offensive and realised that by keeping this going at whatever the cost he could keep the Germans occupied physically and mentally. Haig did not dare tell Lloyd George of the mutiny, for he knew only too well what happens when politicians are given information in the strictest confidence. Even the French government was kept in the dark. Instead it was told that though Nivelle's offensive had been temporarily checked, it would be resumed again as soon as possible. Meanwhile Pétain, for whom this was perhaps a more important moment than Verdun, set to work to assess and limit the damage. He toured the French front, listening to complaints and identifying the ringleaders. The malaise in the French army was not entirely based on the fact that the soldiers felt that they were being herded into a slaughterhouse, but also because their food was bad, leave was short and unfairly allocated, and leadership from above was indifferent to the sufferings of the ordinary soldier.

55 ringleaders were shot, and the causes of the more serious grievances removed. Surprisingly quickly the mutiny subsided and the French army was in being again. However, as Pétain realised only too well, the situation was frail. The French army was not yet in a state in which it could be used as an effective fighting force: time was needed for that. Haig was informed of something he knew already: the burden of keeping the Germans at bay rested on him and the British army.

Russia, on which the Allies had for so long depended to keep the Germans busy on the Eastern Front, was now beginning to disintegrate, though not entirely because of military setbacks. For several years the Czar Nicholas II and, more particularly, his wife Alexandra (originally a German princess) had been influenced by a dissolute mystic called Rasputin (the name, which was not his real one, means debauchee). In 1905 Rasputin had been brought to the Russian court as a healer with supernatural, perhaps occult, powers. Whatever the origin of his skills, he made a profound impression on the Czar and Czarina for his ability to alleviate the sufferings of their haemophiliac son, Alexis. Rumours circulated that his numerous sexual conquests included the Czarina herself: she certainly employed him as her chief adviser, and as a result many of her courtiers disappeared from their influential positions. As Nicholas II had taken personal command of the army in September 1915 and therefore left much of the administration of domestic affairs to the Czarina, the heart of the Russian empire was clearly in a parlous state. Not surprisingly, the Czarina was suspected of being pro-German. Rasputin was assassinated with considerable difficulty, in December 1916, but the general corruption in the court and outside had now gone on so long that Russia was poised for explosive events. In spite of the existence of a nominal parliament, called the Duma, Russia was an imperial dictatorship, and Nicholas had no intention of it being anything else. However, in the early months of 1917 the effect of huge casualty lists, food shortages, and the threat of impending defeat began to be shown by strikes and protest meetings in the streets. Once begun, the revolt spread rapidly; one imperial regiment mutinied and murdered its officers; the Duma criticised the Czar for not allowing democratic reforms, and then refused to disperse when he ordered it to be dissolved. The peaceful demonstrations in the streets became mobs who lit fires and opened the prisons: chaos ruled. Too late the Czar realised the country was seething with revolution. On 15 March he abdicated: a few days later he was arrested. The Revolution had taken place without any special organisation: the Romanov dynasty and all it stood for had suddenly collapsed from internal corruption.

At first there were indications that a reasonably democratic and benign regime might take over the task of governing Russia, although there were ominous portents in the Socialist Committees, known as 'Soviets'. The liberal and moderate socialists supported Kerensky, an articulate and respected lawyer, who was elected head of the new government.

But if the Revolution had happened almost by accident, there was nothing unplanned about the direction it was now going to take. The Germans noted that Kerensky was going to honour Russia's commitments to the Allies and took steps accordingly. Lenin (real name Ulyanov) who had been living in exile in Switzerland, was permitted to travel through Germany to Russia in a sealed train. Money was provided to assist the Revolution. Lenin had been a Marxist since 1889. In the 1890s he had been exiled to Siberia for expressing subversive opinions. Although he established his so-called Dictatorship of the Proletariat, Lenin was, like many other revolutionaries, of middle-class origins.

Trotsky (Leon Bronstein) was also middle class. He too had been exiled to Siberia, from where he escaped to London; he then travelled widely and was in New York when the Czar was dethroned. He hastened back to Russia where he joined Lenin, with whom he had had differences in the past and would again in the future. The third and most enduring of the conspirators was Stalin (Joseph Dzugashvili) who had originally been destined for the priesthood. These three were determined that Russia should get out of the war as soon as possible and in the meantime worked to ensure that the Revolution took the form which they favoured. The Germans, who watched events in Russia with a benign eye, failed to realise that when the new Revolutionary regime was established they would become the principal enemy.

The Allies, unaware of the gravity of events in Russia, urged Kerensky to continue the war. As this seemed a better policy than having hordes of undisciplined soldiers in the streets, Kerensky agreed. Brusilov was Commander in Chief.

But the Revolution had gone too far. Already there were Soviets in army units and very unwisely Kerensky had sanctioned the appointment of commissars. Even before the offensive began, millions of soldiers deserted.

However, the remainder still mustered some 40 divisions, made up of a mixture of nationalities. After the Russians had made some progress against the Austrians, Germany decided that the time for watching was over. Having stiffened their eastern units with a few divisions from the Western Front, they launched a strong counter-offensive. The Russian front crumbled. The

Germans and Austrians then overran Galicia in the southern sector and the Germans captured Riga in the north.

While these disasters were overwhelming the Russian army, the Bolsheviks decided that the time to seize control of the country was now ripe. In October they made their move. Incredibly, the Winter Palace in Petrograd, where the Provisional Government met, was guarded only by a small unit of women soldiers. The Bolsheviks were well aware that their strongest card was their claim that once they were in power they would make peace and save the people from further slaughter and deprivation. Kerensky managed to avoid falling into the hands of his political enemies, and hoped to gather enough support to regain power. But there was no stopping the Bolsheviks and after six months in hiding Kerensky escaped to Europe, where he wrote and lectured. In 1940 he moved on to the United States and died in New York in 1970.

The Bolsheviks lost no time in making peace with the Germans, arranging a truce on 5 December 1917 and signing the Treaty of Brest-Litovsk on 3 March 1918. The terms were so humiliating and crippling that at first even the Bolsheviks found them too severe. However, a threat by Germany to renew the war quickly had an effect. Russia had to give up Finland, Estonia, Latvia, Lithuania, Poland and the Ukraine, and was thus reduced to a smaller size than she had been before the accession of Peter the Great (1682). Observers in the West, some of whom had been toying with the idea of making peace with Germany instead of continuing with the relentless slaughter on the Western Front, looked askance at the harshness of the treaty and decided that there was no alternative to continuing until Germany was defeated.

(In the 1990s there were suggestions that Britain should have made peace with Hitler's Germany in 1940 after Poland and France had been conquered by the Nazis. Presumably, at best, this would have led to a series of Brest-Litovsk type treaties and the extension of the holocaust. Unfortunately, suggestions by revisionist historians, however unrealistic and bizarre, always seem to be uncritically accepted by certain reviewers and journalists whose knowledge of history is incomplete.)

Although the Bolsheviks' seizure of power in 1917 seemed to be complete, the Revolution was by no means secure. The Bolsheviks held an election on 25 November 1917, when voting was by universal and secret ballot, but to their dismay only gained a minority of seats in the Duma. When their resolutions were voted down, they retaliated by closing the Duma, saying it was counter-revolutionary and bourgeois. Civil war now broke out (and would last three years). Various Czarist military leaders organised small counter-revolutionary armies in the Ukraine, Caucasus, White Russia, Baltic and Siberia, but in time all petered out. The Allies gave some not very effective support, hoping that the moderates would be restored and Russia would continue in the war against Germany. More practically they hoped to prevent the Germans seizing or otherwise acquiring huge stocks of arms and supplies that had been despatched to Russia earlier in the war.

Owing to the drive of Trotsky and some Czarist officers who had gone over to the new regime, a Bolshevik 'Red' Army was now created. It received support from the peasants who had been given land when the old Czarist estates were broken up and who now thought they might lose it again if the Bolsheviks were defeated. Working closely with the Red Army was the 'Cheka' (from which the KGB would evolve). The Cheka had been set up by Lenin to suppress saboteurs and counter-revolutionaries and was soon arresting and shooting anyone who looked like threatening the new regime. In 1922 it changed its name to the OGPU, but its methods and motives remained unaltered.

Although all this appeared independent of the war elsewhere, there were still close links and influences. If the Allies had been more successful on the Western Front in 1917–1918 they would have been able to prevent the Germans imposing the treaty of Brest-Litovsk on Russia and would also have had troops to spare to bolster up Kerensky's offensive.

Furthermore, the possible effects of what was happening in Russia were noted by the Allies who wondered if their own soldiers might be tempted to mutiny (as the French had already done) if the war continued much longer. Communism had great popular appeal. According to the proponents it would end wars, as wars were caused by capitalist countries competing for markets. After a short period of 'dictatorship of the proletariat', during which private ownership would be replaced by communal ownership of land and goods, they would be able to cooperate, rather than compete, with other Communist countries. In July 1918 the Russian Socialist Federated Republic (RSFR) was established. In theory, this was a genuine democratic regime: in practice, as was soon apparent, it was ruled by the Communist party which now numbered no more than one in every hundred Russians, but whose power was soon absolute. In the same month as the establishment of the RSFR, the Czar, his wife and his five children were all shot in the cellar of a house in Ekaterinburg.

Although Russia had ceased to be an effective fighting force in July 1917, this did not mean, as we have noted, that it had ceased to exert its influence on the war, although this was now a negative one; not least was the fact that Germany could now withdraw its armies from the east and use them in the west. Although America had now come in on the Allied side, it would be months before her help could be effective and meanwhile the French army was virtually useless. There were disquieting stories that the Italian armies were apparently being influenced by events in Russia too. In May 1917, some Italian units in the Isonzo sector surrendered, saying they would no longer fight in this capitalist war. There was a minor mutiny in the Austrian navy, which was quickly suppressed, and minor trouble in the German High Sea fleet.

Nevertheless, whatever happened on the secondary fronts, the key to victory was France. In view of what had happened to Nivelle's offensive, the options here were limited. Future offensives would have to be in the Ypres area, which Haig knew well, and also favoured, although he was not unaware of its special difficulties. Unfortunately, two factors were going to make the forthcoming battle a military nightmare. Earlier battles in the area had left the Germans in possession of the points from which the city of Ypres could be observed and shelled, and the Belgian summer that year was to be exceptionally wet. The desired objective for the British forces was Roulers, an important junction which lay a few miles beyond the Passchendaele Ridge. Haig estimated that if he could gain possession of the village of Passchendaele (now spelt Passendale by the Belgians) there would be little to stop him reaching Roulers and then he could release his cavalry to stream across the Belgian countryside, liberating Ghent and the Channel ports, and perhaps reaching Cologne. Capturing Passchendaele seemed a minor problem in comparison with the difficulties of the Somme battle, where the Germans had prepared so long and carefully. In fact, on a lesser scale, they had prepared numerous gun-sites and blockhouses in the Ypres area too, as would soon be disclosed. What Haig did not know, although surprisingly the French did, was that the Hindenburg Line (the Siegfried Stellung) which had defeated Nivelle, had been extended up into Belgium, where it was called the Flandern Stellung. It was said that Foch had mentioned this vital piece of information to Wilson, relying on him as the liaison officer between the two armies, to convey it to Haig. This Wilson failed to do. The tragedy of Passchendaele (known in military chronicles as Third Ypres) was that it was wrongly assumed to have been fought in vain. Even if the British forces had taken Passchendaele before the winter set in, they would have faced another campaign before they came anywhere near to capturing Roulers. However, Passchendaele, a battle of appalling misery which caused some

250,000 British casualties and even more German, absorbed German attention to such a degree that they never tested the French defences after the Nivelle debacle. Had they done so, they would have found them fragile and would no doubt have concentrated their efforts in that sector. By doing so they might well have achieved the victory which had eluded them in 1914. Passchendaele was therefore perhaps the most important battle of the war, for it held the line while the French recovered and the Americans settled in.

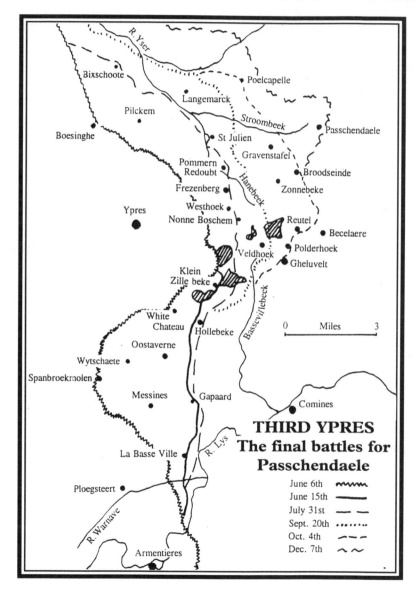

THIRD YPRES
The final battles for
Passchendaele

June 6th	⌇⌇⌇
June 15th	———
July 31st	— —
Sept. 20th	••••••
Oct. 4th	––––
Dec. 7th	⌒ ⌒

0   Miles   3

The benefits of Passchendaele were seen the following year, when the French and the Americans were able to play their part in the final victory.

That being said, it was still one of the most appalling battles in history. The German historian, Kuhl, a former Chief of the German General Staff, wrote:

'The sufferings, privations and exertions which the soldiers had to bear were inexpressible. Terrible was the spiritual burden for the lonely man in the shell hole and terrible the strain on the nerves which continued day and night. The "Hell of Verdun" was exceeded by Flanders. The Battle of Flanders [the German name for Passchendaele] has been called "The greatest martyrdom of the World War".

'No division could last more than a fortnight in this hell. Then it had to be relieved by new troops. Looking back it seems that that which was borne here was superhuman. With respect and thankfulness the German people will always remember the heroes of Flanders.'

Ypres stands at the western end of a low-lying plain surrounded on all sides by low, wooded, hills. Some seven miles to the east of the British positions lay a low, curved ridge, in the middle of which was the village of Passchendaele itself. The plain in between is intersected by canals and streams which form a complex drainage system. These are the result of centuries of work of reclamation of land which is virtually at sea level. This drainage pattern is so precarious that any interference with it, either by natural forces such as unduly heavy rain, or by man, quickly transforms the whole area into a morass. In the second half of 1917 it suffered from both, and the results, inevitably, were chaotic.

Haig's offensive at Passchendaele had been planned to begin on 23 July but was postponed till 31 July to allow French artillery, which was to be used in this battle (and for whom this was regarded as an important morale-boosting exercise), to be completely ready. The bombardment of the front, which as we have already seen was considered a necessary preliminary to any attack in this war, had begun on 22 July and employed 3,000 guns. Four and three quarter tons of shells were thrown at every yard of the front. Inevitably, this completely ruined the drainage system by breaching the canal banks, and silting up the channels. While the guns were pounding away, the air above Flanders was seeing the most vigorous battles of the war, in which the Royal Flying Corps established superiority. In spite of this, Crown Prince Rupprecht, the German Army Group Commander and General Sixt von Arnim felt that their numbers and disposition were adequate to cope with any attack. One of the oddities of this war was that Prince Rupprecht, like the Kaiser, was related to the British Royal family and would have had a plausible claim to the British throne if he had cared to make it.

The British knew very well what would happen when the rains began, for they had been warned by the Belgian Public Works department. However, the weather forecasters did not expect rain till mid-August, by which time Haig hoped that most of the important objectives would have been secured. After the war, his strategy was heavily criticised, often by people who were too young to fight in the First World War and for various reasons unable to take more than an administrative post in the Second, but none of them ventured to suggest alternative methods or tactics. Haig's appearance, personality and background made him the perfect scapegoat for the enormous cost in lives of the First World War. His demeanour was austere, he was a poor public speaker, and he appeared to lack the warmth of Generals 'Bobs' Roberts, Sir John French, Plumer and even Kitchener, even though the last was no expert in public relations either. Nevertheless it is absurd to claim that Haig conducted battles from 50 miles behind the lines and was indifferent to casualties. He often came into the front line, and in the earlier battles his presence had had a very positive effect on morale. However, he was by no means without faults. In the Battle of the Somme he had relied too much on the unsubstantiated reports of his Army Commanders, listened too much to Kiggell, his Chief of the General Staff in France who had no battlefield experience, and naively trusted General Charteris whom he himself had selected to be Chief of Intelligence.

Although the offensive was not launched until 31 July, the Passchendaele battle had begun with the explosion of nineteen mines under the ridge at Messines. Although the Ypres countryside was so waterlogged that trenches were often half full of water, the soil itself possessed an unexpected characteristic. On the surface (in which the trenches were dug) was sand or sandy loam; below that was a layer of half-liquid sand and clay. Below that was a deep seam of blue clay. Earlier mining had been begun (by both sides) in the second layer where revetted tunnels replaced the semi-liquid clay. Mining in the third layer, which meant penetrating right through the blue clay, was the brainchild of an engineering contractor who was also an MP; it soon became a massive operation. Six deep tunnels were driven forward under the German positions and the total area excavated underground extended over 5,000 yards, could sleep 6,000 men, and shelter 10,000. On 7 May a million pounds of ammonal exploded in nineteen mines with a noise that was even heard in London. It destroyed all the positions the Germans had carefully constructed on this vital ridge. Although nineteen huge mines had exploded, two had failed to do so, but this did not make any difference to the overall effect. One exploded years later in a thunderstorm; the other remains dormant to this day.

Although the mines had a devastating effect, causing 23,000 casualties and resulting in the capture of 7,000 prisoners, the Germans made a typically vigorous counter-attack as soon as they had recovered from the initial shock. Intrepid troops occupied some of the craters and proved difficult to dislodge. This limited the size of the Allied success, although it was considerable.

Astonishingly, there was no follow-up to this success and no major action for six weeks. The explanation preferred for the delay is that Haig did not believe that the German army was sufficiently weakened to be on the point of surrender and that only after being drawn into the Flanders sector and pounded by British artillery, would it be willing to do so. Certainly, if the British had taken Passchendaele during July there would still be many German troops, some coming from the Russian front, to block the way to further progress. And it is, of course, true that attention was diverted from French weakness but the price seems to have been excessively high. Although Passchendaele weakened the German army, it did not bring it anywhere near to the point of surrender. There seems little doubt that the tragedy of Passchendaele was largely due to the poor quality of the intelligence and staff work. Intelligence failed to discover the strength of the forts which the Germans had been assiduously building, and completely underestimated the difficulties of road-building. The assumption that flooded areas could be crossed easily by stone or log roads proved hopelessly incorrect. Shellfire quickly transformed the whole area into a vast evil-smelling swamp, full of quicksands into which men, horses, guns and conventional road-making materials would disappear and leave no trace. Methods such as revetting with sandbags, which had proved successful in other sodden areas, proved to be useless at Passchendaele. Here and there were ridges on the battlefield where the ground was firmer, but the Germans were in possession of them and could only be driven off by further shellfire.

To an impartial observer it must seem incomprehensible that the British army should have been placed deliberately in these appalling circumstances. The conditions on the battlefield were certainly worse than had been anticipated but that was an unexpected misfortune. The German High Command would have understood Haig's strategic thinking perfectly. From the beginning of known warfare, possibly some 2,000 BC, military commanders had learnt certain vital tactical lessons. Many of those lessons were encapsulated in the principals laid down by Sun Tzu, writing in China in 500 BC. He emphasised the importance of making the enemy fight on ground of one's own choosing. 'It is only one who is thoroughly acquainted with the evils of war that can thoroughly understand the profitable way of carrying it on.' The 'evils of war', as was subsequently shown in many different countries by widely-varying commanders, often involved sacrificing large portions of one's own army in order to lure the enemy into a trap, in which their strength and morale might be destroyed, in order to facilitate final victory. Medieval warfare saw this happen on numerous occasions. It was clearly recognised that commanders needed to be ruthless, but while being so, they usually took many of the risks themselves. Later we had Frederick the Great urging on his soldiers, 'Dogs, would you live for ever?' and Napoleon of his own elite troops, 'They will not retreat and it will take a long time to kill them all.' Even allegedly compassionate commanders, such as Field Marshal Montgomery in the Second World War, were quite prepared to sacrifice men by sending them through an uncleared minefield. As Wellington said, 'Next to a battle lost the greatest misery is a battle gained.' However, whatever the cost, ultimate victory must be gained. Up till the present century the majority of people killed in a battle died after victory had been won. It was not always the defeated who died either: many of them, cornered or facing the loss of all their possessions and all they had fought for, turned and fought to the death to kill their pursuers, the victors.

War is, of course, barbaric but once it has begun there is no time for half-measures. Russian troops in the Second World War fought superbly and were greatly motivated to do so by the fact that if a member of a section displayed a less than whole-hearted commitment, his comrades were advised, or probably urged, to kill him. When British or French or German soldiers were killed, their next of kin would be informed: when Russians were killed, they were simply replaced by other Russian soldiers: there were no nominal rolls.

In this context, the slaughter of the First World War, even at Passchendaele, becomes more understandable. Similarly, the attempts to humanise war: treatment of prisoners, the wounded, and not bombing 'open' cities, seem great achievements rather than partial failures.

However, it must not be overlooked that in war between civilised countries considerable humanity is sometimes displayed between lower ranks in the treatment of the enemy. Doctors tend the enemy wounded with care and compassion, once the fury of battle is over. Western nations are compassionate towards their prisoners, unless they have been infuriated by the discovery of atrocities. But this did not happen in the First World War when the Turks took prisoners, nor in the Second when the Japanese did likewise, and in the 1990s the warfare in the Balkans seems barbaric by any standards.

As the conditions in the battle of Passchendaele were probably the most appalling in the history of warfare, and as it took place in an area which is now easily accessible to tourists, it is described in some detail here.

Zero hour had been fixed for an hour before dawn on 31 July 1917. By this stage in the war attacks were not usually timed to begin precisely on the hour or half hour but at intervals in between on the basis that this might provide some element of surprise. Zero hour might be 10.25, 11.50 or 12.55, for that purpose.

Owing to the portrayal of war in films and on television, there has grown up an entirely natural belief that First World War attacks consisted of infantry leaping out of trenches and walking or running towards the enemy lines. Eventually, of course, they did that, but it was not as haphazard as it appears. Before battles began there were elaborate rehearsals of tactics on models (often involving large areas) *behind* the battlefield. Most of them practised the capture of specific known objectives and required the coordination of trench mortars, rifle grenades, and Lewis guns. Some explanation of these weapons is necessary. Grenades were used in huge quantities in trench warfare. The two most famous were the British Mills bomb (the 36 grenade), which was shaped like a small pineapple and was filled with amatol, and the German stick bomb, which was shaped like a jamjar with a stick protruding from it. Both had delayed action fuses, which varied between four and seven seconds. Once the pin was removed, the bomb release was held merely by a lever. Having pulled out the pin, the soldier held the lever down while he threw the grenade with a bowling action which was less dangerous than an ordinary throw (which might cause it to slip through his fingers and fall on the ground). An exploding grenade had a lethal range of some 25 yards although on hard surfaces, like roads or concrete, this would be greater. Rifle grenades were developed for anti-tank work as they could be aimed more accurately and would sometimes penetrate a gun aperture. Mills bombs had been invented by Sir William Mills in 1915, but in earlier centuries tall soldiers had thrown explosive projectiles (having lighted the fuse) and been given the name grenadier. Grenades can take many shapes and contain a variety of lethal substances, such as phosphorus, which sets the surrounding area alight.

Trench mortars were another highly effective weapon. The original trench mortar was German and consisted of a steel tube held in a simple frame. A bomb was dropped down the two-foot long, 90mm diameter tube, at the bottom of which a firing pin set off the charge and sent the bomb wobbling through the air at about 45° until it landed on the target and exploded. The original German mortar was named the Minenwerfer (known to the British soldiers as the 'moaning Minnie'). The Minenwerfer was soon copied by the British and in a redesigned form became the Stokes Mortar. This was lighter and even more lethal than its German predecessor. Wilfred Stokes, incidentally, was the Managing Director of a firm which in peacetime produced lawn-mowers but which, like many other manufacturers of domestic products, had been turned over to weapon-making. Although mortars were perfected in the twentieth century they (like grenades) had a long history and were known as bombards in the early development of gunpowder in medieval times.

Unlike the first day of the Somme, the first day of Passchendaele went well for the British. Land from which the Germans had long dominated the British positions, notably part of the Gheluvelt plateau, was captured and although fierce German counter-attacks later meant that some of it was subsequently lost, the overall gain gave much satisfaction to the Higher Command. If the succeeding days went as well as this, they felt, the Passchendaele offensive would soon be seen to have justified itself. Disconcertingly though, in spite of favourable forecasts, it began to rain in the afternoon and during the evening the rain developed into a relentless torrent. The immediate effect was to change the whole character of the battlefield by separating the newly-established front line from the rear areas by a swamp two miles wide. There were still one or two roads across this artificial lake but they were mostly cratered by shells and in any case were inadequate for the volume of traffic they were expected to sustain. In order for the Gheluvelt terrain to be tenable it was now necessary to press on and capture a line of guns further back which had it within close range.

But until some provision could be made for laying fresh roads, or the rain stopped, a further attack could not take place. Meanwhile the Menin road was quickly acquiring the reputation of being the most dangerous road in France. On 9 August the rain at last stopped and an attempt was made to capture the part of the Gheluvelt plateau which the Germans still held. With almost superhuman courage and determination, the British forces pressed forward and captured more ground, although most of it seemed to consist of black slimy mud littered with broken tree trunks. However, having reached it they were trapped, for the Germans concentrated a barrage behind them, cutting them off from reinforcements, food, water and ammunition.

On 14 August there was another heavy thunderstorm and the attack scheduled for that day was postponed till the 16th. Gradually, in the face of determined German counter-attacks, the line was pushed forward, although here and there hard-won territory was lost again. The attack was meant to be halted on the 17th, but suddenly the rain stopped and the sun shone. This seemed an unexpected stroke of good fortune – except perhaps to the men doing the fighting – and the Higher Command decided that the attack should be continued while it lasted. The rain began again on the 22nd.

The suffering by both sides on this battlefield now exceeded everyone's worst nightmare. In one sector infantrymen had to stand for ten hours up to their knees in mud and slime when they reached their objective: all that time they were being shelled. Haig and his commanders now agreed that the best policy was to delay further attacks until 20 September, when reinforcements of men, guns, ammunition and stores would have become available, roads would have been constructed, and, hopefully, the rain would have stopped. Much of September was fine and the roadmakers, who were now relying on log and plank surfaces, were able to work successfully. But all this time the Germans were well aware of what was pending and used the possession of the higher pieces of land, and observation posts, to shell the British lines relentlessly. Roadmaking was done at night but as the German gunners knew exactly where the roads were being made, they shelled them method-ically. Nevertheless, roads were made. Ironically road-making was done by engineers, pioneers, and men of the Labour Corps: the last two of these cat-egories are usually held in low esteem by the remainder of the army, a rep-utation which lingers on from the past when they worked in rear areas out of range of danger. A member of one of these road-building parties at Pass-chendaele recalled: 'We must have presented a fine target. Our roads ran practically at right angles to the trenches so that an enemy gun placed in line with our road had a simple task. So long as the aim was right, length did not matter. If the range were too long for the working party the probability was that a portion of the newly made road would suddenly leap skyward. Thus it was a case of building and repairing over and over again until our patience was almost ended. All the while the slow but steady increase in our casual-ty list was disheartening.'

The artillery which both sides used to pound each other was of consid-erable variety but in general was of two main types: guns and howitzers. 'Guns' were long barrelled weapons which discharged their projectiles at great velocity on a low trajectory. Howitzers had a shorter, stubbier barrel and fired at a much steeper angle, a fact which made them particularly suitable for use against blockhouses and trenches. The most famous British gun, many of which may still be seen flanking war memorials of the First World War were 18-pounders: they had a four mile range. There were, however, plenty of larger guns.

German weapons were roughly equivalent to those of the Allies. Both sides soon learnt to recognise what type of weapon the enemy was using by the sound the shell made as it came through the air. It is said, 'It's the one you don't hear which kills you' and this was broadly but not invariably true. The German 5.9 was particularly disliked and so was the Minenwerfer howitzer, which fired twenty rounds an hour of high-explosive shells, each weighing 200 pounds.

In the circumstances of misery such as Passchendaele it might be thought that men would lose all individuality and would simply regard each other as fellow soldiers (or victims) slaving for a common cause. But the resilience of human beings to adverse circumstances is rarely better shown than on the battlefield. One man who left his reminiscences (Franklin Lushington) described some of the men in his battery. 'One treated every contingency of war as a pleasantry devised by fate for his special entertainment and amusement. With his large mouth and cheerful grin this youthful mathematician used to juggle successfully with figures while the skies rained shells. Next to him was Gunner Thomas, a Welshman whose superior education had turned sour inside him. He suspected all those who were superior to him in military rank, if not in mental ability, of bearing him a personal grudge. All officers and sergeants came automatically into this category. In the morning he would allow no smile of greeting to relax his melancholy features, but invariably produced some dismal prophecy about the weather or some well-founded complaint about the discomfort of life in wartime.'

There were plenty of men like Gunner Thomas who felt more animosity to some of their fellow soldiers than they did to the Germans. Even the possibility of a swift and messy death did not prevent some NCOs or even private soldiers treating their fellow soldiers with callous indifference. Fortunately they were the exceptions: most men settled down to acceptance that life was bad enough anyway without their doing anything to make it worse. It was, of course, necessary to preserve discipline, to make sure that rifles and equipment were as clean as possible and that everyone did his fair share of the work. Some soldiers managed to turn almost everything into a joke.

But there was little to joke about: 'It was still raining, and guns and howitzers had to be manhandled over the sodden spongy ground. Now and again they would sink to their axles, and lines of tired, blaspheming, men would heave and heave under the remorseless downpour. The blinding flash of a shellburst would light up their glistening helmets and bowed forms and etched against the surrounding blackness you saw a sudden picture of the slowly moving howitzer, the sandbags and the shattered trenches, the dismembered stumps of blasted trees, and caught the green shimmer of water in innumerable shellholes. Straining at the ropes, like beasts of burden condemned to unremitting toil, they would lose all fear of death in the hopeless misery of living and, when daylight broke, would sink to sleep in the mud, unmoved by shellfire or rain.'

Once in action, men were tired most of the time. Sentries who stared into the darkness beyond their trenches were liable to hallucinations but forced themselves to stay awake in the knowledge that to fall asleep at one's post was likely to result in an immediate court martial and a possible death sentence. By the time a man had been in the line for a few weeks he became dulled to the sight of horrors, pieces of decomposed corpses or freshly killed comrades and no doubt the feeling of perpetual tiredness acted as a narcotic.

There was no time to be sensitive. Lushington recalled 'Merridew and Cooper were binding up the wounded in the Battery Command Post when a direct hit landed on the roof. There were ten men inside and instantly eight of them were blown to shreds. The other two, the two officers, staggered out from under a heap of human flesh, shattered sandbags and twisted iron, miraculously untouched. A few moments later another shell landed in a detachment dugout killing all the occupants and overturning the gun alongside.'

In spite of the endless rain, all water for drinking and washing had to be carried. Although every man was spattered by mud and probably wet too, he would not dare to take water out of pools to wash the mud off, for it would be contaminated by the corpses lying underneath and also by the gas shells which were used by both sides.

On this and other battlefields, roads, intersections and woods were given nicknames, usually by the regiments using them, but which were soon made permanent. Tyne Cot, a huge cemetery, acquired the name because some buildings on the hillside looked like Northumberland cottages. Among many others were; Piccadilly, Clapham Junction, Lancer Farm, Bitter Wood, Tower Hamlets, Daring Cross, Stirling Castle, Calgary Grange and, more significantly, Hellfire Corner.

Attitudes to life were rarely changed, however horrible the circumstances. Copies of society papers like *The Tatler* were avidly read in squalid dugouts.

Some commanding officers were more interested in the social background of newly-joined subalterns (lieutenants) than in their previous experience and training. One man, temporarily attached to a Guards regiment recalled the following conversation when he met his commanding officer:

"'Are you a regular soldier?"

"No, sir."

"Were you at Eton?"

"No, sir."

The colonel then appeared to lose interest.'

No doubt the colonel felt he knew where he was with Etonians (who had very high casualties in the war) or regulars: no doubt that the newly-joined officer would make a suitable attempt to reach the high standards of the regiment, but he could hardly expect the colonel to be interested in him. This episode must strike a modern reader as bizarre but the facts, as proved in this and other wars, show that this closed world of an exclusive officer caste and highly trained, equally self-confident guardsmen, produced the finest fighting regiments in the world. Guardsmen may not be dearly loved by other regiments, but if it is a question of having them next to you, or in front of you, in a tight corner, there's no doubt about one's gratitude for that fact.

Snobbery about regiments, schools, whether one was a 'regular' or not (when life expectation might be days or weeks) was not limited to the British Army. The Germans and Austrians and Russians and French had much the same outlook. In general British officers seemed to have been more concerned about the welfare of their men than were the officers of other countries.

After the assault on 20 September had been more successful than expected, Haig gave the order for the next attack to take place on the 26th. The Australians and New Zealanders would take a prominent part in the attack. During the war the Australians and New Zealanders made up the Anzac Corps and although the members were well aware of their separate countries of origin, nobody else seemed particularly concerned. For practical purposes they were all described as 'British'. Earlier in the war the Anzacs had acquired the reputation of being good in the assault but less effective when required to be on the receiving end of heavy bombardments or sustained attacks. Passchendaele showed the error of such thinking for the Anzacs endured the conditions as well as anyone, although these were far removed from anything within their previous experience.

Needless to say, the initiative did not lie entirely with the allies and on the day before the next planned attack (26 September) the Germans put in their own. They chose 5.15am to launch their assault (between Menin Road and Polygon Wood), using the heaviest barrage yet seen: it included a number of gas shells among the high explosives. But the attack went badly wrong. Most barrages were timed to creep forward at an agreed pace so that the soldiers would be attacking opponents still stunned from the torrent of explosives which had just passed over them. This 'creeping barrage' manoeuvre is more complicated than it sounds and here the synchronisation was so poor that many of the shells fell among the leading German infantry. Being shelled by the enemy is bad enough; realising that many shells are coming from one's own guns is far worse. The assault was soon called off.

The British attack went in at 5.50am the next day. Astonishingly, although the lower ground was still a sodden swamp, the upper slopes of the Gheluvelt plateau had dried out in the recent sunny weather and the shells which landed there threw up a cloud of powdery dust. The Australians who were prominent in the attack therefore found that instead of having their visibility affected by rain or fog it was now hampered by dust storms. Some areas were won and lost again, changing hands several times between attack and counter-attacks: in the process thousands died. These desperate, murderous battles represented an attempt by the Allies to reach the village of Passchendaele while the weather was reasonably sunny, and a similar dogged resistance by the Germans to ensure that they did not do so. The next big 'push', as the saying was in those days, was set for 4 October. It would use tanks on the new roads and drier spots.

Once ground was captured there was a tendency to take short cuts, for example to climb out of trenches and cross ground in the open to save time. Snipers on both sides were always waiting for such moments, and also for the men who cautiously peeped over the parapet. Snipers sat or lay in their positions for hours on end watching a portion of an enemy trench in which a soldier might occasionally show himself. Invariably snipers were accurate shots with quick reactions which enabled them to respond immediately to the merest shadow of an opportunity. Because of their high success rate they had certain privileges and, of course, avoided the routine fatigues like carrying ammunition, stores or rations, or repairing trenches, which fell to their fellow soldiers.

In spite of the return of rain, the attack on 4 October was successful, although it did not gain as much ground as had been hoped. It was followed by another one five days later. It was still raining unfortunately, but the long-sought Passchendaele village was now almost within grasp. To reach the starting point of the attack, the troops had to march two and a half miles over duckboard tracks, some of which had now sunk so much that the men using them were usually ankle-deep in mud and sometimes knee-deep. One division, having struggled in darkness over the log road, (being shelled all the time), found they now had to advance over a 50-yard wide sea of mud which was waist deep in the middle. This area had originally been drained by a small stream. One hazard in this area was that the advancing troops might leave gaps in their line through which the Germans might infiltrate and create havoc in rear areas.

Stretcher-bearers won universal admiration, here and elsewhere on the battlefield. Under normal conditions two men can carry a wounded man on a stretcher, here it took sixteen in relays of four at a time. In general, stretch-er-bearers were not fired on deliberately, but the fact that they were walk-ing, or rather stumbling through mud, made them particularly vulnerable to shellfire. Sometimes, having carried a man back to the casualty clearing sta-tion they would find he had already died. They would then go back to col-lect other wounded men.

Some areas were now completely impassable, as the floods, on them were too deep. But the attacks, like the rain, continued.

On 6 November the 1st Canadian Division finally entered Passchendaele and during the next four days pushed along the ridge, which the Germans were still trying to defend; the last resistance ended on the 10th.

It was, by now, too late in the year for the success to be exploited. The official view was that this battle had been a success, but as it still left Bel-gium in German hands, and the Germans still strong enough to launch a massive offensive the following Spring, it is difficult to see what their crite-rion of success was. The final casualty lists were roughly similar for both sides, about 250,000 each. Of those, one third were already dead, and many of the remainder would die later, probably from the effects of gas. Few of those who survived would get over the mental effects. The Germans con-sidered that the British had been right to fight the Battle of Passchendaele, for although the German army was not broken it had suffered severely, and in the long run that would count. The Germans could have made matters easier for themselves if they had retired to their Flandern Stellung, but they thought the terrain of Passchendaele was ideal for destroying the British army, just as the British were thinking the same about them. Unintentional-ly, by accepting battle in the area where the British were offering it − and cer-tainly the Passchendaele area seemed to favour the defender − the Germans had allowed their attention to be diverted from other parts of the line, i.e., French-held sectors, and by so doing had allowed the French to recover.

With the virtue of hindsight we can see now that the First World War was a conflict of attrition, rather than tactics, except for certain secondary areas. The French had tried to wear out the Germans in 1915 and as a result had suffered badly themselves. Visitors to the French war museum at Péronne will see that, for the French, 1915 was reckoned the worst year of the four. Certainly Verdun was a great strain, and Nivelle's offensive was the last straw, but it was the blood-letting of 1915 which had broken the French strength. The British had lost most of their regular army by 1915 and then proceeded to lose their 'Kitcheners' in the Battle of the Somme, but the Germans, by their incorrect tactics, managed to throw away all the advantages they had in the Somme area, so that at the end of it they were more exhausted than the British. By the end of 1917, everyone was exhausted, but this did not mean that one country or another would not gear itself up for a final effort. In the event, it was the Germans.

But before the Passchendaele battle had been won, alarming news was received at Allied GHQ. On 24 October the Germans had routed the Italians at Caporetto (now Kobarid, in Slovenia), taking 265,000 prisoners: the survivors had fallen back 50 miles. The British cabinet decided that the Italians must be helped at all costs. Haig, struggling desperately to finish the Battle of Passchendaele before the winter set in, was told he must send two divisions to Italy at the earliest possible moment. Soon afterwards, he was ordered to send another three and then received the unwelcome news that one of his most able generals, Plumer, would have to follow them to take command.

As we saw earlier, the Isonzo sector between Italy and Austria, had seen a series of inconclusive battles. A breakthrough on this front would take the Italian armies into the Austro-Hungarian plain. The Isonzo region was formidable by any standards, but General Luigi Cadorna, a 67-year-old veteran, decided that this was the best area in which to launch his attacks. By May 1917 he was engaged in the battle and made some gains, though at high cost in casualties. He was less worried by the amount of casualties than by the fact that some of his soldiers appeared to have been affected by propaganda from Russia and surrendered or deserted. He decided that the best antidote to communism was more fighting and successes. In August he appeared to be proved right for the Italians drove deeply into the Austrian positions. The effects were rather more serious than he had anticipated: the Germans became alarmed that Austria might be invaded and collapse and in consequence decided that the danger from Italy must be eliminated.

Ludendorff now had an important decision forced on him. He had been planning a drive into Moldavia which he thought would finish off the Russ-

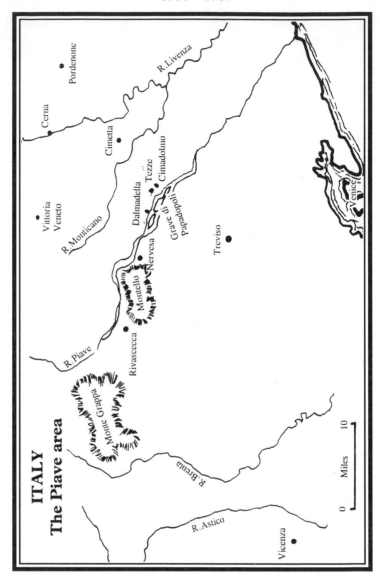

**ITALY
The Piave area**

Pordenone

R.Livenza

Cerna

Cinetta

Vittoria
Veneto

R.Monticano

Dalmadella

Tezze
Cimadolmo

Grave di
Papadopoli

Venice

Treviso

Nervesa

Montello

R.Piave

Rivasecca

Monte Grappa

R.Brenta

Treviso

0   Miles   10

R.Astico

Vicenza

ian army, but the reports coming from Austria suggested that Russia had a lower priority. On the other hand, until Russia had been forced out of the war and German divisions could be withdrawn from that front, his own resources were very limited. At best they only consisted of six divisions and that seemed hardly enough to tip the balance against an Italian army which was now full of confidence. Although Germany was doing well in Russia, mainly because of the revolution, there was little to engender confidence elsewhere. Initiative in the Middle East had passed to the Allies and German armies were being pushed back at Passchendaele. At home, discontent over food shortages was growing alarmingly and the submarine offensive which was meant to bring the war to a quick end had not only failed to do so but had instead helped to draw America into the war.

The plan which led to the Italians' undoing was not, in the event, German but Austrian. The Austrian staff had decided that there was a weak sector on the Italian front, on either side of Caporetto, and this could be exploited if a joint Austro-German force made a sudden swoop across the Isonzo river from Tolmino. Ludendorff despatched his expert in mountain warfare, General Krafft von Delmensingen, to investigate the possibilities. He discovered that the terrain was difficult but far from impossible and that the sector was very thinly garrisoned (two battalions to the mile). He quickly mustered twelve assault divisions and 300 guns in a combined Austro-German force. Although Cadorna was not informed of the presence of this force until it was marching into its assault position, once it was in place he obtained a very good idea of its composition and strength from deserters and spies. His subordinate, General Capello, a somewhat volatile personality, wished to attack immediately but Cadorna hesitated to do so, thinking he might be drawn into a trap. Capello, commanding the Italian Second Army, scorned this cautious approach and rather than reinforce the thinly-held Caporetto sector, would have preferred to press on his own already successful attack until it secured an easily defensible position. But by the end of October the Austro-German force had been reinforced by another three Austrian divisions.

The attack began, as usual, with a bombardment; it included four hours of gas shells and one of high explosives . In spite of this preliminary warning, the actual attack achieved surprise, as it was launched in a mixture of snow, rain and mist. The attackers did not have it all their own way but while the Italian flanks held, the centre, at Caporetto, proved less durable and gave way. Soon there was a huge gap in the Italian defences, leaving Cadorna no option but to pull back the whole line to the river Tagliamento. Here the Italian army endeavoured to stabilise the line, regroup and, possibly, be reinforced by stragglers. It was soon clear that the Tagliamento could only be a temporary stop, for the Austrians had already crossed the river with one division higher up at Cornino. Furthermore there was a strong chance that another Austrian force might make a swift push down from Trentino on the west and come in behind the Italians at the Tagliamento. There was no option but to fall back to the river Piave. Cadorna now gave way to General Diaz, who was younger and more in touch with the rank and file.

However, when the Austrians made their move from Trentino it was blocked. By now British and French reinforcements from France were arriving, although they did not go into action immediately. Meanwhile the Italians rallied with commendable resolution and brought the next German attack to a standstill in the Piave sector and, after two days, the invaders decided that they had achieved enough for the time being. The French then took over this sector and the British deployed at Montello. Surprisingly, the Austro-German armies then agreed that enough ground had been won in this area and that in future their efforts would be confined to the north-west (Asiago and Grappa), where their lines of communication were shorter. It was said that the victors of Caporetto subsequently lost much of their impetus when they encountered Italian storage depots, which were in sharp contrast to their own. Six months later there would be similar problems for the German commanders in France, when advancing troops fell eagerly on various items discarded by the retreating Allies and decided that the resources of the enemy were so copious that in the long run he must he unbeatable.

At the end of the Caporetto campaign the Germans claimed to have captured 275,000 prisoners, 2,500 guns, and a huge quantity of stores, including food. Prisoners of war were a mixed blessing, for they had to be fed when food was short in the captors' country. The most important factor was that the Italian threat to Austria had now been entirely removed and Ludendorff could concentrate on other areas without anxiety about his Austrian ally. Although the arrival of French and British troops had done much for Italian morale, it must not be overlooked that after a disastrous beginning the Italians had rallied and saved themselves. Vittorio Orlando now became Prime Minister of Italy; as such, he would be one of the big four (Clemenceau, Lloyd George and Woodrow Wilson were the others) at the post-war peace conferences.

One other important development which emerged from the Italian crisis was the establishment of a Supreme War Council on 5 November 1917, originally based on Rapallo but later transferred to Versailles. The suggestion came from Lloyd George and the aim was to formulate war policy between the Allied countries, so that priorities were agreed, troops allocated in the appropriate theatres and political and military leaders should see the war from the same standpoint.

The year 1917 saw progress in two other 'sideshows'. One was the embarrassing situation in Salonika. There the nominal Commander in Chief was a French general named Sarrail: he was far from popular. The diplomatic situation was complicated because the Salonika enclave was on Greek soil, but the Greeks were by no means whole-hearted supporters of the Allied cause. On 9 May 1917 Sarrail had launched an attack on Bulgaria, who had proved a useful ally to Germany, but the attack had petered out. This was very disappointing, as he had a sizeable force at his disposal (nineteen divisions: six French, six British, six Serbian and one Italian). The defeat of Bulgaria would have paved the way for the liberation of Serbia. The British, under General Milne, had played a useful part, but Sarrail's army, like many international forces, was more concerned with internal intrigues than beating the enemy, who had been stiffened with a number of excellent German troops. When the offensive was called off, the Serbs felt particularly disappointed and aggrieved.

However, a month later the situation in Greece improved considerably for the Allies when King Constantine was deposed and replaced by the pro-British Venizelos. The new government came onto the Allied side with nine divisions and on 29 June declared war on Germany, Turkey and Bulgaria. The Salonika front now stabilised, waiting for the next favourable opportunity for action, and in December General Guillaumat replaced Sarrail, to widespread satisfaction.

Salonika acquired an unenviable reputation as being one of the worst areas of the war for malaria; it was calculated that everyone suffered from it at one time or another. Malaria is carried by the bite of the anopheles mosquito, whose attentions are normally blocked by mosquito netting, greasy skin creams, or quinine. It lives in stagnant water, which may be in an old tree stump or forgotten drain. Much was learnt about the treatment of this debilitating disease during this campaign, but the general conclusion was that prevention is better than cure and that the breeding grounds should be eliminated wherever possible. Strict discipline is also needed to make sure that anti-malarial precautions are not neglected. The town of Salonika became notorious for its somewhat debauched night life; once it was nearly burnt down. Soldiers, when not incapacitated with malaria or other ills, played football, often in full view of the Bulgarians, who did not trouble to shoot at any unmilitary activity. There were two packs of foxhounds, mostly supplied from England. When the hounds strayed over the boundary into the Bulgarian lines they were always returned to their owners.

Meanwhile a campaign of much more vigour and certainty was beginning in Palestine. As we saw earlier, in 1916, the British forces from Egypt

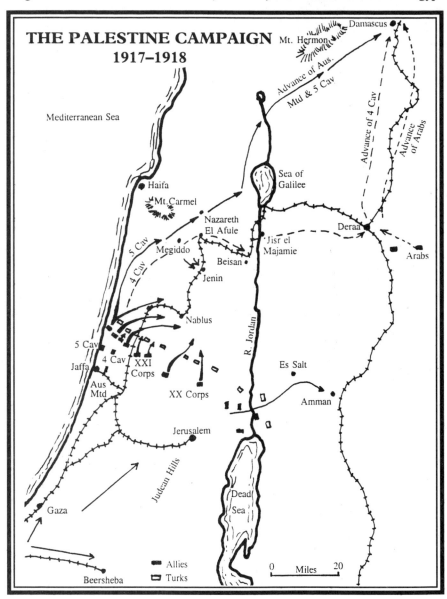

THE PALESTINE CAMPAIGN 1917–1918

had reached the Palestine border. British is perhaps too limited a word to describe the force, which included Indians, Australians, and several other nationalities.

Although neither the British public, nor even the government, realised it, the Middle East was still an important theatre. Even though the Turks had been defeated in Mesopotamia, their previous victories at Gallipoli and Kut and the humiliation they had inflicted on the British prisoners gave them considerable prestige in neighbouring Arab countries, notably Egypt, Persia and India. All these countries had large Moslem populations and if suitably inspired by Turkey could become centres of trouble rather than valuable allies. This fact was lost on people in Britain, who could not understand why so much effort was being expended on what appeared to be a remote and unimportant area. Opinion would, of course, change rapidly if oil supplies were lost or even seriously threatened. Then, of course, the government would be blamed for not having taken the necessary precautions.

The Allied High Command now felt that the best way to settle the Turkish problem, once and for all, was to inflict a crushing defeat on the Turkish army and in the process capture Jerusalem. The loss of the prestigious Holy City would be a blow from which Turkish morale and influence would be unlikely to recover. Jerusalem, although a symbolic Christian city, ranks closely behind Mecca on the list of places sacred to Islam.

Meanwhile Turkish morale had received a considerable boost from the fact that a special force, the Yilderim, had been formed and was being trained in Syria. It was under the command of the German general Falkenhayn, and the recapture of Baghdad was intended to be the first of its many victories. From there it would proceed triumphantly as far as the Suez Canal. By that time it would have cut off all oil supplies from the Allies. In this volatile area any local army which made victorious progress was likely to be joined by many sympathisers, some of whom would already be placed behind its opponents' lines. The Allied High Command were not unmindful of this potential threat and decided that attack was the best form of defence.

The opening stage in the Palestine campaign required the capture of Gaza. General Sir Archibald Murray had made two attempts to capture Gaza in 1917: the first, in March, came very close to success but was muddled at the critical stage, and a second, in April, found the Turks fully prepared and dug in. Gaza was not taken, but Murray's force lost 6,500 against the Turkish casualties of 2,000.

At this stage, Murray was replaced by General Sir Edmund Allenby, who had distinguished himself while commanding Third Army at Arras. Before that he had fought in the Bechuanaland campaign of 1884, and the Boer War of 1899–1902. Allenby was a large, intimidating man, whose nickname was 'The Bull'. It was thought that his overbearing manner might be too much for the Australians and New Zealanders to stomach, but they found his personality impressive: in a brief space all the troops under his command had decided they were now on a winning side. Not least of his qualities was his ability to obtain reinforcements of men and material when he needed them. His only son had been killed in France but he never allowed that to affect his concentration. When he detected inefficiency he would explode, and the word would go round 'The Bull is loose', but when not on duty he would talk fluently on politics, flowers, or ornithology, of all of which he had considerable knowledge.

The plan of attack had been formulated by General Sir Philip Chetwode, Commander of XX Corps, the previous May, and required very little modification. To approach Jerusalem, it was necessary to capture Gaza and Beersheba, the former of which was on the coast and particularly well-defended. Beersheba must also be captured, but in view of the lack of water in the region it was assumed that this could not be taken before Gaza had fallen. Allenby's plan reversed this thinking and instead made Beersheba the first target and Gaza the second. But to cross the waterless area and capture Beersheba meant taking a tremendous risk: if the plan failed the Allied force would be in a worse position than it had been in the previous Spring. And although it was possible to make abandoned camps look as if they were still occupied, it was obvious that once large-scale movement began the Turks and Germans would realise there was an attack in the offing. The deception therefore had to be extended to make it seem that the main attack would be on Gaza, but that there would also be a much smaller operation in the direction of Beersheba. But on the night of 31 October the Desert Mounted Corps and XX Corps, also cavalry, with infantry behind, made a dash across the desert and occupied the latter town. Before the Turks had recovered from the shock of losing Beersheba, they found another attack was being launched on Gaza. It was heavy, and successful, though costly. While the Gaza battle was in full spate, Allenby switched a proportion of his force and drove forward into the space between the two towns, right into the Turkish centre which had been weakened by sending troops to reinforce Gaza on one side and to prevent the victors of Beersheba moving onward from the other.

The Turkish army had now been effectively split into two halves, one north of Gaza and one west of Jerusalem, but was still a highly effective fighting force. Allenby realised that the key to winning the campaign was to keep up the momentum of the attack. The Australians were particularly well adapted to this form of warfare. They were mounted on walers, which were horses imported from New South Wales whose origin was rather unusual, for they were bred from exported English racehorses which had failed to come up to the expectations of their owners and backers. Although they had been acquired cheaply, they were ideal saddle horses for up-country stations in Australia – hard, compact, and full of courage and endeavour. During the campaign they displayed quite astonishing stamina, at times being fed on a mere nine and a half pounds of grain a day, combined with watering once in every 36 hours: some had, in fact, only been watered at 72-hour intervals, which previously would have been thought impossible if they were to survive. However, the British cavalry and most of their horses were second to none in this campaign.

Although there was no shortage of artillery and rifle fire in Allenby's army, many of the successful attacks seemed to belong to an earlier era. Leading squadrons charged with the sword: following squadrons did not carry swords but instead used rifles and bayonets. Very often the second and third squadrons dismounted before reaching the trenches. At the rear there would probably be a mere two machine-guns to deal with any counter-attacks.

The drive into Turkish territory now took the campaign onto the plains of Philistia, originally the home of the Philistines. Meanwhile Anzac units had occupied Ramleh and Jaffa (formerly Joppa and later Yafo – the port from which oranges are shipped). Progress towards Jerusalem was steady but casualties on both sides were high as the Turks frequently counter-attacked. However, by 17 December 1917, the Allied forces had closed around Jerusalem and in consequence the Mayor came out under a flag of truce and surrendered the keys. It was a historic moment, for the Holy City had not been in Christian hands for 600 years. Allenby made his official entry on 11 December, 1917, through the Jaffa gate, which by tradition is only opened to conquerors of the Holy City. In appearance he lacked something of the presence that such an event might have required, for he was dressed in worn service khaki and carried a cane.

The capture of Jerusalem was not, of course, the end of the campaign but it had several important effects. It signified the end of all danger to Mesopotamia, it encouraged the Arabs to continue their efforts to harass the Turkish lines of communication, it disposed of the boasted invulnerability of the Yilderim, and it was an event of enormous moral significance. But the Turks were by no means finished, even in this area. They counter-attacked with three divisions on 26 December in an attempt to recover Jerusalem. Their efforts were unsuccessful, but they displayed remarkable courage. They lost over 1,000 soldiers killed and 500 prisoners for no territorial gain whatever.

At this point Palestine assumed greater importance in the eyes of the Allied High Command. Previously it had been regarded as an area of minor strategic value using troops which many thought would have been employed more usefully in France. But now Allenby's successes had opened up the possibility of knocking Turkey right out of the war. After the humiliation of the Dardanelles this would be some consolation to hurt British pride, but the main consideration was the opportunity to destroy one of Germany's most valued allies. The Germans were not unmindful of this happening and had already despatched German and Austrian troops to fight alongside the Turks in Palestine.

Allenby's force had sustained 18,000 casualties against 25,000 Turkish. He had taken 12,000 prisoners and captured 100 guns. But the next stage looked like being difficult, as the Turks were strongly established in highly defensive positions in rocky country.

The war in Palestine would continue until October 1918, although the Turks would suffer many crushing defeats before that time. We shall return to this scene later.

CHAPTER 8

1917 — 1918

We left France in order to take in the battle of Caporetto and its aftermath in Italy, and from there looked at the situation in the other two 'sideshows', Salonika and Palestine. But meanwhile in France there occurred a battle of historic importance, for it was the first occasion tanks were used as the main means of attack. Their employment in this way was highly controversial for there were many in the armies of both sides who felt that once the novelty of their appearance had worn off, their vulnerability to artillery fire, their mechanical unreliability and their ponderously slow speed (in relation to cavalry) would soon relegate them to a minor role. The reader will recall that aircraft had met considerable opposition before they proved themselves by results. Although Cambrai eventually seemed to have been a very moderate success for the British, it made a great impression on the Germans and gave them the inspiration for the Blitzkrieg of 1940, when the Panzer units tore through the British and French armies.

Haig has often been accused of neglecting aircraft and tanks but although his military thinking was by no means infallible, these two criticisms are unjustified. He was planning the Cambrai battle even when the Passchendaele campaign with infantry, artillery, mud and gas, was relentlessly grinding to its end. Tanks had, of course, been employed at Passchendaele, even though the terrain was hopelessly against them. However, west of Picardy there was dry, flat, ground. If the British High Command was conservative in its military outlook, the Germans were even more so. Having seen the performance of tanks at the Battle of the Somme, they had concluded that the weapon had limited potential and that the Allies would reach the same conclusion and quietly abandon them. Even though an Irish prisoner, who had been captured by the Germans some days before the Cambrai battle began, had given them a detailed account of British preparations, they felt no apprehension, thinking it was probably an ingenious deception exercise. When, therefore, on 20 November, ten days after the end of the Battle of Passchendaele, they were attacked by 381 tanks, followed by small numbers of infantry, they were disagreeably surprised. The battle began on a fifteen-mile front between Moeuvres, three miles to the north of Cambrai, and Banteux, twelve miles to the south.

Before approving of this innovative tank battle, Haig had had long talks with the experts, who were Brigadier General Hugh Elles, Lieutenant Colonel J. F. C. Fuller, and General Sir Julian Byng, commander of the Third Army, in whose area the attack would be made. As the victor of Vimy, Byng's opinion carried considerable weight and when he said there should be no preliminary bombardment, his views were accepted.

Byng was well aware that the area in front of his Third Army had been well fortified by the Germans, and that the beginning of any bombardment would serve as a warning that all forward defences should be fully manned

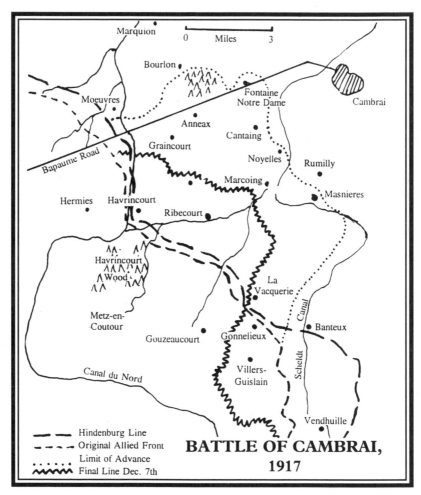

Marquion

0 Miles 3

Bourlon

Moeuvres

Fontaine
Notre Dame

Cambrai

Anneax

Cantaing

Graincourt

Bapaume Road

Noyelles

Rumilly

Marcoing

Masnieres

Hermies Havrincourt

Ribecourt

Havrincourt
Wood

La
Vacquerie

Metz-en-
Coutour

Canal

Banteux

Gouzeaucourt Gonnelieux

Canal du Nord

Villers-
Guislain

Scheldt

Vendhuille

— — Hindenburg Line
- - - - Original Allied Front
.... Limit of Advance
∿∿∿∿ Final Line Dec. 7th

**BATTLE OF CAMBRAI,
1917**

as an attack was probably imminent. He knew from the experience on other fronts in the war that once the initial breakthrough had been made while the Germans were too surprised to know what was happening, they would soon rally and counter-attack to regain lost ground. It was therefore necessary to have heavy artillery in reserve to destroy the second and third line of German defences and also to inflict heavy casualties among their reinforcements, 1,000 heavy guns would be allotted for this purpose. Seven infantry divisions would follow the 381 tanks, and there were four cavalry divisions ready behind the infantry, waiting to pour through any large breach in the German line.

The opening stages were a dramatic success. The Germans, astonished to be confronted by this mass of mobile firepower, gave up their first line without making much resistance. The cavalry was then ordered forward but made little progress. The 5th Cavalry Division could not advance against the concentrated machine-gun fire of the German second line and the 1st Cavalry Division was held up by a bridge which one of the tanks had accidentally destroyed at Masnières. However, one cavalry regiment, the Poona Horse, subsequently reported that they had gained their objective and could have gone much further if the Higher Command had given them the necessary permission. It soon became clear that the principal weakness of the battle was the lack of adequate means of obtaining and conveying news of the progress made. Even the information which was readily available does not seem to have been conveyed to the right quarters. The British should have been aware that the Germans were busily reinforcing their front with troops from the Russian front; they included twenty-three divisions. But the main reason why the Germans were so successful in their counter-attack was their use of low-flying aircraft against the British infantry. If the British had used their own aircraft to assist the advance of their own tanks, their efforts would have been more successful. In 1940 German successes owed much to the scores of low-flying aircraft which preceded the tanks and bombed possible obstacles.

In the event, the 381 tanks were not enough. 179 were out of action by the end of the first day and although some of them were repaired and brought back into action, others were not. The second phase of the attack achieved little, and on 30 November, ten days after the beginning of the battle, the Germans regained the initiative by using gas in a fierce counter-attack.

The conflict dragged on till 5 December, by which time Byng's Third Army had sustained 47,000 casualties and the Germans slightly less.

Although the battle had shown fresh thinking and had demonstrated the way in which tanks should be used, its material gains were negligible. Unfortunately it was also a Public Relations disaster. When the first reports of success came in, the Northcliffe Press, which included *The Times*, decided that these must be heavily trumpeted as a boost to public morale. The normally cautious 'Thunderer' talked about a 'bewildering success' and everyone behaved as if the war was already won. When the facts began to filter back, and the reporters were writing about the German counter-attacks, Northcliffe, instead of feeling humbled and penitent, was furious. Self-righteously he claimed he had been deceived by both the Army and the Government. The War Cabinet decided an investigation was required and set up a Court of Enquiry to discover what had gone wrong. It soon put the blame on Charteris, Haig's Chief of Intelligence, who was well known for producing premature, over-optimistic reports. Haig was therefore ordered to dismiss Charteris, which he did with reluctance. However, Charteris' replacement, who had little love for Haig to whom he had once been senior, was just as unsuitable.

Another change at this time was Kiggell, Haig's Chief of the General Staff, whose health had now broken down under the strain of his responsibilities, though they had never taken him anywhere near the battlefield. It was reported of Kiggell that, after resigning, he visited the edge of the Passchendaele battlefield and as he gazed at it with awe-struck horror, remarked: 'Did we really send men to fight in this?' An accompanying staff officer remarked grimly, 'It's much worse further in.' Kiggell is said to have wept (he was, of course, a sick man). The story has been denied, but is probably true.

Lloyd George's ambition was to oust Haig but he knew that the public, not to mention Haig's many highly-placed friends, would not tolerate this. He therefore concentrated on removing as many of Haig's closest supporters as possible. The next on the list was General Sir William Robertson, the CIGS, who was unswervingly loyal to Haig and detested Lloyd George, even though his own background was similar to the latter's. Robertson was finally edged out on 9 February, and was replaced by the arch-intriguer Wilson.

Lloyd George's motives and attitudes were understandable. He considered that Haig, though competent in a traditional way, lacked the imagination to produce the masterstroke which might finish the war. Haig, for his part, considered that Lloyd George's ideas on strategy were so wild and fanciful that to try to implement them would produce a worse series of disasters than Gallipoli. Lloyd George suspected that Haig and his staff had ceased to regard the manpower of Britain as human beings, but merely as so many companies, battalions, brigades or divisions. Apart from humanitarian considerations Lloyd George felt that if the losses continued at their present rate there would not be many able-bodied men left in Britain, but before the supply was totally exhausted the final contingents would launch a revolution on the Russian model. Although at an earlier period in the war Lloyd George had been a very good Minister of Munitions and had also done his best to support Haig's Western Front strategy, he had never been convinced by it. He simply did not believe that victory could be achieved through hammer blows on the enemy trenches in France. Unfortunately that view was not shared by the German Higher Command who were now busying themselves by building up a huge force in order to achieve victory before the Allies had received the promised support from America. At that moment the advantage lay very strongly with Germany. Although their army had taken a fearful battering at Arras and Passchendaele, it was every day receiving reinforcements from the Russian front. The advantage of the latter was that they were all trained, experienced troops of high morale who saw themselves as victors. By contrast the Americans had no experience of battle, or even of Europe, and were still completing their training. Added to that was the fact that they were not arriving at the speed which had been expected. Whereas the Americans needed to travel thousands of miles to reach France, the Germans from the Russian front only had to travel a few hundred miles.

By mid-February 1918, the Germans had two armies positioned to attack between Ypres and La Bassée, and five more between Arras and Reims. Apart from the right flank, which was held by the French Sixth Army, the Germans would be opposed by British armies which were now spread so thinly, in order to cover a wider area, that they were outnumbered by nearly three to one in both soldiers and guns. From aerial observation, prisoners of war, and spies, the deployment of the German armies was well enough known to the Allies: the only doubt was where the first blow would fall. Wherever that should be, it would test soldiers who were veterans of Passchendaele, Arras, the Somme, and lesser encounters. They had taken over a burden from the French who had fallen out: they were experienced, but they were also exhausted from these grinding encounters.

All doubts were resolved on 21 March. On that day, under cover of a dense fog, the German offensive was launched against Gough's Fifth Army and Byng's Third Army in the Somme area; the heaviest blow was between Arras and St Quentin. The Germans had left nothing to chance. At 5.00am a bombardment by 6,000 guns opened up on the British positions on a 40-mile front. There had never been such a concentration of high explosives before and whole trenches and battalions disappeared without trace. Intense shelling went on for two hours, destroying everything it fell on: communications, guns, headquarters and forward ammunition dumps, the latter added to the conflagration. Mixed in with the high explosives was gas and in the fog it was impossible to detect which was which until it was too late. Those unlucky enough to be gassed stumbled around blinded and coughing: the lucky ones were killed by the intense shellfire which ranged up and down the target area. Even so there were survivors sheltering in the remains of dugouts or trenches, ready for the infantry assault which was expected once the guns lifted and directed their shells on to targets further back.

This was the first part of Ludendorff's plan: the second matched it. Two out of the three assaulting German armies were of a different experience and quality from those in France. One was fresh from the Caporetto victory and the other from the Eastern front. These were not infantrymen who would plod to the trenches, cut the wires and bayonet the defenders: they were highly mobile, fast-moving, shock troops. They would be used as such. Ludendorff had anticipated that, after the bombardment there would be no wire, no strongpoints, and no resistance worth consideration. It was identical to the situation which Haig had hoped to achieve on the Somme, two years earlier, but this time there were no deep dugouts and caves to protect the defenders from artillery fire. The attacking German infantry tore through the fog, leapt over the trenches which should have been full of troops but which mostly held corpses, slipped past any strongpoints which looked like holding them up, and moved on. Later waves of infantry could deal with any stubborn resistance points. There were more of the latter than had been anticipated. When the fog began to clear and the British troops could see the advancing infantry, they cut them to pieces with machine-guns. That too was like the Somme, though it was quicker. Although they had experienced a nightmare of annihilation in the fog, British survivors still had plenty of fight left in them, and with the desperation of the doomed, counter-attacked. Now the Germans were made to pay for their gains. Whenever German infantrymen showed themselves in front of British machine-guns, or exposed their flanks as they tried to slide past, bullets cut into them. The disadvantage of attacking in close order is that you are scythed down in droves; however, if the infantry reaches the objective it holds a continuous line. Infiltration in smaller groups means that soldiers lose touch with the supporting units and at the same time leave gaps for a counter-attack if any of the enemy are still able to make one. Almost unbelievably, they still were. Where possible they dug fresh trenches, although these were too shallow to be much protection, and they used up every round of ammunition they could lay their hands on. Any messages they received from the rear were not of the imminent arrival of reinforcements or relief but brisk instructions to fight to the last round, which they were doing anyway.

The first German thrust broke through in the south, but that in the north was held up near Arras. The stubborn defence in the northern sector irritated Ludendorff and caused him to make a tactical mistake. Instead of grasping the magnificent opportunity offered by the greater success in the south, which he should have concentrated on exploiting, he decided to teach the British a lesson by crushing them at Arras, where they believed themselves to be at their strongest. Once Arras and the surrounding region fell into German hands, he reasoned, the morale of the British army would be broken. Success there would enable him to execute a giant pincer movement which would slice through the British-held areas. To achieve this objective he ordered the Eighteenth Army, which was enjoying great success in the St Quentin sector, to pause for two days before once more driving forward towards Amiens. In the meantime he ordered his Seventeenth Army near Arras to launch a further attack in the Arras area, while the Sixth Army attacked between Vimy and La Bassée.

The flaws in this tactical plan were soon apparent. The British Third Army in the northern sector was commanded by Byng, the victor of Vimy, and from the beginning of the German onslaught he had been resolutely strengthening the defences, particularly in the rear area. When the German Seventeenth Army launched the next attack, it came as no surprise and did not have the advantage of the fog which had made the earlier attacks easier. Ludendorff soon became aware that progress in the northern area was going to be exceptionally difficult, so belatedly he decided to concentrate his efforts further south. He had defied a classic military maxim: 'Always reinforce strength, never reinforce weakness.' And while he had been purposelessly hammering away in the north, the British in the south were taking advantage of the respite given them by the Eighteenth Army and were strengthening their defences. When therefore Eighteenth Army resumed the attack, resistance had hardened and progress was slower.

Nevertheless the British Army had taken a fearful blow, was on the edge of disaster, and was desperately trying to make sense out of a chaotic retreat. Within the first week of the attack they had been pushed back 40 miles, lost 975 guns, and had their numbers depleted by the 80,000 prisoners the Germans had taken, most of whom had fought until their ammunition was exhausted and then surrendered. In addition to these, some 200,000 had been killed or wounded. And even the Third Army was now giving ground.

The prevailing emotion both in France and at home was shock, verging on disbelief. After years of being locked into struggles for a few hundred yards of ground, which they had painstakingly captured over the years, the British and French had come to terms with the fact that the German advances were now in miles, rather than yards. Paris was now coming under fire from guns with a range of 75 miles. On the brighter side was the fact that the Royal Flying Corps was steadily harassing the German infantry with low-flying attacks and this was undoubtedly slowing them down. Nevertheless German progress was still alarmingly fast.

Pétain transferred eleven divisions to the British front with some reluctance. He thought the main German thrust would soon be directed towards Paris and that his army should be reserved for that likely contingency. Ludendorff had correctly suspected that if he could put the Allies under enough pressure the French and British might develop a mutual distrust: Haig had no doubt that if matters became worse Pétain would abandon coordinated strategy and group his armies around the capital: Pétain thought that the British valued the Channel ports more highly than Paris and would give priority to their defence. Haig reflected bitterly on Lloyd George's policy of retaining as many troops as possible in England, rather than despatching them to Haig to use – or, as he thought – misuse, in France. Many of them were now being despatched at speed, but it all took time when delays meant further disaster.

The much maligned Haig was now responsible for a move which was one of the most effective in the war, although he cannot have been happy about having to propose it. He requested the presence of the Secretary of State for War, Lord Milner, and his bête noir, Wilson, at the Doullens Conference of 26 March, at which Poincaré, the French President, was Chairman. Others present were Clemenceau (the French Prime Minister), Foch, Pétain, Lawrence and the French Minister of Munitions, Loucheur. Pétain did not endear himself to Haig by saying to Clemenceau that the Germans would now beat the British in open warfare (that is, away from the trenches). His demeanour suggested that they would beat the French too. Foch was more optimistic, and Haig suggested that if Foch offered him strategic advice he would take it. From this grew the proposal that there should be a unified command and that Foch should be the overall commander. A conference at Beauvais a week later (3 April) extended Foch's powers to the direction of

military operations, rather than merely their coordination. General Pershing, CinC of the American Army, added his assent. Although this might
seen to be a replica of the previous arrangement when Nivelle had been put
above Haig, it had an essential difference: Haig was not simply subject to a
French commander but to a Supreme Allied Commander. The other difference was that whereas Nivelle had been incapable of handling the opportunities he had requested for himself, Foch was well suited for his enormous
responsibilities. One of his first moves was to order Pétain to divert divisions
to the support of Haig, even though it meant weakening the shield in front
of Paris.

Two weeks after it had begun, the German attack had lost its impetus,
though it still posed a great danger to the Allies. The German armies were
tired, had outrun their artillery, and had taken heavy casualties (more in fact
than the Allies), but a new thrust was still a distinct possibility. But the
British were in a worse case. The casualties of the last fortnight were
replaced by conscripts who were either too young or too old, more of the
former than the latter, and not enough of either. A casualty of a different sort
was Gough, who had commanded the Fifth Army through the swamps of
Passchendaele and in this battle had tried to hold the southern sector.
Unfortunately for Gough, much had gone wrong with the attempts to coordinate the defence, and if a culprit had to be found it must obviously be him.
Orders came from the British government that Gough must be replaced.
Haig did not relish having to dismiss a loyal subordinate who had done as
well as anyone could have in the circumstances, but the War Cabinet, probably egged on by Wilson in his new capacity as CIGS, was insistent. Gough
protested and asked for an official enquiry into the reasons for his superses-
sion. It was refused. His replacement was Sir Henry Rawlinson, an able
enough commander but one, it will be remembered, who had given Haig
bad advice about the German defences on the Somme in 1916. In those
days he had commanded the Fourth British Army and now, when he took
over the Fifth, decided to take the old number with him. This was unfair on
the Fifth, for it left the impression that the latter was battle-weary and must
have performed badly to lose its old number – of which many were proud.

On 9 April Ludendorff launched the second phase of his attack, this time
on the twelve mile front between Armentières and La Bassée. If this went
well it would probably drive a spearhead right through to Boulogne, but
even if it only reached Hazebrouck, an important railway junction, it would
still have captured a vital pivotal point. From Hazebrouck a thrust could be
made in almost any direction, and the Channel ports would be under dire

threat. Once again the attack was preceded with a massive bombardment, but when the German infantry went in, they had a very different reception. The troops on the German right wing made slow progress against intense British fire, those in the middle encountered inexperienced Portuguese troops who soon fled from the scene, but were then held by a Scottish division which rushed up to plug the gap. Nevertheless, the situation was highly dangerous because Amiens could easily be the next major town to fall. Haig's chief worry was that he had no more reserves to commit. Foch therefore tried to reassure him that all was not lost if Amiens did fall, for he was deploying French reserves behind the town. But by 12 April Haig had thrown his last troops into the battle without preventing the Germans advancing an average of ten miles and drawing close to Hazebrouck. It was a desperate moment. Haig, not noted for producing stirring Orders of the Day in the manner of many generals, now issued the following statement:

'With our backs to the wall and believing in the justice of our cause each one must fight on to the end. The safety of our homes and the freedom of mankind alike depend upon the conduct of each one of us at this critical moment.

'There is no other course open to us but to fight it out. Every position must be held to the last man.'

The Germans were being made to pay dearly for their gains, especially by the Royal Flying Corps, who bombed and machine-gunned the advancing infantry relentlessly. Nevertheless they swarmed into the Passchendaele area where British troops had gained victory at fearful cost some six months earlier, captured the Messines ridge and came close to Ypres itself. They also extended their line northwards into the area between Ypres and the coast but here they met a major setback: the Belgians, defending their last strip of unoccupied territory, had been reinforced by four French divisions. Had Foch not been overall commander, it is unlikely that those divisions would have been there at all, for Belgium's predicament was of less interest to the French than their own. Nevertheless all was not entirely satisfactory. After the key point of Mont Kemmel had been lost by fresh French divisions (after being held by weary British divisions), the British launched a counter-attack in which the French refused to join. The outlook for mutual confidence did not seem good. Although the French now seemed to have recovered the confidence they had lost during their mutiny, they were still not as reliable as the battered British divisions. Foch was well aware of his overall responsibilities and was meticulously fair in his disposition of troops. This, however, did not stop Pétain accusing him of sacrificing French troops, and perhaps Paris, for Belgium and the Channel ports.

On 29 April the Germans made a final effort in this area. They began with a massive bombardment of high explosives, but after two hours began saturating the area with gas shells. The infantry went in at 5.40am. The Germans also knew better than to attack precisely on the hour or half hour. They were met by a combined Anglo-French force, which stopped them by unexpectedly concentrated and heavy fire. This became known as the Battle of the Lys. The Germans made a few small gains but the expected breakthrough never occurred. For the moment at least the Channel ports were saved. Any further advance in the area could only be gained by long battles of attrition and these were not wanted by Ludendorff with the thought of more American troops being available every month. He looked elsewhere for a quicker means of achieving victory and inevitably his eyes fell on the southern sector. Success there would free more of his troops for the northern sector and with luck he could then have a final drive for the Channel ports.

Meanwhile, his advances in the north had squeezed the British into a small vulnerable area which could be pounded by German aircraft and artillery. The British air force would protect the area by day, but at night the bombers would certainly get through.

Overall the situation was still desperately dangerous for the Allies. The French troops were performing well now but still fell short of what they had been earlier in the war: Clemenceau had doubts about the internal political situation, knowing that some of the major industrial cities in France were excited by the news from Russia and inclined to follow suit. He took the precaution of retaining four cavalry divisions to deal with any sudden insurrection.

Haig's divisions were shadows of their former selves even though they still kept their fighting spirit. By now, men who previously would have been thought unfit for overseas service were taking their place in the line. They were joined by others hastily transferred from Palestine, where Allenby was still locked in the conflict with the Turks. It was a critical moment, as both sides knew. The Germans realised they must win soon or face a humiliating defeat and probably revolution at home. The British and French realised that they were at the end of their resources. But before we follow the events of the next six months of the war we must look at the progress on the other fronts, not forgetting the one at home.

CHAPTER 9

April 1918

While the armies in France were waiting for the final decisive phase of the years of warfare in the trenches, a very different but no less important battle was being fought at sea. The fact of being an island has been an enormous advantage to Britain and has often saved her from being invaded: however, in modern warfare being a small island leaves her in an extremely vulnerable position because more than half her food-stuffs and raw materials need to he imported. Much of this vital traffic came from America and German submarines had taken a grim toll of it over the years. Now that America herself was in the war, that traffic would be increased by troop transports. Surprisingly, no American troop transports were ever sunk.

Although by January 1918 there was confidence in the British Cabinet and the Admiralty that the U boat threat was now being effectively countered by the convoy system, there was always the possibility that the Germans might produce a new type of submarine or weapon which would swing the balance back in their favour again. Ironically, this was the period when the British invented the magnetic mine, which was then neglected by Britain but used to great effect by the Germans in the opening stages of the Second World War.

Some idea of the delicacy of the balance in sea warfare may be gained from a look at the figures: in January 1918, 306,000 tons of Allied shipping were sunk by German submarines: this was considered an acceptable figure.

In March it jumped up to 342,000 tons, but this figure exceeded the speed at which it could be replaced. However, it settled down to less than 300,000 tons a month for the rest of the war. Fortunately for the Allies, the Germans were losing submarines slightly faster than they could be replaced, and every month saw an improvement in the Allied counter-measures.

As we saw earlier, the Dover Patrol was one of the great success stories of the war. 20,000,000 soldiers crossed the English Channel as the transports took them to France, brought them back on leave or wounded, and then, if still fit to fight, back into action. It was based at Dover and Dunkirk and had such a high combination of morale and expertise that German coastal shipping was reluctant to try any venture which would bring it into contact with the Patrol. Mistakes did sometimes occur. On 13 February 1918 a German destroyer took a chance and undetected, owing to signalling mishaps (and the belief that any surface craft heard or seen in the dark must be friendly), sank eight small British craft which were guarding the nets. Another attempt was made in March, but met less success.

Nevertheless, the British Admiralty was very concerned by the base which the Germans had built up around Zeebrugge, which they suspected was full of submarines and other dangerous craft. The base consisted of a fortified triangle of which one side was the coast between Zeebrugge and Ostend, another the ship canal to Bruges itself, and the third the canal system linking Bruges to Ostend. Apart from the main canals, there were minor waterways and important dockyard installations. Here submarines, destroyers and other small craft could shelter when not preying on Allied shipping. There was always the chance that a large raid from this base could break through the Dover barrage and destroy troop transports.

Although it seemed unlikely that the German Grand Fleet would venture out to sea again, it was by no means certain. If, however, it did, it would need a host of minor craft for such duties as mine sweeping and reconnaissance. Mine sweepers were also of vital importance for keeping the boat routes (well known to the Royal Navy) clear of mines. In consequence, the Germans maintained 30 submarines and the same number of destroyers and torpedo boats in the Zeebrugge area. After that rather embarrassing raid on the barrage in February, it seemed appropriate to the Royal Navy to take steps against this base from which the destroyer had emerged and from which, no doubt, others could be expected.

On 24 February 1918 Vice Admiral Roger Keyes, an intrepid 45-year-old, had proposed to the Admiralty a scheme for blocking Zeebrugge and Ostend. All thought this seemed almost impossible, but it was approved. If it entirely succeeded, it would seal up a German naval base which represented a great threat to the Allies. Even if it was only partly successful, it would raise the spirits of the British public, which were at that moment being depressed by the gloomy news from the Western Front. It would also improve the morale of the Royal Navy which, at the beginning of April, had relinquished control of all air force matters except the design and construction of airships and aircraft carriers to the newly-created Royal Air Force (the combined Royal Flying Corps and Royal Naval Air Service). This meant that nearly 3,000 aircraft and 67,000 men trained to fly and maintain them, as well as 103 airships had passed from the Royal Navy to the new Royal Air Force. The transfer could not have come at a worse time for the Navy. If the raid was as successful as had been hoped for, there would be scores of German craft boxed up in the Zeebrugge triangle which could then be bombed to pieces by the Air Force. (In the event, after urgent pleas to the Air Ministry, only one RAF squadron was allotted to the task, and that a month later, when most of the German craft had managed to disperse.) However, the Royal Navy had a lengthy experience of battling against adverse conditions and were determined to show that even after being stripped of its air components it could achieve the near-impossible.

The raid was scheduled for 23 April (St George's Day). Attacking a well-fortified port from the sea would be a difficult enough task in any case, but at Zeebrugge it was complicated by the fact that the artificial harbour was created by a one-and-a-half-mile-long mole (the longest in the world) which jutted out to sea in a north-easterly arc. The mole was joined to the shore by a causeway 300 yards long and, though the Germans did not expect it to be attacked, they had taken suitable precautions in case it was. Twelve heavy guns (some 5.9 inch) anti-aircraft guns, machine-guns, blockhouses, barbed wire, a seaplane base, four hangars, a submarine shelter and a garrison of 1,000 men were all ready in case anyone should be foolish enough to attack Zeebrugge. Unless some ingenious device for diverting German attention could be found, this concentration of firepower would destroy the attacker as it passed alongside the mole on the way into the harbour.

The plan, though ingenious, was simple. Three obsolete cruisers, loaded with cement, were to proceed into the entrance to the Bruges canal, and then scuttle themselves: they would sink quickly and be difficult to remove. But unless an appropriate diversion could be arranged, they would be sunk long before they reached their destination and their purpose would therefore be nullified.

The 'diversion' was to be provided by another obsolete cruiser, HMS *Vindictive*. *Vindictive*'s task was to proceed up to the mole under cover of smoke screen laid by a host of escorting craft (mainly motor launches), another halfway along it, and land demolition parties to destroy the German guns. It would be accompanied by two ferry steamers specially brought from the Mersey, which would press up alongside and keep *Vindictive* close to the mole. The two ferry boats (*Iris* and *Daffodil*) would also carry assault parties which would also land via the *Vindictive*. In order to preserve secrecy, vital to this operation, the inhabitants of Merseyside, who were not pleased when they saw their ferry boats departing, perhaps never to return, were told they were being used to transport American troops. In the event, both did return and were greeted with pride and joy by their former passengers.

The attacking party was well aware that the smoke screen through which the ships were to approach the mole would not give them complete protection. A freshening wind, or a change in its direction, could leave them completely exposed to all the firepower the Germans could bring to bear. In any event they were certain of a frenzied reception as they closed up on the mole.

The planners were well aware that as soon as the *Vindictive* closed up on the mole and began to unload the assault crews, the alarm would be raised on the shore and reinforcements would be rushed across the causeway, which ran on top of a viaduct. To prevent this happening, two old 'C' class submarines, loaded with explosives, were allotted the task of proceeding up to the arches of the viaduct. They would force themselves as far under the arches as possible, discharge their crews onto a picket boat which was standing by, and, hopefully, be clear of the area before the submarines blew themselves and a substantial portion of the viaduct, high into the air. If they were not clear when the explosion took place, they would be dead men. In the event, only one of the submarines reached its target, but the effects were extremely satisfactory. A wide gap was blown in the viaduct and the first victims of it were a German cyclist battalion which, peddling hot foot for the mole, came to the gap in the dark and bicycled straight into the sea.

The key to the success of the operation was, of course, the assault by the *Vindictive*. Unfortunately, just before she reached the mole the wind changed and began to blow the smoke screen away. When the Germans concentrated their searchlights, and also fired star shells, the *Vindictive* was seen as clearly as if it was full daylight. It seemed as if nothing and no one could survive the onslaught of German fire, but fortunately neither steering nor engine room was hit, and she closed the last few hundred yards to the mole, all her own guns were pounding the German positions on the mole.

Scenes of superhuman sacrifice and courage took place as the landing parties fought their way ashore. Landing was difficult enough in itself, for the swell caused the scaling ladders to slip, and made securing gangways exceptionally difficult, even without the stream of machine-gun bullets which were sweeping across the decks. Wounds, such as broken arms and fractured jaws, which would normally have checked men in their stride, were ignored as desperate attempts were made to reach the German gun positions. Shore batteries soon joined those of the mole in pounding the *Vindictive* and the host of supporting craft. Meanwhile the Germans, who had seen the three blockships and realised their purpose, concentrated fire on them too. The leading ship *Thetis* ran into anti-submarine nets which she took with her but was then hit so often that she began to sink. As she settled down, demolition charges blew out her bottom. However, she had cleared the main channel and drawn enemy fire onto herself while the other two, *Intrepid* and *Iphigenia*, passed by without serious damage, reached their appointed stations and scuttled themselves. Here, as elsewhere, the ubiquitous motor launches, indifferent to their own vulnerability, were at hand to take off the crews, many of whom were wounded.

The battle lasted 80 minutes. 214 sailors and marines were killed, 318 were wounded, and sixteen were taken prisoner. Eight Victoria Crosses were awarded, two of them posthumously.

Simultaneously with the Zeebrugge raid a lesser one was carried out on Ostend. It included a total of 59 ships, of which eleven were French. It failed because of an ingenious piece of German deception. Although for the most part the Germans had removed the marker buoys from the hazards round the Belgian coast, they had left a few in position around the harbour entrances. At Ostend they had gone a step further and repositioned a marker buoy, thus creating an additional hazard for any craft trying to enter the harbour without the knowledge and approval of the German command. This completely deceived the two incoming blockships, *Sirius* and *Brilliant*, which promptly ran aground. The crew was evacuated by the motor launches (under heavy gunfire) before the blockships were blown up. The only benefit of this raid was that the Navy learnt by bitter experience that any future operation which relied on enemy marker buoys should be preceded by a careful aerial reconnaissance.

The commanders of both the Ostend blockships begged to be allowed to make a second attempt at Ostend and this was permitted on 9 May. This time the *Vindictive*, which miraculously had been able to make its way back to England after its tremendous battering at Zeebrugge, was now allotted as one blockship and *Sappho* as the other. Unfortunately, the veteran *Sappho* blew a hole in one of her boilers just before starting out and had to be left behind. *Vindictive* reached the entrance to the harbour in thick fog but while this was an advantage in one way it prevented her finding the exact position intended for blocking the canal. In order to disperse the fog, a flare of a million candle-power was ignited but this, of course, also exposed the *Vindictive* to all the firepower the Germans could muster. This did so much damage that the old cruiser was not quite able to reach the most favoured position but the one she did reach caused the Germans considerable inconvenience. After the war, it was learnt that the Bruges–Ostend canal was too shallow for submarines, though they used the harbour.

Naturally enough, the German propaganda department tried to make out that the Zeebrugge raid was a complete failure, although aerial photographs showed that the reverse was the case. In fact, as was subsequently discovered, not only was the Zeebrugge canal completely blocked but several German submarines which were inside stayed there until the end of the war.

The success of the Dover barrage in preventing submarines taking the quicker route to the Atlantic caused the Allies to embark on a larger and more ambitious project to block the North Sea outlet between the Orkneys and the Norwegian coast, some 300 miles as compared with the 21 of the Dover straits. This was begun in May 1918 and continued until November. 56,171 mines were laid by American ships and 13,546 by British. It did not completely seal the route but undoubtedly it caused casualties and discouragement among the U boats.

The Allies were gaining the upper hand on other seas. Earlier we noted that the battlecruiser *Goeben* and the light cruiser *Breslau* which had infuriated the Allies by slipping out of the Mediterranean in 1914 and joining Turkey, had done considerable damage to Russian ports around Sebastopol. However, for the rest of the war they had been penned up in the Black Sea. In January 1918, they decided to attempt a break-out through the Dardanelles. The *Breslau* struck a mine and blew up and sank; the *Goeben* also struck a mine but was damaged less, she managed to reach the shores of the Dardanelles. Here she was damaged further by British aircraft, but managed to struggle off again and reach Istanbul.

The Adriatic was already sealed, but there was room for improvement and this was achieved by reinforcements from the US Navy. Nevertheless, the following June (1918) the Austrians attempted to break the barrage with a substantial fleet which included battleships, cruisers, and destroyers. However, when an Italian motor launch torpedoed and sank the pride of the Austrian navy, the *Szent Istvon*, the attempt was called off.

The American navy was now becoming a considerable force in this war. Of the 2,000,000 American troops transported to Europe, US ships carried just under half: the rest were carried by British craft. America also deployed some 400 naval aircraft, many of which were employed in anti-submarine warfare.

Although the Zeppelins still posed a threat (their March raid on the Midlands and Liverpool had given evidence of that), the air war was gently tilting in favour of the Allies. However, in April 1918 the Germans supported their grand offensive very effectively with aircraft designed for that role. Otherwise their machines, the Fokker Dr I, Albatross D III and Pfalz D III, were outclassed by the British SE 5a, the Sopwith Camel, and the French Spad 13. All these Allied aircraft mounted two machine-guns, and were fast and manoeuvrable. The Germans relied heavily on 'J' class, ground attack aircraft, one of which was the Junkers J 1, a large, slow (95mph) biplane, and another the Junkers J 10 monoplane. Another very useful aircraft was the Halberstadt CL IV, which carried three machine-guns and could reach 103mph. Undaunted by reverses elsewhere, the Germans still hoped to regain air superiority and in 1918 were developing the Fokker D VII, which would eventually (but too late) become the best fighter of the war with a speed of 124mph and a ceiling of 23,000 feet. These began to arrive in April 1918, but production was slow.

The workhorse of the German bombers was the Gotha G IV, which had a ceiling of 21,000 feet, a range of 300 miles, and a bomb load of 1,100 pounds. It had two 260hp Mercedes engines and could protect itself with two Parabellum machine-guns. These bombed London and other British towns during 1917–18. At the end of the war the victorious Allies insisted that all production of military aircraft in Germany must stop, but in the early 1920s the Soviet Union made a private arrangement with Germany that German pilots could be trained at an airfield near Moscow. From that the Luftwaffe which pounded Russia (and other countries) between 1939 and 1945 was born.

Although the Americans had entered the war in 1917 with negligible air resources, and had to rely on British and French aircraft, they produced first-class pilots and developed an excellent Liberty engine and training facilities.

As Paris had been attacked by German bombers in 1914, the French built up their own bomber force of Voisins, which at first restricted itself to military targets in Germany. However, as the war progressed, it was inevitable that, probably by mistake, the Germans would bomb 'open' (i.e. undefended, civilian) towns in France. Mistake or not, the French decided to give the Germans a taste of their own medicine and deliberately launched attacks against German towns.

Italy maintained a substantial force of Caproni bombers which they used strategically against Austrian targets, of which the main one was the Austro-Hungarian naval base at Pola.

Although victory in this war would be decided by the ground armies in France, the navies and the air forces had reached a decisive point in their development in the Spring of 1918. By then, Britain had over 2,000 operational aircraft, the French over 3,500, the Italians 800, the Germans over 2,500 and the Americans approximately 1,000. Although the bomb loads were light by later standards, they did considerable damage to military installations and even more to civilian morale. Night raids sent people to the London Underground, and although this probably had a minimal effect on war industries, it had a depressing effect on the spirits of people already lowered by shortages, disrupted lives, losses in battle and various forms of rationing.

CHAPTER 10

Women in the War

By 1918 the status of women had changed beyond the wildest imaginings of anyone at the outbreak, four years earlier. Although at various periods of history, women have managed to attain an independent, even dominant, rôle, that certainly did not apply to the early years of the twentieth century. Nevertheless, from the outbreak of war there were a number of dauntless women who defied every form of authority and bureaucracy to serve at the front in a humanitarian rôle.

Perhaps the most surprising development was the way Emmeline Pankhurst, dynamic leader of the Suffragettes, led a drive to get women to work in the factories. The Trade Unions, which had fought long and hard for their rights, were far from pleased at this unpredictable intrusion into their territory. But the response of women was enormous and it soon became clear that after the war they would never be pushed back into their subordinate positions. In the General Election of 1918, sixteen women offered themselves as candidates, although women had not yet achieved the right to vote.

Although the war brought the emancipation of women, it was only the culmination of a process which had begun a hundred years earlier. In the middle of the nineteenth century women had taken the first steps to becoming doctors and to achieving academic qualifications. It was a hard struggle but gradually the foundation of women's colleges at Oxford and Cambridge ensured that they could be educated there even though they were not entitled to take degrees. Elsewhere, dynamic leaders, such as Josephine Butler, put pressure on Parliament to give women industrial training and better opportunities. The first women's trade union was founded in 1875 by Emma Paterson, and included a miscellany of occupations from dressmakers to shop assistants. Nevertheless, the wages of women were so low that many resorted to part-time prostitution, and hours were so long that slaves would have been treated better, even if only to keep them healthy. Any incursions into traditionally male occupations was bitterly opposed on the basis that it would depress the hard-won wage levels. Many women worked all day at boring jobs in their own homes or in ill-lit, ill-ventilated factories; others on the surface of coal mines or on fish docks at arduous physical labour. There were always vacancies for domestic servants, but here the hours were so long, the pay so low and the job so dependent on the attitude of the employer that many girls preferred to avoid this if possible. Many women married young and with the imperfect knowledge of contraception, had large families which it was a struggle to clothe and feed. Nevertheless most managed to remain 'respectable', which meant scrubbing their floors and doorsteps, mending threadbare clothes, and producing meals from the cheapest possible sources. Even so, few wished their sons to join the Army or Navy, as both these services had acquired a bad reputation for drunkenness and hooliganism in peacetime.

Although the early years of this century now appear to have been calm and peaceful from the perspective of the 1990s, they did not appear to be so at the time. The Boer War had only been settled in 1902, and the French, ancient enemies, seemed as hostile as ever until the Entente Cordiale. There were numerous trouble spots overseas, such as the endlessly fermenting Balkans, which might drag Britain into their wars, and there was clearly going to be trouble from Germany sooner or later, probably the former. With an enormous overseas empire, Britain might be called to defend her interests at any time. Upper and middle class women looked on enviously when their menfolk sailed away to campaign in what seemed like exotic countries overseas and now that nursing (once a very low-grade profession) had become respectable, it seemed to offer opportunities to go too, combining both travel and caring. The First Aid Nursing Yeomanry (Fanys) was formed in 1907 from women who could provide their own horses on which they would ride to the battlefield. 1907 also saw the foundation of the Women's Convoy Corps. In 1910 the Voluntary Aid Detachment, officially approved by the War Office, was organised by the Territorial Army and managed by the British Red Cross and St John Ambulance. Like the Territorial Force it was thought the VADs would only be called out if Britain was invaded, but in 1914, they were asked if, in the event of an emergency, they would consent to serve overseas: most agreed to do so. In theory, VADs could be either men or women, but as their most suitable employment seemed to be as nurses, a VAD soon became a term for a woman nurse. They were, of course, voluntary and unpaid.

In 1902 Queen Alexandra's Imperial Military Nursing Service had been founded as a professional nursing service for military hospitals. It became the Queen Alexandra Royal Army Nursing Corps in 1949 (QARANC).

Usually it was referred to as QA. Queen Alexandra's Royal Naval Nursing Service had been founded even earlier, in 1884, but only gained its present title when it came under Queen Alexandra's patronage in 1902 (like the QAIMNS). Until recently, QA and VAD were all officers, which helped to attract many recruits into what were often dangerous and horrifying tasks.

Accompanying and often leading all these steps to female emancipation was the Women's Suffragette movement, which was founded in 1867 and developed into a National Union of Women's Suffragette Societies in 1898. A more dynamic movement, the Women's Social and Political Union (WSPU) was founded in 1903, with the motto, 'Deeds not Words'. Run by Emmeline Pankhurst and her daughter Christabel, the WSPU resorted to violence. Determined to obtain the vote, they damaged churches and railway stations, set three castles on fire, chained themselves to railings, slashed paintings in art galleries, paying particular attention to nudes, and even damaged the Coronation Chair in Westminster Abbey with a bomb. When arrested by the police and put in prison, they were treated brutally. Their most spectacular gesture was made by Emily Davison, who died when she threw herself under a horse in the 1911 Derby. She may have only been grabbing the bridle, but as she had already tried to commit suicide in Holloway prison, this is debatable. Emily Davison had achieved first-class honours at Oxford and in a less academic moment had once horsewhipped a clergyman under the impression that he was Lloyd George.

Although the first reaction of the women's movement to the war was wary and guarded, this attitude was soon replaced by patriotic fervour. Emmeline Pankhurst urged all women to encourage men to join the armed forces. She said at a meeting, 'The war has made me feel renewed belief in men.' One way in which women might encourage men to join up was to shame them, though this idea did not originate from Mrs Pankhurst but from Admiral Penrose Fitzgerald. He made a speech at Folkestone after which he recruited a group of young women to walk through the streets and present a white feather to every young man they met who was not in army or naval uniform. This misguided movement sent into the Army many students, medical, engineering and otherwise, who should have completed their studies and later performed a more valuable task than being mown down in pointless infantry attacks.

Another fervent recruiter was the now forgotten but once famous romantic novelist, Baroness Orczy, who founded the Women of England's Active Service League with the aim of making men join up. Members agreed never to be seen in public with men who refused to do so. She was a genuine baroness, though a Hungarian one, and was a very talented artist as well as a novelist. Her principal hero was 'The Scarlet Pimpernel', an English baronet who smuggled French aristocrats out of France during the 1789 Revolution.

However, in spite of patriotic fervour, the position of women in the first year of the war was worse than it had been before the outbreak. Unemployment in traditional women's trades had risen sharply as credit was restricted, demand was limited by patriotic self-denial, and other industries took priority. Although there was no reason for them to do so at this stage, food prices had risen sharply: bread in particular had doubled in price, flour and sugar were soon well on the way to reaching the same level, and coal, on which vast numbers of people relied for heating and cooking, was also beginning to edge upwards in price. Heartening though it was to see men volunteering in response to Kitchener's appeal that 'Your Country needs You', the obverse side of it was that their wives and dependants were often reduced to conditions of great hardship. Although there was a National Relief Fund established and there were various charitable organisations, there were often long bureaucratic delays before allowances were handed to those in dire need. Many women had meanwhile taken over their husband's former job.

However, not every woman supported the war, preferring instead to take the part of the conscientious objectors, who had organised a Conscientious Objectors Fellowship. When the leaders of this 'No Conscription Fellowship' were arrested, sympathetic suffragettes took their places. Although Emmeline Pankhurst ardently supported the war, her daughter Sylvia was equally opposed to it.

Belatedly, six months after the outbreak of war, the government established a register of women who were prepared to make themselves available for clerical, agricultural and industrial work. When, a month later, two women, who already worked in the Glasgow Tramways department, were allowed to become conductresses, this was considered to be a significant breach of a bastion of male-dominated society: the work was arduous, it could mean dealing with trouble-makers, it involved handling money in heavy bags, and it symbolised authority. Later in the war there were women lumberjacks – another blow to male self-esteem. But, as with the men who had volunteered for the Army earlier, it was a major task to train, equip, and place the 40,000 women who had registered promptly. However, the shortage of munitions, mentioned earlier, which was hampering the Army on the Western Front, soon brought more opportunities. In May 1915, Lloyd

George became Minister of Munitions in the Asquith Liberal government and, recognising a useful ally when he saw one, gave a government grant to Emmeline Pankhurst to organise a Suffragette demonstration demanding 'Women's Right to Serve'. The movement was directed at Trade Union leaders, and more particularly at employers who were afraid of employing women in case it should lead to strikes by men. The Ministry of Munitions was the pioneer in paying fair wage rates: other factories usually followed suit but often tried to pay less. All women workers were volunteers, although when joining certain organisations such as the Women's Forage Corps and the Land Army they signed a contract committing themselves to a minimum of six months service. All munitions factories operated under government rules and supervision, but there were many other factories employing women on an entirely independent (and sometimes very profitable) basis, though not to the workers. The Ministry of Munitions increased until it had 50 main departments and a staff of 20,000. However, the establishment of crèches for married women came not from the Ministry (though it adopted the idea) but from private individuals working in small factories.

Some women found the work too arduous or too boring and sordid but most persevered. They had little encouragement, often other male workers were openly hostile, even the foremen. Although their treatment seemed petty and unfair, most women realised that the men had an underlying fear that if women liked their factory jobs and became skilled workers, unemployment among men would rocket once the war was over and soldiers became civilians again.

Although the least pleasant and most dangerous of jobs, that of the munitions worker was one of the most prestigious and better paid. Its physical effects could be immediate or long-delayed. Filling shells with TNT (trinitrotoluene) could cause a variety of ills ranging from coughing to vomiting and convulsions. In January 1917 there was a huge explosion at Silvertown, East London, in which an unknown number were killed, including several women. It flattened a square mile of houses and sent a huge fireball into the air. Soon afterwards there was another explosion at Gretna, when a shed full of nitro-glycerine suddenly went up. Fortunately only one girl was killed then, although dozens were injured. Gretna was the largest munitions factory in the country, employing 11,000 women who lived in special hostels. This concentration of women was very worrying for the authorities, who believed that large numbers of young women with no recreational facilities were likely to become the target of undesirable influences. The most likely place for them to go astray, and thus be less effective as a work force, was Carlisle, so the train service between that town and Gretna was strictly curtailed: the last train for Gretna on Saturday night left at 9.30pm. However, in fairness it must be added that 'the authorities' provided club rooms for both men and women at Gretna and some of the girls played football, apparently to an impressively high standard.

Unfortunately there were a number of women who were neither interested in playing draughts in the club rooms or hockey or football outside, and many of them found solace for their boring life in the public houses of the district, which their independence and substantial earnings enabled them to patronise. Whether for the motive of safeguarding the women's morals, or making sure they did not drink so much that they were incapable of doing their vital war work, the government decided to take control. This they did by buying up all the local breweries and public houses. Many of the latter were then closed down and the remainder were managed by civil servants who abolished advertising and other inducements to encourage sales. Food was also served and drinking became more civilised. It was said that drunkenness was abolished by making the beer so thin that no one could drink enough of it, but this appears to have been an exaggeration. Carlisle's state-owned pubs continued until 1973, but were then sold back to the brewers.

Although the voluntary registration in March 1915 had produced a heartening response, it was soon clear that, as with men, a voluntary system would not bring in the numbers required. On 15 August 1915, a more serious step was taken in that a National Register was compiled. Everyone, both men and women, between the ages of fifteen and 65 was listed, with age and occupation. The main need was for manpower, but the scheme had obvious implications in showing which male jobs could be taken over by women as their former holders were sent to the Services. The Liberal government had been reluctant to bring in conscription but when, in 1915, it was replaced by a National Coalition government (still leaving Asquith as Prime Minister), a step towards it was taken by the 'Derby Scheme', in which men agreed to serve if they were required. Lord Derby was then Director-General of Recruiting.

Although the Derby Scheme produced its quota, it was clearly inadequate and on 5 January 1916 Asquith reluctantly brought in the Military Service Bill. As this only provided for the conscription of single men, and most men were married, it fell short of requirements again. In consequence, the Universal Conscription Bill was passed in May 1916. Although women were not conscripted, then or later, for military purposes, they could be compelled to work in certain types of civilian employment if necessary. In January 1917, a National Service Scheme, covering both men and women, signalled the end of a voluntary system or, for that matter, avoidance of service. In terms of numbers this meant that the war years had seen an increase in employed women of approximately 2–3,000,000 but, of course, they now operated in very different capacities. Dressmakers were now making aircraft fuselages, domestic servants were filling shells rather than coal scuttles, and teachers were working in armament manufacture. Many women did jobs which were well below their intellectual abilities. In general, women were resented less if they worked in one of the less masculine type of jobs. Needless to say they had their own preferences and these did not often accord with men's ideas of what were suitable jobs for them.

One profession in which women made considerable inroads was the preservation of law and order. Large numbers of women police were employed at munitions factories, but they took on general duties too, often more successfully than their predecessors. Not least of their responsibilities was keeping a look out for activities hostile to the state.

A notable step forward was taken in January 1917 when the Lawson report, commissioned by the War Office, recommended employing women in the Army in France in jobs similar to the ones which they were doing in England. This, of course, would release many men for services at the Front. It was a controversial proposal, much debated, and not until the following July did the Women's Army Auxiliary Corps (WAAC) come into being. Although run on army lines, different rank titles were used in the WAAC: officers were to be controllers and administrators, NCOs were to be forewomen. Like soldiers they had their own uniform, which included two pairs of khaki stockings, two pairs of combinations, two pairs of dark coloured knickers (nicknamed 'passion-killers'), and two strong nightdresses. There were four areas of employment: Cookery, Mechanical, Clerical and Miscellaneous. When serving in Britain, WAACs might be allowed to live at home, but not if they were cooks (in case they were tempted to divert some of the official rations to their own domestic needs). Initially there was friction between the WAACs and the VADs, of which over 8,000 were now serving in France and doing vital but often horrific jobs, but gradually this settled down. When one looks at the thick clothing and long, cumbersome, skirts in which women were expected to perform their tasks, and did, one can only marvel at their ingenuity and adaptability.

Many people who felt themselves to be guardians of morals were greatly concerned about the temptations (for both sexes) which overseas service presented. Although women could not be guarded all the time, there were strict regulations ensuring that the living quarters of both sexes were separate and under supervision. Segregation was not invariably successful. Not surprisingly, many women became engaged or married in France, although inevitably a high proportion were soon widowed.

There was, of course, a good proportion of women who regarded the rules for their moral welfare as something to be ignored rather than respected. Others approved of the regulations and felt that more should be done to protect them from the unwelcome attentions of soldiers with whom they had to work: VADs often had cause for complaint.

The Women's Land Army abounded with problems. Farmers often resented having to employ women because their physique prevented them from tackling some of the tasks easily performed by the men they had replaced. There were complaints that they fraternised with German prisoners of war, who were also employed on farms. Supervision was difficult and absenteeism was often reported: sometimes land girls ran away and disappeared altogether. Some of them failed to apply themselves to learning their jobs with the enthusiasm their instructors required. However, as their hours ranged from 7.00am (after breakfast) to bedtime at 9.30pm (after supper), it seems hardly surprising that they sometimes kicked over the traces: the miracle was that so many women buckled down to milking cows, shearing sheep, picking potatoes, cleaning out cattle sheds, hoeing root crops, sowing and harvesting. Life on a farm went on winter and summer, hot or cold, rain or snow, and animals were more awkward to manage than factory machinery. A story which was quite popular in the Land Army was that at the start of the war when women were presenting men with white feathers, one had targeted a farm, gone up to a man milking a cow, waved a white feather at him, and asked aggressively, 'Why aren't you at the Front?' Astonished and bewildered, he answered: 'Because there's no milk at that end.'

In March 1918 there were 6,023 WAACs serving in France. It was widely rumoured that promiscuity was rife, and well-meaning women of influence put pressure on Parliament to investigate this and put a stop to it. In consequence, the Minister of Labour appointed a Commission of Enquiry: all the appointed commissioners were women. It reported that out of the total of 6,000 WAACs, only 21 had become pregnant and only twelve had contracted venereal disease. Of the former, two were married and most of the others were already pregnant when they arrived in France. The rumour that soldiers were contracting venereal disease from WAACs was found to be wildly untrue, in fact the reverse was likely to be the case. Venereal disease was a massive problem for the Army in France, and it was said that there were never fewer than 20,000 men being treated for it at any one time. The figure is hard to verify, but the number was indeed high and undoubtedly most disease was contracted from prostitutes in the rear areas: men considering they might be killed on their return to the trenches are unlikely to be too finicky about the objects of their attentions. However, it would be completely wrong to assume that all the soldiers resorted to prostitutes or that all the French women who for one reason or another slept with soldiers were diseased.

Even with the dangers and changed environment of war, Victorian attitudes died hard. Although skirts became a little shorter, they still remained long; hardly above the shoes. Munitions workers often wore slacks, and land girls breeches, but they were seen as necessities for their jobs rather than signs of emancipation. Cosmetics were still regarded as signifying 'fast' women, probably prostitutes, but began to be used by girls of impeccable morals. Although upper class and working class women paid little attention to accepted ideas of morality (exerting common sense and prudence, rather than religious convictions), the middle class girls were more likely to hang on to their virtue until Mr Right came along. Sadly, most of the Mr Rights were killed in the fighting, with the result that at the end there were 2,000,000 more women in the country than men.

The year 1917 had seen the introduction of the Women's Institutes, prevalent in North America but new to Britain. They were officially encouraged, for they taught the best use of home produce and also of preventing waste. They also acted as a useful forum for women's opinions.

Many of the reforms to women's status, earned during the war, were not confirmed until after the Armistice, but within a month of that event the Coalition government under Lloyd George had brought in a Sex Disqualification Act. This took the first step to making women eligible for National Insurance benefits, and also admitted them to the legal profession and full membership of Oxford and Cambridge. Apart from these formal steps there were changes in attitude to women employees, particularly to domestic servants. Perhaps the most remarkable change in attitude had been shown by the Foundation for the National Council for the Unmarried Mother in February 1918. No longer were illegitimate children God's punishment for sinners, but people who needed help and care.

During the war women had shown they could be as brave as men. When the Military Medal was introduced for soldiers in 1916, it was also available to women and several won it. Nobody could doubt the courage of nurses and ambulance drivers. They had often shown themselves to be braver than men.

Least enviable were the women who had married Germans or Austrians, or who had other family connections with them. They came from all levels of society. Some of the former departed to Germany with their husbands; others stayed in Britain (where their spouses were interned).

The Royal family, of course, had as strong a German connection as any, and although King George V was one of the most ardent patriots in the country, his German background and family name of Saxe-Coburg-Gotha did nothing for his popularity. All the old German titles had to go: the Royal family now became the quintessentially British House of Windsor. As he had married Princess May of Teck, who was given the more English name of Mary, he had an embarrassment in that his brothers-in-law were the Duke of Teck and Prince Alexander of Teck. This situation was rectified by making the former the Marquess of Cambridge and the latter the Earl of Athlone. That still left his cousins, the Battenbergs, Prince Louis and Prince Alexander, but that problem was overcome by the relatively small change of Battenberg to Mountbatten, and the conferment of the title of Marquess of Milford Haven on the former and Marquess of Carisbrooke on the latter. Prince Louis of Battenberg, who had long severed his German connection, was a naturalised Englishman and was also First Sea Lord. No one could question Prince Louis' patriotism: he had alerted the Fleet at the outbreak of war, but public indignation at the thought of a German as the senior member of the Royal Navy was so vociferous that it was discreetly suggested to him, by George V on the advice of Churchill, that it would be advisable to resign. The presence of a German dynasty in Britain had been accepted as being right and proper as stemming from the royal line under normal conditions, but these were not normal conditions but war with a particularly ruthless enemy. Unless the provocative aspects were handled carefully, there was no knowing where this loose talk might lead: the word 'republic' was mentioned more than once.

Lower on the social scale, though not of importance, were the families of the City of London merchants, many of whom also happened to be Jewish. The fact that most had been naturalised long before did not save them from opprobrium: it merely suggested they were more deeply cunning than might have been suspected. Even in those days many firms dealing with chemicals, banking or engineering had international ramifications and these were thought by the more paranoid members of society to be being used for espionage. In fact, many of the leading industrialists were so keen to show how British they were that they exceeded the average native Englishman in their patriotism.

Even soldiers fighting in the trenches against the Germans were not above suspicion. Robert Graves, quoted elsewhere in this book, had German and Danish relations on his mother's side and had been christened Robert von Ranke Graves. Even at school before the war, this had led to taunts of 'German Jew', although he was neither. When the war came, he was in Harlech and enlisted in the Royal Welch Fusiliers, although he was not Welsh either. His first job in the army was guarding prisoners: seamen arrested on German vessels in Liverpool harbour, waiters from big hotels in the north, an odd German band or two, harmless German commercial travellers and shopkeepers. 'Many were married, had families, and had lived peaceably in England for years.' Later, in France, he often thought of his distant cousins, fighting perhaps in the opposite trenches.

Understandably, many families with German names changed them to the literal English translation or adopted an approximation. Kaufman became Kay, Schutz became Sterling. Arthur Schloss, a distinguished sinologist and translator who had been born in London and educated at Rugby and Cambridge, decided it would be prudent to become Arthur Waley, and Ford Hermann Hueffer, an internationally-famous novelist and critic, born in England, who fought in the British Army until he was gassed in the trenches, changed his name to Ford Madox Ford after the war. Not least of the reasons for the despair of many soldiers with German names was the fact that their wives were often nicknamed 'Hunwives'. But not every German married to an Englishman felt quite the same about her country of origin: D. H. Lawrence's wife was one of them. Born Frieda von Richthofen, and a cousin of the soon-to-be-famous 'Red Baron', she had first married Professor Ernest Weekley, who had taught Lawrence at University College, Nottingham, but had left him for Lawrence in 1912. She travelled around Germany with him for two years and then married him in England in 1914. Frieda is said to have been his inspiration for *Lady Chatterley's Lover*, although that book did not appear (privately printed in 1928) until two years before he died.

However, in 1914 Lawrence was already well known from his novels and poems when war broke out, and when later they went to live in Cornwall, where Frieda used to dance ostentatiously on the beach, and both of them used to sing German songs, they became less than popular. Frieda made no secret of her admiration for her cousin's feats in the air, and the Germans who flew in Zeppelins or went to sea in U boats. The Lawrences were already friends of Lady Ottoline Morrell, who used her home at Garsington Manor, near Oxford, as a refuge for conscientious objectors and pacifists, including

Bertrand Russell, who strongly opposed all things military, as well as others of similarly unorthodox views. When conscription came in in 1916 Lawrence was called up but failed the medical. The pair were now thoroughly distrusted and were directed by the police to live well away from the coast. Undoubtedly the Lawrences went out of their way to draw attention to themselves and their unpopular allegiances, but many who tried to behave as good, loyal, British citizens did not always receive the understanding they deserved. One who did was a naturalised German maid who lived and worked at No 10 Downing Street. Asquith, as a Liberal, was bound to let her stay, even though common sense might have suggested moving her to a less sensitive area. Asquith was not very security conscious. While Prime Minister he wrote a series of letters to a girl half his age, with whom he was having an affair; they abounded with interesting gossip from Cabinet meetings.

Not only people, but places experienced a change of name to rid them of any foreign association. The quintessentially English Coburg Hotel off Berkeley Square became the Connaught. It was, perhaps, unfortunate that the English language had Anglo-Saxon origins.

Unfortunately the general animosity to all things German was extended to many people whose only crime was that they sounded, and were, foreign: Serbs, Poles, even Italians, among others, were dismayed to find they were classed with Germans, whom they had every reason to hate, and did. Even dead composers like Handel, Beethoven or Wagner, or cherished possessions like Bechstein pianos were not admired as they once were. The music of Johann, and the other two Strauss composers, suddenly seemed to have become less infectiously cheerful.

These emotions were mirrored in France, where there was also a massive response to appeals for women to work in war industry. They were less marked in Germany and Austria, perhaps because these were aggressor countries.

CHAPTER 11

The Final Stages

May 1918 saw the beginning of the last traumatic six months of the war. Russia was out of it, Austria and Hungary were hard pressed, the Turks were being pushed to the brink of defeat, and the Germans in Tanganyika were grimly holding on; every belligerent was feeling the strain on the home front, none more so than the Fatherland. Although German losses had been high in the Spring offensive (348,300 casualties) it was clear to Ludendorff that he must press on, for this was the vital moment when victory would be won or slip away for ever.

He realised only too well that time was running out for Germany. He had received a valuable addition to his Western army when he had been able to incorporate the divisions which had returned from the Russian front. They were fresher than his other troops which had been fighting in France, on and off, for the previous four years, enduring the battles of the Somme, Arras, and Passchendaele, and the relentless strain of trench warfare.

But he must strike again quickly before the Allies received large reinforcements from America. He decided that, although the British had been gravely weakened in the Spring offensive, the best spot to attack now was in the French sector. He was well aware that Foch had sent French reserves to help the British and reasoned that, if he could break through in the French sector, there would be little to check his rapid progress. His eye fell on the Notre Dame Ridge. Although this was held by the French, it also contained the British IX Corps, which had been sent there to rest and recover from their earlier fighting. The corps contained five divisions. Haig had informed Foch that these divisions were in no condition to be used again as front-line troops.

However, when Ludendorff opened his offensive on 27 May with the usual devastating bombardment, those divisions were in an action as severe as anything they had previously encountered. After the bombardment came massed infantry attacks. Within five days the Germans had reached Château Thierry on the river Marne. The situation was as bad as it had been in the worst days of 1914. British losses, including prisoners, were 28,703; French losses were 98,634, but Haig, Weygand and Foch all suspected that many of the French had surrendered too easily.

By now American troops were arriving in substantial numbers. They were new to battle and Foch thought that the best way for them to gain experience was by plugging gaps in the French sector: Haig disagreed. Instead, some American units were attached to British units to gain experience of trench warfare. This was good, sound sense but General Pershing, the American commander, was anxious to keep all the American troops together and to go into action as an army.

Foch now began to alarm his allies by taking an autocratic approach: he assumed that as Commander in Chief he could move troops as and when he pleased. As he had decided that the French sector was the most vulnerable, he now began moving both British and French divisions from the northern to the southern fronts. Lloyd George, who had strongly favoured Foch's appointment, now began to be alarmed by these moves and called a conference to discuss the matter. Foch emphasised that he had the authority to move any troops, British, French or American, at short notice, according to where they were most needed. Although Haig agreed with this in principle, he felt that it should not be done without consultation, however rapid, with the national commanders concerned. Clemenceau, while supporting Foch's right to do as he thought fit, nevertheless insisted that he must not move troops from Haig's area of command without first stating his intention.

As invariably happens when armies are in danger of defeat, there was a tendency to criticise the tactical dispositions of allies. Certainly the Chemin des Dames was an unfortunate choice for a defensive position and gave the Germans very little trouble when they came to it. By June they were on the Marne, which they crossed. But they were paying a high price, some of it extracted by the Americans. On 6 June the American 2nd Division had counter-attacked and retaken much of Belleau Wood as well as the village of Bouresches. The gains themselves were not of great importance, but the fact they had been made by Americans did wonders for their own confidence and that of their allies. It also caused Ludendorff to revise his opinion of American soldiers, which he had thought would be too brash and raw to be effective for many months; by that time he expected to have won the war.

There were, of course, in the great retreat of 1918 many occasions when certain units had far exceeded anything which might be expected of them. One of then was the 2nd Battalion of the Devonshire Regiment which, on 27 May, was holding the last trench north of the Aisne at Bois des Buttes. At dawn on the 27th, the 2nd Devons numbered 581 which included 29 officers. Six hours later there were 50 left, but they had halted an entire German division.

Before the attack began the Devons were told that not a foot of ground must be given, but they were not told anything of the strength of their potential attackers, nor even why this area was of such vital importance. There was nothing particularly unusual about that. In the general retreat many units had been allocated vital sectors which they had been told they must hold to the last round and the last man. Often such orders were altered as the situation on another part of the front altered drastically. This time there would be no counter order.

The attack began at 1.00am. Two gas shells came first, then the high explosive shells from 2,000 guns followed. The gas made it essential to wear masks in the trenches, but many men had already been trapped in dugouts by the shellfire which had closed the entrance. British artillery behind was responding to the German onslaught but unfortunately for the gunners they had taken positions recently vacated by the French artillery and the Germans had the details of the gunpits, and the range of the guns, so it was not difficult to silence them one by one. During the night the Devons hoped there would be more counter-fire from British or French artillery, but waited in vain. By dawn, many of their trenches had been destroyed but an infantry attack must obviously be imminent, so the companies were deployed in the open. As the barrage was still continuing, it was impossible to know whether all the soldiers had reached their allotted positions. A thick morning mist covered the flat land and was made even more impenetrable by the smoke and dust from the shellfire.

The Commanding Officer was left in complete ignorance of the direction from which the next enemy attack might be expected. In fact they were advancing on each of his flanks and, unknown to him, some of the companies were already in action. When the barrage lifted to let in the attacking German infantry, the mist seemed to clear. The Devons then saw their opponents. They were advancing in lines, and bringing with them transport and guns. Overhead were a few aeroplanes, mostly spotting for artillery but often descending to machine-gun the Devons. When the German soldiers came into range, the Devon Lewis gunners mowed them down easily, but when the Germans realised what they were up against they took cover and used their rifle grenades. Most of the Devons were beginning to be worried that they would run out of ammunition, as the number of Germans advancing like automatons seemed endless: even so, they did not yet realise they were confronting not a mere battalion but a division. One section of the

Devons decided to try a bayonet charge before they entirely ran out of ammunition. Unfortunately it did not take them very far for they were held up by barbed wire which had been there so long that it was now hidden in thick undergrowth: here they were pinned down and raked with enemy machine-gun and mortar fire. Most of the Devons were firing at any Germans they saw without any particular animosity, but one officer in particular was taking a particular delight in killing as many as possible; his only child had been drowned when a German submarine sank the *Lusitania*. He moved around, encouraging his platoon, and showing no trace of fear. Then he too was killed.

Certain factors made this heroic stand by the Devons particularly disconcerting for the Germans. The attack was partly taking place through a wood, and as the original trenches had been destroyed, the Devons were now firing from unexpected angles. Although they had lost their own trenches, there were remains of other trenches in the neighbourhood, and these were used to full advantage. There were so many Germans that it was almost impossible to fire without hitting one. The Devons' Commanding Officer, Lieutenant Colonel Anderson-Morshead (aged 28) had trained this battalion and took enormous pride in it. Now it was being slaughtered in what by any standards was an impossible task. But his orders were to stand to the last man, to hold up the enemy as long as possible so that other troops could form a line behind him. He knew there was no chance of retreating to better positions, so he thought there was no point in withholding the truth from his men. He told them they were surrounded and announced with the simplicity that men of his type at that time used in making such statements: 'Your job for England, men,' he said, 'is to hold the blighters up as much as you can to give our troops a chance on the other side of the river. There is no hope of relief. We have to fight to the last.'

Completely indifferent to the bullets and high explosives around him, Anderson-Morshead moved around encouraging the small groups remaining. His orderly (Lance Corporal Jordan), who survived, looked up and saw a large force of Germans moving down the road from Juvincourt. He pointed it out to the Colonel, who, surrounded by dead and dying and flying bullets, calmly took a pipe from his pocket and lit it and remarked, without a trace of emotion in his voice, 'Ah well, Jordan, we shall have to make the best of it.'

They already had. The toll they had taken of the Germans, out of all proportion to their own numbers, had helped to slow down and disrupt the offensive. It had not yet been fully checked but rearguard actions, such as this of the 2nd Devons, were ensuring that that moment would soon come.

Remarkable and unexpected efforts had already come from units much less organised than the Devons. When the German infantry had made the first breakthrough in their offensive, Gough had ordered that every man, able-bodied or not, would fight as an infantryman. All had, of course, fired their rifles a few times, but those who had gone on to become mechanics, pioneers, or specialists in one of the many trades required by the army had probably never fired one since. Now they had to. Cooks, storemen and others who never dreamt they would ever shoot to kill, now found themselves hastily drafted into units and doing something they had thought impossible.

One unexpected effect of the German successes in the 1918 offensive was on morale. Although German soldiers were elated by driving British and French troops ahead of them, they began to doubt their chances of ultimate success when they saw the quality of the equipment discarded by the Allies. Apart from weapons, everything seemed greatly superior to their own possessions. If this was the quality of goods the Allies could throw away, what must they have in reserve, they asked themselves.

On 9 July, Ludendorff made his final effort. His troops crossed the Marne and occupied ground on either side of Reims; they paid a high price for doing so, for the French artillery were prepared for them. Although he had now made substantial gains, Ludendorff decided that his positions on the far side of the Marne were probably untenable, and ordered a withdrawal. But before this withdrawal could take place, his worst fears were realised. On 18 July the French General Mangin's Tenth Army was launched at the right flank of the German army with the Sixth French Army supporting it. At the same time, the Fifth and Ninth French Armies were launched from the east and south. The German army was hurled back to its former position along the Vesle River from Reims to Soissons. This became known as the Second Battle of the Marne, but has never been accorded the recognition it deserves. It showed that the French army had now fully recovered from its traumas of 1917 and Foch's reputation was assured.

In this last few months of the war, the Western Front was seeing a different form of warfare from that experienced in the earlier years. Loos, the Somme, Artois, Champagne, Arras, Ypres, Verdun, had all been localised battles, even though they had involved huge numbers, cost many lives, and usually been supported by diversionary attacks elsewhere. This was different. This time the action swung from one end of the trench line to the other, and was nearer to the open warfare which both sides had envisaged before the outbreak.

Ludendorff's unsuccessful drive to cross the Marne and reach Paris had used up his reserves. This meant that if the British army could now launch an offensive in the central sector, and break through the German defences, Ludendorff would theoretically be unable to contain it. The Fourth Army (formerly the Fifth, but now renumbered by its new commander, General Rawlinson) was concentrated in front of Amiens. It mustered a substantial force consisting of thirteen infantry divisions, three horsed cavalry divisions, 456 tanks, and 2,000 guns. It was supported by seventeen air squadrons. On its right was the French First Army.

The date chosen for the counter-attack was 8 August, and the direction was to be along the Somme east of Amiens, after which this battle was subsequently named. Rawlinson was, of course, familiar with this area from past experience. He was allotted the Australian Corps, commanded by the redoubtable Sir John Monash, which contained five divisions; and the Canadian Corps, commanded by General Sir Arthur Currie, which was no less eager to give the Germans a taste of what the Canadians had received from them. When the offensive began, there would be a diversionary attack by the British III Corps, which had not yet fully recovered from the mauling it had received five months earlier but was still strong enough to confuse the Germans about the main British intention. This time there would be no preliminary bombardment to warn the Germans what was coming, but when the attack was launched the British and French artillery would saturate the German positions minutes before the infantry went in. Although most of the tanks were the heavy Mark Vs, there were also 96 Whippets which, though lightly armed, had a top speed of 8mph (twice that of the Mark Vs). This would enable them to exploit any gaps left in the German defence – classical cavalry tactics.

The attack began at 4.20am on 8 August in early morning mist and the troops had reached all their objectives by noon, in an advance of five miles. 14,000 prisoners and over 300 guns were captured. However, the cavalry aspect of the battle was disappointing. Two-thirds of the tanks were knocked out or broke down mechanically and the supporting horsed cavalry made little headway against concentrated machine-gun fire. But the success of the attack was enough to make Ludendorff write in his book *My War Memories*, published in 1919: 'August 8th was the black day of the German army in the history of this war. This was the worst experience I had to go through.'

Although the attack was continued on the 9th and 10th, progress was slow. As had been shown so often in this war, the Germans were quick to recover from a surprise and, if unable to counter-attack, would defend stubbornly against further attacks. However, Fourth Army gradually pushed on and was joined by the French Third, which was deployed on the right of the First, thus lengthening the front. By the 12th, the Germans had been forced off their valuable salient on the Oise, a loss which badly affected morale. When Haig halted Fourth Army, it had increased its advance to twelve miles and taken 22,000 prisoners.

At this point there was a slight but unsettling change in Haig's relationship with Foch. Haig thought that Fourth Army had done enough for the moment and should be allowed to recover and regroup. This did not fall in with Foch's plans, and he expressed strong displeasure. Haig suggested that if it was important to keep up the momentum of the attack this could be done by using Byng's Third British Army to attack in the La Bassée–Arras sector. Foch disagreed completely, and gave a direct order to Haig to continue the attack by Fourth Army as part of the overall plan to push the Germans out of France.

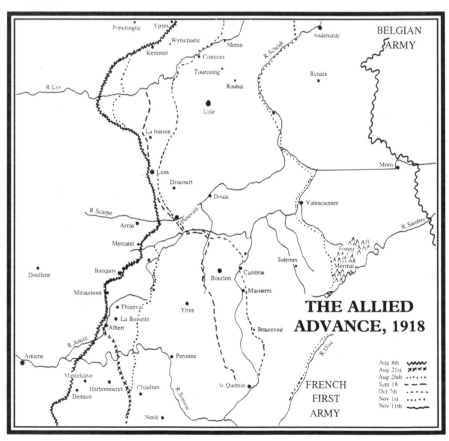

THE ALLIED
ADVANCE, 1918

Aug 8th	
Aug 21st	
Aug 26th	
Sept 18	
Oct 7th	
Nov 1st	
Nov 11th	

Haig thereupon went to Rawlinson and told him that previous orders were cancelled and that he must continue his attack. Not surprisingly, Rawlinson was indignant and angry. 'Are you commanding the British army or is Foch?' he demanded. It was a delicate situation. Although Foch was Commander in Chief, his appointment did not entitle him to give direct orders to the components of the British Army. Haig was well aware of this, but did not wish to damage a relationship which up till this moment had been working smoothly and whose harmonious continuation was essential to the successful conclusion of the war. Even so, he agreed that for Rawlinson to continue the attack with his army in an exhausted state would probably bring heavy casualties with small gains. He therefore agreed with Rawlinson that Fourth Army should not carry out the order.

Foch, with other armies committed, was furious. He repeated the order that Fourth Army must continue the attack.

Haig was now in an embarrassing situation. He decided to go and see Foch personally at his headquarters. As he arrived, he was greeted somewhat brusquely with the question 'When is Fourth Army going to attack?' Haig was patient but firm. He replied that though Foch was responsible for overall strategy, he himself was responsible to the British government and people for the handling of British forces. Much to his surprise, Foch replied very mildly and said all he really wanted from Haig was information about his intentions so that he could coordinate his plans with those of the other armies. He agreed that Haig was right to take the stand he had. Meanwhile, the Germans had assumed that Fourth Army would attack again and concentrated most of their scanty reserves in that sector. This enabled the French Tenth Army to launch another offensive on the sector opposite them in the south.

Haig was surprised to receive a visit from Clemenceau four days later to confer on him the Medaille Militaire. Although this may have been mere coincidence, it seems likely that the initiative had come from Foch, who realised he had overstepped his authority as GOCinC and wished to ensure that the British commander was not nursing a sense of resentment. Happily for Allied cooperation, all seemed to have ended harmoniously. The history of warfare is beset with examples of victorious commanders quarrelling among themselves and in consequence losing gains they have acquired at great cost.

The attack which Haig had now planned for Byng's Third Army began at dawn of 21 August and advanced nearly five miles, taking 5,000 prisoners. On 21 August Fourth Army, rested and revived, came into the offensive again and made further gains. This was followed by an attack by the British First Army, for Haig was determined that the Germans should have no chance to recover and the best way to make sure of that was to hit them with one massive blow after another. He suggested to Foch that the Americans should now be brought into the attack. Foch thought this was an excellent idea, as Americans had given ample demonstrations of their fighting ability in this campaign; however, when he proposed that they should be put under French command, the American commander, General Pershing, objected strongly. Eventually it was agreed that the Americans should go into action as an independent command. Although abounding with fighting spirit, the American commanders lacked experience of offensives on this scale, and this attack, between the Meuse and the Aisne, failed badly.

German prisoners were now telling their captors what the latter had long wanted to hear, that discipline was beginning to break down in the German army. This appeared to support what Haig was already deducing from the success of his recent attacks and encouraged him to believe that if the British army could make one supreme attempt it could crash through the remaining German defences and bring the German army to the brink of surrender. But for this he needed reserves. He knew well enough that there were plenty of troops in England, including those for anti-Zeppelin duties, and he did not believe for one moment they were needed any longer there. He decided that the only way he could obtain them was to go home and talk to the Cabinet himself. This would mean leaving the front at a critical time, but he decided it was essential. Alas for his hopes, his journey was in vain. Lord Milner, a Cabinet Minister with a notable record for inflexibility (he was of mixed German and English extraction) flatly opposed the idea that Haig should now drain England of reserves. He was, of course, simply reaffirming the policy of Lloyd George, but both he and the Prime Minister showed a complete misunderstanding of the tactical situation at that time. The French appeared to have recovered fully from the traumas of the past, while the Germans faced the grim reality that their last great offensive had failed, they were steadily being pushed back, and there was unrest at home. The core of the matter was that Lloyd George did not trust his Commander in Chief. Subsequently he acknowledged that he had been mistaken in this attitude. Milner told Haig that the army he was commanding was the last one that Britain would be able to produce, and that there would be no more reinforcements. It is not clear how Lloyd George expected Haig to achieve victory at this critical stage if he was going to be short of troops for the final moves he was planning.

There was, of course, an element of risk, and Haig was probably more aware of it than Lloyd George. The next stage was to break through the Siegfried Stellung, the fortification on which the Germans had been lavishing such care over the last few years. It was a hazardous operation and might prove disastrous.

The assault began on 18 September, when the First, Third and Fourth British Armies swept forward to reach the outer fortifications of the Siegfried Stellung. In doing so, they captured another 116,000 prisoners but not without heavy losses to themselves. The stage was now set for the final assault. It was to be in the form of a huge pincer movement. The northern claw would consist of the Belgian army and the British Second Army, the central attack would be made by the British First, Third and Fourth armies, and the French Fourth Army; and the southern claw would be Pershing's American army.

In order to deceive the Germans about the purpose and direction of the attack, the assault was planned to come in sector by sector. The French Fourth Army would begin in the Champagne sector, a scene of bitter memories, and the Americans would tackle the Argonne. The following day, the British First and Third armies would launch attacks through the line of the Canal du Nord, and the next day the Belgian army and the British Second Army would set off with the object of liberating Bruges and Brussels. Not until the 29th would the British Fourth and French First armies be committed in the centre.

Nobody was under any illusion that this great battle would lead to an easy victory. Although German morale had been dented by gloomy news from home and other fronts, such as Palestine and Mesopotamia, it was now revived by the thought that German armies were now fighting a battle which might finally break the Allied armies in France.

The Germans had nothing to learn about defensive warfare. Sometimes they would appear to yield and then, when the enemy was disorganised, could attack with ferocity which completely disorganised opponents who thought they were winning. At other times they would arrange a mixture of hard points and soft points. Attacking troops would be held up on the hard points, but would find they could slide by them easily through apparently weaker sections. This would upset the cohesion of the attacking force and frequently led to a situation where the infiltrations could be enfiladed or even cut off completely. There was nothing original about such tactics: medieval castle-builders, particularly the Normans, had used them with great success. However, the difference between the medieval past and the

1918 present was that the Germans had more effective weapons and greater expertise.

The Americans, who had been pressing for an important and difficult sector to attack, now received it. The Argonne had been in German hands for four years. It was tactically important because while they held it the Germans were in an excellent position to outflank the Fourth French Army as it advanced. However, it would be difficult terrain because the Argonne forest is spread over ridges which lie between the Aire and upper Aisne. It is full of deep ravines which make it impossible for tanks (of which the Americans had 189) and it was full of wire and netting, much of which was now concealed in deep undergrowth. To shell a forest like this merely made it more impenetrable, for the broken tree trunks then blocked all possible paths. Apart from the problem of making headway in the forest, there was a formidable problem of supply. Immediately behind were the battlefields of Verdun where all roads, villages and the drainage system had been systematically destroyed by bombardments. This 'scorched earth' had been extended to the east of the forest, in the area over which the Americans were likely to approach. Here towns and villages had been set on fire, all roads and railway bridges demolished, embankments and cuttings blown up by explosive, wells and water supplies polluted, and an elaborate array of booby traps prepared. The innocuously-named 'booby traps' caused both casualties and delays. A discarded German helmet or a useful-looking pistol, particularly attractive as souvenirs, often concealed explosives for killing the unwary. Even a well-sited sniper's platform in a tree might have been wired up as a death trap. Lurid magazines, apparently flung down carelessly on a chair, could conceal contact explosives. The Germans were nothing if not methodical, but such hazards were not created out of vindictiveness, but for their military value.

Pershing's First American Army consisted of fifteen infantry divisions and one cavalry division, each being twice the size of the British or French counterpart. As the assigned front was only 22 miles long, only nine divisions could be used in the initial attack.

Although lacking in experience, the Americans abounded in enthusiasm and although their casualties were high their results were impressive. In the middle of their area was the town of Montfaucon, which was so well fortified, as well as being on top of a hill, that it was thought to be impregnable against infantry attack. The Americans bypassed it on the first day and captured it on the second. In doing so they incurred many casualties, for it was surrounded by camouflaged machine-gun posts on platforms in the trees.

The only surviving building at the time of its capture was a château which Crown Prince Rupprecht had used as an observatory in 1916. From the basement 30 feet below ground he had watched the attacks on Verdun through a periscope which was in turn protected by a concrete cylinder. (The periscope is now in the Museum at the US Military Academy, West Point.) The Americans were in action continuously between the opening of the Argonne campaign and the end of the war, a total of 47 days: it rained on 40 of them. Two Americans who were to become famous during the Second World War earned distinction in the Argonne campaign. One was Colonel S. C. Marshall, who would be Chief of Staff in World War II and who would also originate the Marshall Plan for rebuilding Europe in 1948; the other was George Patton, who was wounded here. Patton was the originator of the classic saying: 'No one ever won a war by dying for his country but only by making some poor bastard die for his.'

In spite of the difficulties of the terrain the Americans coped with their problems and made advances which surprised and pleased Foch. However, Ludendorff was not prepared to surrender this important area lightly and soon switched whatever divisions he could spare to this sector. Consequently, the advance of the first few days soon slowed down. The forest could not be bypassed but had to be cleared, often by infantry moving from tree to tree in rain and fog. Sometimes this meant that quite large units were virtually lost. One battalion became surrounded and to make matters worse came under its own artillery fire. Its commander's only contact with the rest of the army was by carrier pigeon. Thousands of carrier pigeons were used in this war, as they could often get a message through when all other means had failed. This one was called 'Cher Ami', but was in fact British, being one of a consignment of 600 sent by British pigeon fanciers to the American army. The Germans, who had already shot down three of its predecessors, made a desperate effort to do the same to this one. One bullet broke its leg, another damaged a wing and the third broke its breastbone, but after appearing to fall it regained height and set off with its vital message. Although it became a national hero, 'Cher Ami' only survived another year, but after dying was stuffed and put on display in the Smithsonian Institute in Washington. It was a minor incident in a major war, but had a distinct effect on morale.

Pigeons, of course, were not the only non-human message carriers of this war. Dogs were also used and were also able to lay signal wires from drums strapped on to their backs.

Not surprisingly, the American army produced various soldiers who would have been regarded as a strain on human credibility if they had appeared in Hollywood films. One was Corporal York. When called up by the army, York, who belonged to a religious group which emphasised the commandment 'Thou shalt not kill', had originally refused to serve. Fortunately for the army, his prospective commanding officer was able to match biblical quotation for biblical quotation until York confessed himself convinced. Although York did not believe in killing humans, much of his early life had been spent hunting in Wolf River Valley, Tennessee, so he had no problem with his military tasks.

On 8 October 1918, York's platoon was advancing towards the Decauville railway when it encountered heavy machine-gun fire from all sides. Although the platoon managed to infiltrate and capture a German regimental headquarters, it then ran into heavy fire which accounted for half its numbers. This left York as the senior rank. He therefore told the rest of the platoon to guard the prisoners they had taken earlier while he went ahead to 'investigate'. Investigating consisted of crawling up to an outpost (using his hunting skills) and shooting the occupants with his revolver. He said he found it 'easier'n shooting turkeys'. A German major, not realising that all the shots were coming from one man, decided his unit must be surrounded and would be well advised to surrender before they were eliminated. He therefore raised a white flag and handed over the remains of his command, a total of 132. This remarkable feat made York something of a national hero, but York proved a great disappointment to those who tried to lionise him. He refused to appear in a film, he refused to make speeches, and he refused a lecture tour, for all of which he was offered enormous fees. He merely said: 'It's all over: let's forget it.'

By this time there were over 1,000,000 Americans in the battle area, and the numbers were still pouring in. A second army was created on 10 October and both were almost continuously in action. But there were few spectacular successes. The Germans were beaten but not broken, and the Americans were made to pay dearly for their advances. Nevertheless, by the time the war ended they had done more and better than anyone had expected. Although their casualties were low in relation to those of the other combatants, being only 264,092 when others were over the million mark, it should be borne in mind that the Americans were only in action with a full-scale army for less than two months, whereas the others had experienced four years. Although the Americans relied heavily on their allies for weapons, using French 75mms, 155mm howitzers and cannons, Chauchat automatic rifles and Hotchkiss machine-guns, and, British Stokes mortars, Newton 6in mortars, 6in howitzers and Enfield rifles, they were also beginning to produce excellent weapons of their own in the shape of Browning machine-guns and automatics. Added to this was the fact that the best light machine-gun of the war was the invention of an American colonel, I. N. Lewis.

In following the Americans, we have moved ahead of the fighting in the other sectors.

The British task was to advance towards Cambrai and St Quentin and at the same time sweep through the Flanders area (the north claw). For this part of the battle, both the British Second Army under General Plumer and the Belgian army set off on 28 September 1918 through the Passchendaele area which had seen so much misery and bloodshed. This time the attackers raced through the old battlefields in a day. This was not surprising: the Germans had only five divisions to spare for this area which they now had to regard as being of secondary importance. The British First Army were already in action along the Canal du Nord and this was no mean undertaking, for the canal was approximately 100 feet across, was half full of water and was defended by a line of machine-guns. Although casualties were high, the canal was crossed, the Germans were driven back five miles (on a twelve mile front), and 4,000 prisoners and 100 guns were captured. On 29 September, Third Army reached Cambrai, two days later First Army had bypassed the town on the northern side.

The Siegfried Stellung proved less formidable than had been feared. Third Army had already breached the northern end, and Fourth Army pushed the Germans back over the Scheldt Canal. There was, however, a formidable line of defences to the north of St Quentin, known as the Masnières–Beaurevoir line. However this too was cleared by Fourth Army between 3–5 October. Surprisingly the Germans had been ejected from their supposedly impregnable defences in the course of nine days and in doing so had lost 67,000 prisoners and 680 guns. Nevertheless they were still fighting rearguard actions, even if it now seemed that defeat was inevitable.

Remorselessly the Allied offensive pushed through towns and villages which in the past had been fought over for months, and in some cases now only existed as names of piles of ruins. By 18 October, the Belgian army had reached Bruges and Zeebrugge, and the British were holding a line along the Lys. But even though they were being forced back, the Germans seemed to have time to carry out an extensive programme of demolitions. This not only delayed the progress of the advances but also made life infinitely worse for the civilians who were now trying to return to their homes. Surprisingly, the British cavalry, which had waited so long to take its part in this war, and had often been used as stop-gap infantry, was now given a task well within its means. As the warfare was now much more open, cavalry squadrons could sometimes gallop into enemy lines and deal with German engineers who were blowing up roads and bridges. They were also destroying many installations which had no military use: even the shopping centre in Douai was flattened.

By 1 November, the British had reached the Scheldt and the Oise, and Valenciennes was captured. On 4 November, three British armies, First, Third and Fourth, attacked on a 30-mile front from Valenciennes to the river Samborx. German prisoners were now being taken in their thousands. On 9 November the British troops crossed the Scheldt, reached Tournai and approached Mons where the war had begun for them, though not, of course, for the unfortunate Belgians.

In Germany itself the end of the war had been anticipated for weeks. Even as early as 4 October, the Chancellor, Prince Max of Baden, had sent a note to President Wilson of America saying that Germany was now prepared to make peace on the lines of Wilson's Fourteen Points. Although there was nothing revolutionary about the Fourteen Points and they merely reiterated principles which idealists for generations had suggested were the basic requirements for universal peace, they were immensely important in bringing this war to an end and forming the peace settlement. In 1918 they seemed to augur a new and better future. The fact that they had now been stated as policy by the President of the one country which had benefited from the war and which alone now had the money, energy and, hopefully, the will, to establish a decent, viable world order, made them appeal strongly to countries which otherwise would have been tempted not to lay down their arms but instead to battle on in a desperate, hopeless manner. We shall examine the Fourteen Points and their effects more closely in due course. Wilson, who was a former Professor of Political Science, lacked the charisma to enthuse his allies. Clemenceau remarked: 'The Good Lord only gave us ten commandments: the American President has given us fourteen.' However Wilson was not so naive as to imagine that the Allies would now take German promises on trust. He knew there were plenty of prominent Germans who could be blamed for launching and continuing the war which was now grinding to its end, and that the Kaiser was only the symbolical figurehead for German intransigence and aggression. In fact, Ludendorff would have been a more justifiable target.

In November the news of the collapse of Germany came in steadily. First the German fleet at Kiel mutinied; rumours had been circulating that it was under orders to put to sea and perish in a heroic but unequal battle with the British and American fleets. This aroused considerably less enthusiasm on the lower deck than among the admirals. Attempts to arrest the ringleaders and stop the mutiny were unsuccessful. On 8 November there were revolutionary riots in Munich and on the following day there were similar riots in other German towns. The Kaiser, who had been pressed to resign, announced that he was prepared to renounce his title of German Emperor (there was now no German empire), but he must be allowed to retain his title of King of Prussia. However the German Liberals had had enough of Prussia, from which they felt most of their troubles stemmed, and opposed him. Realising that his situation was hopeless, the Kaiser then fled to Holland (still neutral) on 10 November.

When Germany had made her final, desperate offensive in the Spring of 1918, her allies in the 'sideshows' had heard the news of her successes with relief and jubilation. The relief came from their belief that if Britain and France were being knocked out of the war they themselves would soon become victors in their own particular theatres. However, their jubilation was tempered by speculation about their Teutonic ally's future attitude towards themselves. Would the Germans be gracious and grateful victors, rewarding their allies who had supported them so well in the past, or would they now use their supreme power to extend their domination, ignoring the claims of those who had helped them?

Bulgaria had for long had misgivings about joining in on the side of the Central Powers. They were not equipped for a long war of attrition. On 1 September 1918 they had been attacked by the British near the river Vardar, and a week later the Greeks had attacked them near Struma. In the middle of the month the French and Serbs attacked them too and while they were trying to repel this thrust the British and Greeks renewed their attacks. Confused by these tactical switches, the Bulgars did not realise that the principal threat came from the Franco-Serb force until it broke through into Macedonia. French cavalry occupied Uskub, thus splitting the two main Bulgarian armies. Those opposing the British fell back into the Struma valley. Hopelessly outmanoeuvred they now asked for peace before the Serbs and Greeks should enter Bulgaria and exact a fearful revenge for the atrocities inflicted on both peoples by Bulgarian troops earlier in the war. When the Allies offered an armistice on 30 September, the Bulgars accepted with alacrity. Four days later King Ferdinand of Bulgaria abdicated in favour of his son. The Serbs were now able to return to their own country. The news of the Bulgarian collapse caused a panic on the German stock exchange.

Although Russia had been effectively out of the war since the Treaty of Brest-Litovsk, Britain and France realised only too well that there were large dumps of Allied arms in Archangel: they had been sent for the use of the Russian army but now might be used for unpredictable but probably anti-Allied purposes. On 16 July 1918, the Bolsheviks had massacred the Czar Nicholas and his entire family at Ekaterinburg in the Urals. Up till this point the Romanovs had been living in reasonable comfort in Siberia. It seems that the Bolsheviks feared that there might be an attempt by the White Russians to rescue them and use them in the fight against Bolshevism, even if only symbolically. They were therefore moved to what was thought to be a more secure location at Ekaterinburg but apparently were assassinated in a cellar in a panic-stricken reaction. In 1993, after the collapse of the Soviet regime has released many closely-guarded documents to the world, attempts are being made to find out exactly what happened.

The assassination left no doubt in the minds of the Allies what might happen if the Bolsheviks got their hands on the arms which had been intended for Russia when she was fighting as an ally. In consequence, on 2 August 1918, a force commanded by Major General Frederick Poole landed at Archangel (Arkhangelsk) and took it, without serious opposition. This was by invitation of the White armies, who said they did not recognise the Brest-Litovsk treaty but were pro-Ally and anti-German. Poole established a form of military law and cancelled a number of resolutions passed by the Bolsheviks. Appropriately his force contained Poles, US Marines, Royal Marines and a French battalion.

However, after the war Archangel passed back into the hands of the Soviets and became one of their most important and secret bases. Severodvinsk, where Russian nuclear submarines were built and based, is nearby.

There were other matters, nearer home, to occupy public attention at this time. Leading amongst them was the extraordinary epidemic of influenza which became known as 'Spanish flu', though it seems to have originated in China, or perhaps India. Whatever its source, there was no mistaking its virulence. Over 2,000 deaths a week were being caused in London alone and it was reported to be killing US soldiers more rapidly and effectively than the Germans ever did. Although 'Spanish flu' was said to be the result of wartime privation, it killed just as easily in countries which had been unaffected by the war. No exact total of the deaths was ever made, but they were thought to have far exceeded the entire number of those killed in the fighting.

It was the era of republicanism. Czechoslovakia proclaimed itself a republic at the end of October, and Hungary announced its independence from the Austro-Hungarian empire on the same day.

Germany had become a republic on the day the Kaiser abdicated. Austria, which had signed an armistice with the Allies on 3 November, became a republic too when the Emperor Karl abdicated on the 11th of the same month.

The collapse of Austria had come after one of the most spectacular victories of the war at Vittorio Veneto on 29 October. We left the Italians recovering from the battle of the River Piave, grateful that the Joint Austro-German threat had not continued. But now that Germany was too hard-pressed herself to do more for her ally, the Italian General Diaz decided that a swift drive towards the town of Vittorio Veneto would split the Austrian army into two halves. He had three armies under his own command for this move. Of the three, the British (Tenth Army) was the most effective and in the last week of October crossed the Piave, the Monticano and the Livenza, leaving the way clear for the Italians to occupy Vittorio Veneto, which they proceeded to do on 29 October. Negotiations had already begun for the armistice which was signed on 3 November. Although a 'sideshow' battle, Vittorio Veneto was the most dramatic victory of the war, for it signalled the complete collapse of the Austro-Hungarian army which had now lost 500,000 prisoners here, and 7,000 guns. Although ostensibly an Italian victory, it would not have been possible without the substantial British contingent.

The most frustrating (to the British) of the other sideshows was that in East Africa. Von Lettow-Vorbeck had proved himself one of the most skilled and resourceful generals of the war but even he could not exist without further supplies of ammunition and explosives. In November 1917 a German Zeppelin had flown from Bulgaria with supplies of those vital commodities, but was only half way across the Sudan when it learned that von Lettow-Vorbeck had left East Africa. It therefore turned back and reached Bulgaria successfully.

Von Lettow-Vorbeck had decided that his best course now would be to operate from the remoter region of northern Mozambique. On 25 November 1917 he crossed the river Rovuma with an 'army' of 300 Germans and 2,000 Askaris. His fellow general (Tafel), no mean guerrilla leader either, attempted follow, but was cut off and had to surrender. Von Lettow-Vorbeck had noted that the Portuguese were not strongly motivated to pursue guerrilla leaders and took care to avoid, rather than confront them. His plan was to allow the British to supply the Portuguese with arms and ammunition, while himself avoided all contact, until a moment arrived when he could make a surprise raid on a Portuguese depot and restock his own troops. In the event, he underestimated the forces opposing him; a joint British/Portuguese force pursued him inland, far away from the coastal areas. But, resourceful as ever, by July 1918 he had moved to the neighbourhood of Quilimane where the Zambesi flows out into the Indian Ocean. He then turned north again, weighed up the possibilities of replenishing his supplies in British Nyasaland (now Malawi), but decided the local opposition might be too strong, and instead recrossed the Rovuma back into Tanganyika. However, this was clearly not an area in which to linger, so he now moved into Northern Rhodesia (Zambia) with the aim of reaching the Belgian Congo. The vast size of these remote territories made these adventures possible, but his luck now ran out. On 9 November 1918 he learnt that the Kaiser had abdicated and he therefore surrendered at Abercorn, Northern Rhodesia, just to the south of Lake Tanganyika. By this time his forces were down to 150 Germans and 1,200 Askaris. Chasing von Lettow-Vorbeck over East Africa had involved 100,000 Allied troops, among whom casualties from battle and disease probably amounted to some 20,000. The East African operation was criticised at the time and later for absorbing so much in the way of human and material resources, but it is difficult to see what the alternatives could have been. Von Lettow-Vorbeck was not the sort of man who could be left to his own devices in the hope that the threat from him would gradually fade away. He was undoubtedly highly skilled as a guerrilla leader; however, his achievements were negative rather than positive, such as those of Lawrence.

We left the Palestine campaign at the point when the War Office had suddenly decided that it was now an important theatre and that a Turkish defeat there would help to shorten the war. Allenby was ordered to renew the offensive as soon as possible in 1918. (Jerusalem had been captured in December, 1917.) He was promised reinforcements which duly arrived. Later he would have to exchange some of his veterans for less experienced troops when the Germans began their Spring offensive in France, but that time was not yet. In February he moved north-east of Jerusalem, and captured Jericho on the 21st. He also succeeded in crossing the Jordan and establishing a bridgehead at Goraniye. This move effectively secured his right flank against a sudden Turkish attack, and gave further protection to Jerusalem. However, any advance further north would have to confront a formidable, well-armed Turkish force which was positioned between the hills and the sea. The area was only ten miles wide and a breakthrough would require an enormous effort, costing many casualties, unless alternative tactics could be employed.

Allenby decided that there was no other way forward than this but that the Turks might be deceived into thinking that the attack would come not from his left, but from his centre and right. To create this impression he made a forceful threat in the direction of Amman during the last two weeks of March. Bad weather and the rocky terrain of the mountains of Moab delayed this thrust, and although it reached El Salt, it failed to capture Amman. This, of course, was when the German offensive in France looked like ending the war there and then, so Allenby had to despatch two complete divisions and a number of separate battalions to plug the gap. To replace them he was sent a number of inexperienced troops who needed training before they could be put in the battle. Nevertheless he kept up the deception of the Turks by pushing XXI Corps into the foothills of Judea. This involved keeping a force of cavalry in the Jordan valley during the summer. There they were shelled by Turkish long-range guns but that was the least of their troubles. The average daytime temperature was 110° Fahrenheit, the floor of the valley consists of dust, stones and rocks, and the whole area is full of snakes and scorpions. Hot winds, full of choking dust, completed the picture. Not surprisingly, the place was known as 'The Valley of Desolation'. Although a few deceptive pushes were made in other directions, it was made clear to Turkish spies that when the next Allied threat came it would be on the right.

Meanwhile, Allenby reinforced the British left wing until it held nearly 45,000 men. The rest of the front was held by less than half that number but as any Turkish or German aircraft which tried to reconnoitre the area was promptly shot down, the Turks remained unaware of the danger threatening them.

On 19 September 1918, Allied aircraft began pounding the Turkish communications and were lucky enough to cut off Liman von Sanders, the German commander in Nazareth, from the Turkish forward position. This aerial assault was followed by a heavy artillery bombardment. A heavy attack on the right of the Turkish position (by the Allied left wing) created a gap which the cavalry divisions were soon exploiting. They rode straight through into the Turkish rear position, one reaching Jenin, another Megiddo, and the third Nazareth, from which von Sanders had to make a hasty retreat. Megiddo, which lies in the middle of the Plain of Esdraelon, was a ruined fortress city (Armageddon in Hebrew), which is now known by the Arabic name of Lajjun. As it lies at the entrance to the Musmus Pass, it was a place of great strategic importance in Biblical times. In the last book of the Bible, the prophetic Revelations, Chapter 16, verses 16–21, the city suffers a very unpleasant fate, in which evil men are destroyed. To Christians it appeared that the prophecy had now come true.

The same day the Allies took possession of the bridge over the river Jordan at Jisr Mejamie, thereby trapping many Turks who were trying to escape that way. The Turkish Fourth Army managed to extricate itself but only after the loss of 28 guns and 5,000 men taken prisoner. An Indian Army cavalry unit swept forward and captured Haifa. Many Turks found that their escape routes had been blocked by sabotage from Arab guerrillas from Lawrence's force.

Damascus was 120 miles away. Allenby's cavalry were now pressing towards it, on the way overtaking Turkish stragglers. On 30 September they reached it, but then found the garrison had no stomach for a last stand, preferring instead to escape towards Beirut. 4,000 Turkish soldiers were caught in the Borada gorge and after being raked with machine-gun fire from all sides decided to surrender.

Allenby's Desert Mounted Corps was now sweeping all before it. It reached and occupied Homs on 15 October, Hama on 20 October and Aleppo on 26 October. Five days later the Turks accepted terms of unconditional surrender.

Although the final stages of the Palestine campaign tend to give the impression that the Turks put up little fight, this is an incorrect assumption: they never gave up without a fight. Their army included reinforcements of Austrians and Germans, and they had skilful commanders in chief, first Falkenhayn then Liman von Sanders. They were, it is true, weakened by disease and shortage of supplies. However, the latter facts must not be allowed to detract from the achievements of the Egyptian Expeditionary Force, who also suffered from short rations, lack of water, and insufficient rest. Malaria and the new scourge, influenza, were taking their toll in the final stages of this campaign to such an extent that some units were unable to carry out their allotted tasks for sheer lack of manpower.

Allenby had shown that he was a general of the highest class. He had welded together a very mixed force, convinced the War Office that he should be given full support, and given an excellent example of leading from the front.

After the war, he was appointed High Commissioner in Egypt and acquitted himself well there too. He died in 1936. At the beginning of the campaign, many people had assumed that Allenby and Lawrence would be unable to work together, but were soon found to be wrong. Allenby realised that guerrilla leaders are probably more successful if they are unconventional in manner and appearance. Although he did not share Lawrence's aspirations to see Arab states constructed from the former Turkish empire, he realised that by enlisting Arab support Lawrence was pinning down a large number of Turks who were trying to defend the Hejaz railway (on which the Turks relied for most of their communications) Allenby therefore made sure that Lawrence received all the money and arms which he requested.

Independently of Germany, Turkey signed a separate peace with the Allies on 30 October 1918. The ceremony took place on HMS *Agamemnon*, the flagship of the CinC Mediterranean. Among those present was the unfortunate Major General Townshend, who had surrendered Kut in 1916 and been a prisoner ever since. The Turks had released him in mid-October and sent him to the Allied HQ; they held the optimistic view that he would be so grateful for his survival that he would negotiate terms favourable to his former captors.

However, this peace treaty was not a final settlement. That would come much later. There was obviously much to be settled over the disposal of the former Turkish empire, and this preliminary treaty, known as the Mudros Agreement, left the political problems to the politicians. It specified that the Allies would now take over the forts along the Bosporus and Dardanelles which had given them so much trouble in the past, that all mines were to be cleared from the straits, all Turkish warships were to be surrendered, all troops were to be demobilised although some units might be returned to areas where the Allies wished them to preserve law and order, and all Germans and Austrians were to be repatriated. Most of the key towns in the former Turkish empire were already occupied by Allied troops. A joint Allied force, consisting of British, French, Italians and Greeks, marched into Istanbul. It was all surprisingly amicable – so far. Life in Turkey, and even in its former empire, seemed to carry on much as it had done for centuries.

But the longer-term future was going to be considerably less amicable. During the war when expediency and, often, unavoidable necessity, dictated policy, various countries had been promised pieces of Turkish territory as a reward for their cooperation. Although the outcome takes us slightly ahead of the rest of this narrative, it is necessary to explain why the terms of the treaty with Turkey (the Peace of Sèvres, 13 May 1920) had such dramatic effects.

On 10 January 1915 Britain, France and Russia had promised the Greeks various parts of the Turkish coastline, including Smyrna (now Izmir). When the Greeks therefore sent three divisions to occupy Smyrna in May 1919, the local Turks bitterly resented their arrival, and the area became the centre of a resistance movement.

On 15 May 1915, Britain had promised Constantinople and the Dardanelles and Bosporus straits to Russia. This was a move of desperation, for if there was one situation which was unpalatable to Britain (and France) it was to see Russia having easy access to the Mediterranean from the Black Sea. British diplomats had devoted much thought and ingenuity to preventing this during the nineteenth century. Then came the revolution in Russia and, by 1918, the idea of handing over the Straits to the Bolsheviks was clearly untenable.

In April 1915 Italy had been offered various territorial concessions for entering the war on the Allied side: they were, of course, at the expense of Turkey. However, in May 1916 (only a year later) Britain and France had signed a secret treaty effectively dividing the Turkish empire between them: Mesopotamia (later Iraq) and part of Palestine would come under British administration: the remainder of Palestine was to be administered by an international committee. Damascus, Aleppo and Mosul were to be areas of 'French influence'. Unfortunately for the secret treaty-makers, who had, of course, informed their wartime ally Czarist Russia of what was going on – on the understanding that the secret would remain locked away in the Russian archives – the Bolsheviks published the agreement when they found it in the state archives. The Bolsheviks affirmed that they did not believe in secret diplomacy, and had done this in order to expose the perfidy of capitalist states, but may well have had the additional motive of wishing to sow discord among the allies who were now openly opposing the new, revolutionary regime. When the Italians learnt the terms of the Sykes-Picot agreement they were furious, for it appeared that the major spoils were going to be divided between Britain and France while they themselves were to be fobbed off with a few strips of unimportant territory. So the Italians had to be placated in 1917 and were offered some 70,000 miles of Turkish territory including Smyrna which, as we saw, had already been promised to the Greeks. Eventually, in the post-war treaty Italy, which had suffered heavily in the war, was given a piece of the Dalmatian coast but not Fiume (which contained many Italians), which she had badly wanted.

When the news of how poorly the Italians were going to be rewarded for the sacrifices they had made during the war came out, there was widespread anger, not so much against the Allies for treating them so badly but against the Italian government which had allowed such an injustice to happen. In consequence, there were riots and acts of terrorism all over the country. A very popular poet and airman, D'Annunzio, organised a group of fighters who called themselves nationalists and flew to Fiume and held it for four months. They were then ejected by a warship despatched by the Prime Minister. In a general state of anarchy there were strikes, temporary Soviets in the factories, and a sequence of bombings and assassinations. From this chaos the one party which seemed to offer stability gained strength and numbers. Its members called themselves fascists. They had an energetic leader called Mussolini, and they beat up their political opponents with sadistic brutality. In 1922, Mussolini seized power and established a fascist state which would rule Italy with an iron hand until 1943. By that time Mussolini would have dragged them into another war, and himself become a Nazi puppet. He was shot by Italian partisans in 1945.

It was soon clear to the Allies that although they occupied Constantinople they did not control the rest of Turkey. The man who would soon do this was Mustafa Kemal, an army officer who had distinguished himself in the Gallipoli battles. Although the creator of modern Turkey and the symbol of Turkish nationalism, he was not Turkish by birth: his father was Serbian-Albanian and his mother Macedonian-Albanian.

We have followed the story of Turkey to the end of the war and into the chaotic conditions that followed. Before leaving the story it is important to emphasise that during and after the peace treaties the situation in what in those days used to be called Asia Minor but is now referred to as the Balkans or even the Middle East, was far from peaceful or stable. Although the recent Great War (as it was then known) had begun because of an assassination in an obscure Balkan state, most Europeans were too concerned with their own problems of finding a job and a house, and a stable life, to be interested in the politics of countries in which some of them had had to live and fight, but which few ever wished to see again.

And if the Balkans, with their apparently never-ending wars, were places which few people ever wished to visit, the new countries carved out of the old Turkish empire were even less interesting. Most Europeans hoped that they would never have anything to disturb their peace of mind from Mesopotamia, Palestine or Syria. They were in blissful ignorance that, apart from the aspirations of the inhabitants of these regions, there would soon be an overwhelming economic factor – oil.

The first country to be disappointed when the war ended was Egypt. Since 1914 it had been made a British Protectorate in order to save it from being reconquered by Turkey, of whose empire it had once been a part. Unfortunately there was no withdrawal of the Protectorate and would not be until 1922. Egypt, of course, contained the Suez Canal.

Palestine, which had now been freed from Turkish domination, was not to be handed over to whatever government the Arabs wished to provide. It was to be a British Mandate, that is a territory administered by a responsible power, in this case Britain, until it should be sufficiently mature, politically and economically, to be a sovereign, independent state. That did not happen till 1948, when Israel was born. In 1918 the Arab inhabitants of Palestine were far from happy to learn that a National Home for Jews was to be established in their country. There were already Jews living in Palestine in harmony with the Arabs, but the thought that thousands more would soon be sponsored for entering the country alarmed and angered the Arabs.

A National Home for Jews in Palestine had long been the vision of the Zionist organisation which had been created by one Dr Hertzl in 1894. Britain had favoured the idea that the Jews, of whom there were 12,000,000 in various countries, should have a National Home and had even suggested that one should be established in Uganda. We have learnt that Lloyd George had promised Weizmann a National Home for the Jews in Palestine (assuming that this would simply be a retirement home for a few elderly Jews in failing health), and on 2 November 1917 (when the battle of Passchendaele was drawing to its close), the British government issued the Balfour Declaration, agreeing to the establishment of this National Home, 'it being understood that nothing shall be done that may prejudice the rights of existing non-Jewish communities in Palestine...'. Subsequently, when Jews came in in thousands to settle in their new homeland, the Arabs who had been Britain's ally in the war, felt betrayed. Although Jews and Arabs each resented the other, they had an even stronger dislike for the British government which grew rather than diminished as the years passed.

The 1919 Peace Conference made Palestine a British Mandate, a responsibility which Britain thankfully relinquished in 1948. Mesopotamia also became a British Mandate: it contained 2,500,000 Iraqis, 500,000 Kurds, and 250,000 Assyrian Christians, and the Mosul oilfields. Soon there would be a pipeline from Mosul to Haifa and Tripoli.

The immediate effect of the announcement that Mesopotamia was to be a British Mandate was murder and revolt. Total casualties were in the region of 10,000. Translated into Arabic 'mandate' means 'domination'. However, after the revolt had been suppressed, the Iraqis were persuaded that the mandate was not simply a move from Turkish to British domination, but a move to give the country independent self-rule. Initially progress was encouragingly rapid, the Emir Feisal was elected King in 1921, and the mandate formally ended in 1932. The monarchy ended with the assassination of King Feisal II in 1958. European powers have always wished that Iraq and its neighbours would gradually develop a democratic government which, using the vast oil revenues which had enriched them beyond their wildest dreams, would develop a high standard of living, a stable government, and mutual tolerance. These hopes have not been realised.

Syria was even more complicated than Iraq or Palestine. The Sykes-Picot agreement had specified that Syria should be an area of French influence and it eventually became a French Mandate. In the meantime, the Arabs had already elected a king (Feisal), who had fought with the Allies. Feisal's nationalist forces were soon at war with the French, demanding immediate independence instead. However, the French won and Feisal was deposed and forced to leave the country in July 1920. The following year Britain appointed him King of their Iraq Mandate. The subsequent troubles of Syria fall outside the scope of this book.

Grateful for the assistance he had provided for Lawrence during the war, Britain installed the Grand Sherif Hussein as King of the Hejaz, now the western region of Saudi Arabia, which contains Mecca and Medina. However, Hussein was soon dispossessed by Ibn Saud, leader of the Wahhabi tribes, extremely devout Moslems from the eastern side of the country. Ibn Saud therefore became the ruler of the independent Kingdom of Saudi Arabia, which extended from the Red Sea to the Persian Gulf and from the Indian Ocean to Syria. As much of the country is barren desert, it has been nicknamed 'the empty quarter', but because it contains vast supplies of oil which is cheap to extract its importance and influence has continued to grow.

Britain was also given a Mandate for the Emirate on the other side of the Jordan, which was originally called Transjordan. In 1946 this became a constitutional monarchy under King Abdullah with the name The Hashemite Kingdom of Jordan. (In the Arab-Israeli war of 1967, Israel occupied all the Jordanian territory on the west bank of the river, including the Jordanian sector of Jerusalem.)

Armenia, which had helped the Allies also, had been promised home rule. The United States was therefore asked to accept a Mandate for Armenia, but refused as it had no wish to entangle itself in Middle Eastern affairs. Left unprotected, the Armenians were massacred steadily by the Turks. The civilised world was appalled by these massacres – and did nothing. In the 1990s the civilised world was appalled by the massacres in Yugoslavia – and did nothing effective to stop them.

Examining the effects of the peace treaty with the Turks has taken us away from the situation we left in November 1918, to which we must now return.

CHAPTER 12

Peace Treaties

A t 5.00am on 11 November 1918 an Armistice was signed with Germany in a railway coach in the Forest of Compiègne. The news of this momentous event was relayed as rapidly as possible throughout the warring armies, and at 11.00am on the same day the guns stopped. Armistice was a convenient word to use for what was clearly a German defeat, but the fact that this was used gave the Nazis a pretext for claiming later that Germany had not been beaten but merely accepted a truce. The Nazis further explained that Germany had only been put in the unfortunate position of having to accept a truce in this war, rather than dictate surrender terms to her enemies as she had done at Brest-Litovsk, because she had been stabbed in the back by Jews. This gave them, as they saw it, an excuse for the policy of genocide which became known as the holocaust.

But Germany had been beaten fairly and squarely on land, sea and in the air. Allied troops now moved up to the Rhine and occupied the bridgeheads: the British at Cologne, the French at Mainz, and the Americans at Coblenz. All German submarines which had not been scuttled were now in Allied hands. The German High Seas Fleet, which still contained eleven battleships, five battlecruisers, eight light cruisers and 49 destroyers, lay at anchor in Scapa Flow, while the Allies were wondering what should be done with them, who should move them, where should they go. This became one of the least of the Allies' problems, for the following June (1919) the German crews opened the stopcocks and scuttled the entire fleet.

The problems confronting the victors were stupendous. At least 8,000,000 people had been killed in the belligerent armies, 20,000,000 had been wounded. At least 12,000,000 tons of shipping had been sunk. Destruction of agriculture and food production had caused famine in many areas. Trading patterns were in disarray and would take years to re-establish. Influenza was ravaging the world, but it was only one of many diseases: typhoid and smallpox were also widespread. The victors now had to draw up a series of peace treaties and set the world to rights. Many people thought the Germans, and to a lesser extent the Austrians, should be heavily punished for the horrors which they had launched on the world: Clemenceau grimly said, 'We must squeeze the German orange till the pips squeak,' and spoke of enormous reparations. Even Lloyd George, likely to be as generous as anyone to the defeated, was full of triumph and led a government thirsting for revenge. The only man likely to take an impartial and reasonable point of view seemed to be President Woodrow Wilson of the United States. He had already drawn up a list of what he thought were the necessary requirements for a lasting peace. They consisted of Four Principles and Fourteen Points. The Four Principles stated:

1. Each part of the final settlement must be based upon the essential justice of that particular case.
2. Peoples and sovereignty must not be bartered about from sovereignty to sovereignty as if they were pawns in a game.
3. Every territorial settlement must be in the interests of the population concerned; and not as part of any mere adjustment or compromise of claims among rival states.
4. All well-defined national elements shall be accorded the utmost satisfaction that can be accorded them without introducing new, or perpetuating old, elements of discord and antagonism.

The Fourteen Points described how these principles should be applied. In hindsight both the Principles and the Points may appear almost naively idealistic, but their appeal to the peoples of many nations was immediate. Unfortunately for their success, Britain and France did not view the problems of Europe in the same way as Wilson, who was not well-versed in European geography, let alone its long tangled history.

It was obvious that France at least would require heavy reparations from Germany for the damage the war had caused to her country. However, that must be a problem for the future.

Wilson did not limit himself to the Four Principles or the Fourteen Points, but also produced 'The Four Ends' and 'The Five Particulars'. But the Fourteen Points were the pronouncement which caught the imagination of the newly-liberated peoples of Europe.

They stipulated:

1. Open covenants openly arrived at [that is, the end of secret diplomacy].
2. Absolute freedom of navigation upon the seas outside territorial waters, alike in peace and war.
3. The removal, as far as possible, of all economic barriers to trade.
4. Adequate guarantees given and taken that national armaments will be reduced to the lowest point consistent with domestic safety.

5. A free, open-minded and absolutely impartial adjustment of colonial claims based upon a strict observance of the principle that in determining all such questions of sovereignty the interests of the population concerned must have equal weight with the equitable claims of the Government whose title is to be determined.

6. All Russian territory to be evacuated and Russia to be given unhampered and unembarrassed opportunity for the independent determination of her own political development and national policy. [This was obviously aimed at the countries who were trying to restore the pre-revolutionary situation and to recover some of their own property.] Russia was to be made more than welcome in the League of Nations under institutions of her own choosing and be given every form of assistance.

7. Belgium was to be restored to its pre-war situation.

8. France was to be evacuated [that is, cleared of all enemy troops] and the invaded portion to be restored. Alsace-Lorraine was also to be returned to her.

9. A readjustment of the frontiers of Italy should be effected along clearly recognisable lines of nationality (that is, on an ethnic basis).

10. The people of Austria-Hungary should be given the freest opportunity for autonomous development.

11. Romania, Serbia and Montenegro to be evacuated and all territories occupied during the war were to be restored. Serbia must be given free access to the sea.

12. The Turkish parts of the former Ottoman Empire to be assured of 'secure sovereignty'. All previously subject nationalities to be assured of security and absolutely unmolested opportunities of autonomous development.

13. An independent Polish State to be established, which should include territories inhabited by indisputably Polish population. It must be granted free and secure access to the sea.

14. A general association of nations was to be formed under specific covenants for the purpose of affording mutual guarantees of political independence and territorial integrity to great and small states alike.

The fourteenth point, the creation of a League of Nations, was to be the tail which wagged the dog. Under its benign rule all nations would protect each other, solve problems in harmony and eradicate the causes of war. It was not a new idea, but an extremely idealistic one. In the event, the League would be destroyed by the greed or apathy of its members, and by ruthless demagogues. By the mid-1930s the main purpose, of preventing rearmament and aggression, would demonstrably have failed; but many of the committees, such as those dealing with health, welfare, and economic problems, would have achieved considerable success. It would be reborn with greater powers and better organisation and finance as the United Nations at the end of the Second World War.

Woodrow Wilson, although an admirable man in many ways, was no diplomat, and had already had his own power curtailed in the United States by a Congressional election in the middle of his Presidential term. European politicians considered he was too naive and ill-informed to control the Peace Conference. The key members were reduced to four: Wilson, Lloyd George, Clemenceau, and Orlando of Italy. Clemenceau spoke French and English fluently, and was determined to make Germany pay huge reparations. Neither Wilson nor Lloyd George spoke French, and Orlando spoke no English.

The Paris Peace Conference had begun its proceedings on 18 January 1919. On 7 May 1919, the German delegates were summoned to Versailles and told the terms of the treaty. They were horrified at the severity of the terms but had no option but to accept it. In France, the Treaty of Versailles did not seem severe enough but in England, which had just re-elected Lloyd George on the grounds of his promise to 'make Germany pay', it seemed reasonable. As we subsequently learnt, some of its provisions made the next war virtually inevitable. Germany would be ruined financially by runaway inflation, and in desperation would allow a demagogue to intrigue and bully his way to power. Once there, that demagogue, the Nazi Hitler, would be able to stay in power and rally the German nation by defying the League of Nations and the provisions of the Versailles Treaty. He promised the German people he would restore power by force. In the latter aim he would be assisted by armaments manufactured in other countries who realised that if one country re-arms, the neighbours will follow suit, and a very profitable arms race will begin. Eventually, of course, the price will be paid by soldiers, sailors, airmen, and civilians with their lives.

However, this is not the place to examine the post-war situation in detail, although it is necessary to give the broad outline.

There were, of course, many other problems than the Treaty for Germany itself. These were addressed in separate treaties, which took their names from suburbs or villages near Paris. Austria, the subject of the Treaty of Saint-Germain, was reduced to Vienna and a small amount of territory on the Danube. The former Austro-Hungarian empire was divided up to create new countries based, as far as possible, on ethnic groups, but sometimes including other people who were settled in the area. Thus Czechoslovakia (Bohemia) consisted of Czechs and Slovaks, but included 3,000,000 German-speaking Austrians, who later became described as the 'Sudeten Germans'. This was a matter of administrative convenience but was relentlessly exploited later by Hitler, who claimed the Sudeten Germans were an oppressed minority whom it was his duty to free by force. 'Freeing' the allegedly oppressed German minorities in countries such as Czechoslovakia and Poland became Hitler's iniquitous crusade in his aim to create a greater Germany. Czechoslovakia was eventually dismembered in the Munich Agreement of 1938. Poland was subjected to the same process of lying and bullying, but was finally 'freed' by being invaded in 1939, thus beginning the Second World War.

Austria was no longer a viable state after losing so much territory but was prevented from joining Germany by a specific clause in the treaty.

Bulgaria's future was settled by the Treaty of Neuilly, and she paid dearly for joining the losing side. Some of her territory went to the newly-created state of Yugoslavia, and some to Greece. However, she was given some Turkish territory in compensation and was allowed to retain her merchant fleet and a small army.

Romania had joined the Allies in 1916 but was quickly defeated by early 1917, losing half of her army in the process. However, she was amply compensated in the peace treaties, gaining Transylvania (from Hungary), Bessarabia and former Hungarian territory containing 1,500,000 Magyars.

Hungary was dismembered even more ruthlessly than Austria, and portions of its land and Magyar population were given to its neighbours. By the time this process had finished she had been reduced from 125,000 square miles to 35,000, and from 21,000,000 inhabitants to 8,000,000. This made her a small, land-locked, agricultural country, her industrial resources taken from her. At the end of the war, the defeated and bitter people of Hungary had sent their King (Karl) into exile and murdered their Prime Minister before declaring themselves pacifist in an attempt to dissociate themselves from the wartime regime. They hoped that this would cause the Peace Conference to feel benign towards them. However, when news of the provisions of their peace treaty leaked out, and they learnt that huge quantities of territory were to be surrendered to their traditional enemies, they promptly elected Bela Kun, a hardline Communist, as President, and announced the formation of a Soviet Republic. However, the Allies were hardly likely to approve the establishment of a Communist republic in southern Europe, and sent in the Romanian army to suppress it. This it did, with brutal thoroughness. At the end of it Hungary was forced to sign the Treaty of Trianon (4 June 1920). A new government was set up by Admiral Horthy, theoretically as a regent for the absent King Karl, but in practice a dictator who was approved by the Allies because he was likely to stabilise the country and act as a barrier to the spread of Russian Communism.

Serbia and Bosnia-Hercegovina, whose politics may be said to have supplied the seedbed for the beginning of the war, were now linked in what was at first called the Kingdom of the Serbs, Croats and Slovenes, and later, Yugoslavia.

However, no country was treated quite so severely as Germany. Alsace-Lorraine, which had been seized by Germany at the end of the Franco-Prussian War of 1870–1 was to return to France, who would also be allowed to take possession of the Saar coalfield for the next fifteen years. Posen and West Prussia would go to Poland. Upper Silesia, apart from a small portion which would go to Czechoslovakia, would become Polish, Danzig and Memel would be administered by an Allied commission. Danzig remained a free city but Memel was soon acquired by Lithuania.

Germany would lose all her colonies (which would become Mandates), her merchant fleet, even control of her own rivers, and her army would be reduced to 100,000 men. (This, incidentally, is only 19,000 less than Britain's army of the 1990s.) She used it for training officers and NCOs for greatly expanded forces later. Her navy was to be reduced to 15,000.

She was to pay a huge sum in reparations (the exact figure to be decided later). To make sure Germany agreed to these terms, German territory west of the Rhine, together with the bridgeheads, would be occupied by the Allies for fifteen years.

Article 231 of the treaty, the 'war guilt clause', stated: 'The Allied and Associated Governments affirm, and Germany accepts, the responsibility of Germany and her allies for causing all the loss and damage to which the Allied and Associated Governments have been subjected as a consequence of the war imposed on them by the aggression of Germany and her allies.'

This claim was bitterly resented by Germany but as the Belgian representative retorted, 'You can hardly claim that Belgium invaded Germany.' The Belgians, of course, had good cause to wish that the finger of guilt should be pointed at Germany. Not only had Belgium been occupied and partly devastated, but in the early days of the war the citizens had suffered appalling atrocities, as may be seen on the memorials in various Belgian towns, including Louvain. There appears to be no truth in the propaganda story that the Germans boiled down corpses to make soap in the First World War. However, there is ample evidence to show that Germans did do that in the Second World War, and also made lampshades of human skin.

Germany had not many colonies to lose: in fact it may be said that she went to war because she felt she ought to have more colonies. However, in Africa she had Tanganyika, which became a British Mandate, and is now independent Tanzania; and German South West Africa which became a Mandate under the supervision of the Union of South Africa, and is now Namibia. Ruanda-Burundi became a Belgian Mandate and is now independent Rwanda. In West Africa, the German colony of Togoland had been captured in April 1914 and later British and French forces took over the Cameroons. Togoland later became a French Mandate and is now independent Togo. The Cameroons were divided and became British and French Mandates, and in 1960 the whole territory became the Republic of Cameroon.

Italy, who had long wished for colonies and would have been happy to receive a Mandate, received nothing.

The situation in the Far East presented diplomatic complications. China had joined the Allied side because the Peking government was afraid that if she was left out of any post-war settlement her old enemy Japan would achieve concessions to China's disadvantage. The presence of these two potential enemies in the Allied team posed difficult problems for the United States, which was suspicious of Japan's motives and favoured China. However, a British/Japanese combined force had besieged and captured the German concession of Tsingtao in 1914 and Japanese warships had occupied the Caroline and Marshall Islands, both of which were German colonies but were undefended. The Japanese navy had also patrolled the Far Eastern seas. At the Peace Conference the Japanese claimed all the former German concessions in China and received half of them. The Chinese suggested that all concessions and extra-territorial rights, which had developed in China in the pre-war years, should now be abolished. Her plea was refused, and as a result she left the conference in disgust.

Australia was given the Mandate for the former German territory in New Guinea, and the Solomon Islands. New Zealand was given the Mandate for the former German Samoa.

The war was over, and the peace settlements were made and would be adjusted over the following years. Unfortunately it was not the war to end wars as everyone had hoped: within a few years there were no less than 23 separate wars being fought in various parts of the world.

CHAPTER 13

The Literature of the War

E arlier in the book we gave a brief account of the idealism which sent young men to volunteer. In these days, when patriotism is a word regarded with suspicion by many, as it has so often been misused to encourage chauvinism, rampant nationalism, and many other undesirable activities, it may be difficult for some readers to understand the patriotic idealism of 1914.

In spite of many disappointments, idealism always seems to flourish, particularly among young people, who are likely to be killed when inspired by it. Nowadays idealism tends to take a different form: it may be that of a protest against what appears to be unjustified authority, oppression, economic hardship, or the policies of governments. Protesters suffer various indignities to prevent the spoliation of the environment, or to try to prevent the manufacture and deployment of nuclear weapons. Fanatical protesters turn to acts of terrorism, such as hijacking aircraft or planting bombs.

One of the results of the First World War was a resolve that such a horror must not be allowed to happen again. In the 1930s there were Peace Pledge Unions, organisations to encourage disarmament, and protests against what seemed false patriotism, for example, the Oxford Union voted that it would not fight for King and Country. The drafters of the motion probably meant that if the youth of the country was to be asked to sacrifice life in the future, it must be for something more realistic than emotive words or symbols. The reaction among the older generation to this 'student protest' was intense and indignant. More serious was the effect on Hitler and Mussolini, who decided that British youth had now become too feeble and decadent to fight. Mussolini therefore decided he could carve out an empire for himself in Ethiopia without hindrance, and Hitler decided he could tear up the Versailles Treaty, rearm, and set off on a quest to become master of the world. Many of those who voted for the motion in Oxford were subsequently killed in the war which followed at the end of the decade.

But even in 1914 idealism was not quite as widespread as the poets would have us believe. It was soon obvious that whereas the 'upper classes' were prepared to sacrifice their sons in the fighting, they were not above hoarding or clinging to privileges and the advantages of wealth.

At the other end of the scale were many who had no wish to fight at all and ultimately had to be conscripted and made to do so. Miners, factory workers, dockers, and others in essential industries learnt they had power and that strikes, or threats to strike, could gain them more money. When asked what the men in the trenches must think of them for restricting the production of essential war materials, they retorted, 'They wouldn't want us to give in to the bosses.' The history of industrial disputes in ship-building during the war is a far from idealistic story. James Maxton and William Gallacher were imprisoned for inflammatory oratory encouraging strikers.

But the poets and writers also lost their idealism once they knew the grim reality of war. Edmund Blunden, the author of *Undertones of War*, described his moment of truth. As a young lieutenant he had marched up to the trenches in the dusk and while doing so noted that there seemed to be a good crop of mushrooms. He was pleased, he liked mushrooms, and looked forward to eating them. In daylight he realised those white objects were not mushrooms but human bones sticking out of the ground.

Robert Graves did not publish *Good-bye To All That* till 1929. He was very proud to be a member of the Royal Welch Fusiliers, a regiment with a distinguished history, but his initial reactions were not so much horror of war as dismay at the unfriendly reception he received in the officers' mess: it was the custom to treat subalterns like dirt, which may have had a good effect on precocious cockiness in peacetime but was pointless when every-one might be dead within the year. The RWF was by no means unusual in the attitude to young officers, but could say, if it had bothered to defend the policy, that it certainly worked in producing a first-class fighting regiment. Although Graves has been criticised for doing so, he had no scruples about describing the rivalry and lack of cooperation with the French, or the atti-tude of regulars to Territorials, and vice-versa. His description of life in the trenches is crisp:

'Cuinchy was one of the worst places for rats. They came up from the canal and fed on the many corpses and multiplied. When I was here with the Welch [not the RWF but the Welch Regiment] a new officer came to the company, and, as a token of his welcome, he was given a spring bed. When he turned in the night he heard a scuffling, shone his torch, and there were two rats on his blankets tussling for the possession of a severed hand. This was thought a great joke.'

After Graves had been wounded, he was sent to convalesce near Harlech. But 'when I was strong enough to climb the hill behind Harlech and revisit my favourite country I found I could only see it as a prospective battlefield. I would find myself working out tactical problems, planning how I would hold the Northern Artro valley against an attack from the sea, or where I would put a Lewis gun if I were trying to rush Dolwreiddiog Farm from the brow of the hill, and what would be the best position for the rifle-grenade section.'

Graves was lucky to have survived but he had not been unscathed. He said he was 'very thin, very nervous, and had about four years loss of sleep to make up. I found I was suffering from a large sort of intestinal worm which came from drinking bad water in France.' In 1919 he felt full of gloom, thinking that the Versailles Treaty would almost certainly lead to another war. He was appalled at the mass unemployment after the war, the injustice to ex-service men who were refused reinstatement in the jobs they had been doing before the war, and at strikes and lock-outs. He had written poetry during the war, but his literary career did not begin till the 1930s. Two of his best-known later books were *I, Claudius* and *Claudius the God*, but his other books and poetry were also of the highest quality. He became Professor of Poetry at Oxford in 1961.

Edmund Blunden, who was eighteen when the war began, succeeded Graves as Professor of Poetry at Oxford. Blunden had a gentler disposition than Graves and conveys the horrors with understatement rather than defiance. He understood the men he commanded and was liked by them. He commented sadly, 'They were all doomed.'

Siegfried Sassoon (1886–1967) was several years older and before the war had enjoyed an upper middle class, sheltered, upbringing. He had become Master of the Atherstone Hunt, which he describes in *Memoirs of a Fox-Hunting Man* (he called it the Packlestone). His subsequent book, *Memoirs of an Infantry Officer* describes the conditions which made him wholeheartedly anti-war. As he had been wounded and awarded the MC, his protests were put down to shell-shock and he was put into hospital, an experience he wrote about under the name of 'George Sherston'. Eventually, having made his protest, Sassoon decided it was hopeless and went back to his regiment: he was also in the Royal Welch Fusiliers and was a friend of Robert Graves during and after the war. However, he never came to terms with his bitter memories. Many years later, when in Ypres, he looked at the Menin Gate, which bears the names of 57,000 dead with no known grave and wrote:

Who will remember, passing through the gate
The unheroic Dead who fed the guns?
Who shall absolve the foulness of their fate
Those doomed, conscripted, unvictorious ones?
Crudely renewed, the Salient holds its own.
Paid are its dim defenders by this pomp;
Paid, with a pile of peace-complacent stone
The armies who endured that sullen swamp.
Here was the world's worst wound. And here with pride
"Their name liveth for ever," the gateway claims
Was ever an immolation so belied
As their intolerably nameless names?
Well might the Dead who struggled in the slime
Rise and deride this sepulchre of crime.

Sassoon never lost his compassion:

When you are standing at your hero's grave,
Or near some homeless village where he died,
Remember, through your heart's rekindling pride
The German soldiers who were loyal and brave
Men fought like brutes; and hideous things were done
And you have nourished hatred, harsh and blind
But in that Golgotha perhaps you'll find
The mothers of the men who killed your son.

and

O German mother dreaming by the fire
While you are knitting socks to send your son
His face is trodden deeper in the mud.

and

"Good morning, good morning," the General said
When we met him last week on our way to the line
Now the soldiers he smiled at are most of them dead,
And we're cursing his staff for incompetent swine.
"He's a cheery old card,' grunted Harry to Jack
As they slogged up to Arras with rifle and pack.
But he did for them both with his plan of attack.

Edmund Wyndham Tennant (1897–1916) was nineteen when he was killed at the Battle of the Somme. He wrote:

> Green gardens in Laventie!
> Soldiers only know the street
> Where the mud is churned and splashed about
> By battle-wending feet;
> And yet beside one stricken house there is a glimpse of grass,
> Look for it when you pass.

As *he* looked at it, it stirred memories:

> I saw green banks of daffodil,
> Slim poplars in the breeze,
> Great tan-brown hares in gusty March
> A-courting on the leas;
> And meadows with their glittering streams, and silver scurrying dace,
> Home – what a perfect place.

But he would never see it again.

W. N. Hodgson (1893–1916), also killed on the Somme, preserved his idealism up to the day of his death:

> By all the glories of the day
> And the cool evening's benison,
> By that last sunset touch that lay
> Upon the hills when day was done,
> By beauty lavishly outpoured
> And blessings carelessly received,
> By all the days that I have lived
> Make me a soldier, Lord.

but the third and last verse ends:

> By all delights that I shall miss
> Help me to die, O Lord.

He was killed two days later.

Most of these poems were by officers, but men, who had never thought about writing poems, were equally observant and full of heart-warming memories, even though many were of industrial towns and deprived lives.

Robert Nichols passed the stage of remembering the past and immersed himself in the present:

Was there love once? I have forgotten her.
Was there grief once? Grief yet is mine.
Other loves I have, men rough, but men who stir
More grief, more joy, than love of thee and thine.
Faces cheerful, full of whimsical mirth
Lined by the wind, burned by the sun,
Bodies enraptured by the abounding earth,
As whose children we are brethren: one.
And at any moment may descend hot death
To shatter limbs! pulp, tear, blast
Beloved soldiers who love rough life and breath
Not less for dying faithful to the last.

Many of the poets came from privileged homes and public schools. R.C. Sherriff, the author of *Journey's End* had experienced neither: he was an insurance clerk. The play, in which the entire action takes place in a dugout, was originally written for a rowing club entertainment, but when staged in London was an instant success. It was soon being performed all over the world, even though its atmosphere and language were entirely British.

Sherriff went on to write a number of successful film scripts: *The Invisible Man* , *Good-bye Mr Chips* and *The Dam Busters*.

One of the most impressive poets of the war was Wilfrid Owen (1893–1918), who was in hospital with Sassoon, then returned to the battlefield and was killed five days before the Armistice. He too had won a Military Cross. Attempts were made to put him into a staff job after he came out of hospital, but he refused this. His 'Anthem for Doomed Youth' shows the range of his powers, and what was lost by his premature death.

What passing-bells for those who die as cattle?
Only the monstrous anger of the guns.
Only the stuttering rifles' rapid rattle
Can patter out their hasty orisons.
No mockeries for them from prayers or bells,

Nor any voice of mourning save the choirs, –
The shrill, demented choirs of wailing shells;
And bugles calling for them from sad shires.
What candles may be held to speed them all?
Not in the hands of boys, but in their eyes
Shall shine the holy glimmers of good-byes.
The pallor of girls' brows shall be their pall;
Their flowers the tenderness of silent minds,
And each slow dusk a drawing-down of blinds.

Owen gave a description of life in the trenches between attacks, when boredom seemed one of the great horrors of war, even when men were dying steadily from snipers or sporadic shellfire.

Our brains ache in the merciless iced east winds that knive us...
Wearied we keep awake because the night is silent...
Low, drooping flames confuse our memory of the salient...
Worried by silence, sentries whisper, curious, nervous
But nothing happens.

The poignant misery of dawn begins to grow...
We only know war lasts, rain soaks, and clouds sag stormy.
Dawn massing in the east her melancholy army
Attacks once more in shivering ranks of gray,
But nothing happens.
Sudden successive flights of bullets streak the silence.
Less deadly than the air that shudders black with snow,
With sidelong flowing flakes that flock, pause, and renew,
We watch them wandering up and down the wind's nonchalance,
But nothing happens.

To-night, His frost, will fasten on this mud and us,
Shrivelling many hands, puckering foreheads crisp.
The burying party, picks and shovels in their shaking grasp
Pause over half-known faces. All their eyes are ice,
But nothing happens.

Owen never forgets the contrast between the beauties of life away from the trenches:

Red lips are not so red
As these stained stones kissed by the English dead
Kindness of wooed and wooer
Seems shame to their love pure
O Love, your eyes lose lure
When I behold eyes blinded in my stead.

Unlike many, Owen never lost his feelings of compassion. He wrote of the people whom others preferred to forget, the men whose bodies had survived but minds had not:

These are the men whose minds the Dead have ravished
Memory fingers in their hair of murders,
Multitudinous murders they once witnessed.
Wading sloughs of flesh these helpless wander,
Treading blood from lungs that had loved laughter.
Always they must see these things and hear them,
Batter of guns and shatter of flying muscles,
Carnage incomparable, and human squander,
Rucked too thick for these men's extrication.

Finally:

Awful falseness of set-smiling corpses
– Thus their hands are plucking at each other:

There were many others who expressed the horror and disillusionment of warfare which was so far removed from the idealism of 1914. Isaac Rosenberg had been a very promising painter and poet before he joined the army in 1915. He was killed in April 1918.

Sombre the night is.
And though we have our lives, we know
What sinister threat lurks there.

Dragging these anguished limbs, we only know
This poison-blasted track opens on our camp –
On a little safe sleep.
But hark! Joy – joy – strange joy

Lo! Heights of night ringing with unseen larks
Music showering on our upturned listening faces.
Death could drop from the dark
As easily as song –

But song only dropped,
Like a blind man's dreams on the sand
By dangerous tides,
Like a girl's dark hair, for she dreams no ruin lies there,
Or her kisses where a serpent hides.

Richard Aldington (1892–1962) attacked pretentiousness and hypocrisy wherever he saw it. His *Death of a Hero* takes middle-class, unwarlike, unassuming George Winterbourne through trench warfare in France where 'he felt a degradation, a humiliation, in the dirt, the lice, the communal life in holes and ruins, the innumerable deprivations and hardships. He suffered a feeling that his body had become worthless, condemned to a tramp's standard of living, and ruthlessly treated as cannon-fodder. He suffered for other men too that they should be condemned to this; but since it was the common fate of the men of his generation he decided he must endure it.'

Winterbourne was killed in the last week of the war when he had suddenly stood up and a dozen machine-gun bullets had gone through him.

'The death of a hero. What mockery, what bloody cant. What sickening, putrid cant! George's death is a symbol of the whole sickening, bloody waste of it.'

Winterbourne was a civilised man who had become disillusioned with the whole idea of war achieving anything useful, and whose family had never been a support to him. They all grieved at his death in different ways: his father became fanatically religious, his mother took a somewhat unwilling, younger lover, his wife consoled herself with 'unlicensed copulation and brandy'.

Although this is fiction, it comes very close to fact. Aldington sees the 'hero' as betrayed by everyone, except by his fellow soldiers, who were also victims. 'Friendships between soldiers during the war were a real and beautiful and unique relationship which has now entirely vanished, at least from Western Europe. Let me at once disabuse the eager-eyed sodomites among my readers by stating emphatically that there was nothing sodomitical in these friendships. I have lived and slept for months, indeed years, with 'the troops' and had several such companionships. But no vaguest proposal was ever made to me: I never saw any signs of sodomy, and never heard anything to make me suppose it existed.

'It was just a human relation, a comradeship, an undemonstrative exchange of sympathies between ordinary men racked to extremity under a great common strain in a great common danger. There was nothing dramatic about it.'

In this, and subsequent, books, Aldington attacks insincerity and bland, false assumptions about war and other situations, made by those without experience. Like Robert Graves, he was a brilliant classical scholar and poet, who produced excellent translations, and biographies, notably of Wellington, Voltaire and D. H. and T. E. Lawrence. He deplored hypocrisy in any form and found plenty of it in the literary world, where his scathing criticisms made enemies.

There were, of course, many others, and even today long-neglected manuscripts and diaries are still being published. Some have distinct literary qualities; other are simply moving documentaries. Readers suspecting that many writers describe war from too low a level – from private soldier up to junior officer to be entirely reliable, were interested to encounter even more virulent denunciation of war in Brigadier General F. P. Crozier's *A Brass Hat in No Man's Land*. This carried much criticism of the staff.

The Spanish Farm by R. H. Mottram describes the war, and the French, from the viewpoint of a hard-hearted French woman, running a farm which takes its name from the long-past Spanish occupation of that area. *All Our Yesterdays* by H. M. Tomlinson ranges more widely (it begins with the Boer War). Henry Williamson in *The Patriot's Progress* describes the feelings of the private soldier. Williamson recovered his mental stability by living in the depths of the country after the war, and in consequence wrote *Tarka the Otter*, *Life in a Devon Village* and *The Story of a Norfolk Farm*. However, the scars of war stayed with him.

Vera Brittain described the thoughts and feelings of a highly-intelligent woman who became a VAD. Her fiancé and all her male friends were killed in the war. *Testament of Youth* is the best known of her many books.

'Perhaps some day the sun will shine again
And I shall see that still the skies are blue
And feel once more I do not live in vain
Although bereft of you

....

But though kind Time may many joys renew

There is one greatest joy I shall not know
Again, because my heart for loss of you
Lies broken, long ago.

Another viewpoint, the Austrian, comes in Cecil Roberts' *Spears Against Us*. Karl came to admire the men he commanded.

'Rough, untutored lads, with calf-like stupidity and clumsiness it seemed shameful to be leading them into the slaughter-house, for they had no quarrel with anyone. They ate, slept, washed, and fought under stern direction. Karl intrigued for their needs, bullied and mothered them as the moment necessitated. He tended their feet, wrote their letters and assisted them with their domestic problems. They kept him from going mad. It was a revelation that he could even feel a moment's concern for a company of illiterate boors. Yet.... he felt their deaths, although he had seen a thousand deaths and had heard the spongy tread of horse's hoofs on the bodies of the slain.'

Herbert Read (1893–1968) had a distinguished literary and artistic career that eventually earned him a knighthood. He served in the trenches for three years. He wrote a memorable account of the confusion which followed the retreat from St Quentin in 1918, and a vivid description of an incident on 10 November 1918 when, in the final stages of the war, a battalion of English troops was marching forward to occupy a village. On the outskirts they encountered a German officer who told them that all German troops had now left the area. They marched on and stopped in the central square. Suddenly machine-guns opened up on them from all the neighbouring buildings, killing over a hundred. The remainder rushed into the houses and bayoneted the machine-gunners.

A corporal then ran to the entrance to the village to settle with the wounded officer who had lured them into the trap. 'The German seemed to be expecting him; his face did not flinch as the bayonet descended.'

In a cottage in the village the British soldiers found the 'naked body of a young girl. Both legs were severed, and one severed arm was found in another room. The body was covered with bayonet wounds.'

This discovery haunted Read until he wrote a series of poems, analysing the thoughts of all concerned, and philosophising on good and evil. Of the German officer he wrote:

The bells of hell ring ting-a-ling
for you but not for me – for you
whose gentian eyes stared from the cold

impassive alp of death. You betrayed us
at the last hour of the last day
playing the game to the end
your smile the only comment
on the well-done deed. What mind
have you carried over the confines.

C. E. Montague, who wrote *Disenchantment*, among many other books, observed the war sceptically without being cynical. NCOs and men soon acquired their own philosophy, without letting it affect their efforts to win the war: 'A man was a fool if he imagined that anyone set over him was not looking after number one, the patriotism of the press was bunkum, the red tabs of the Staff were the 'Red Badge of Funk'.

But, 'while so many things were shaken, one thing which held fast was the men's will to win. It may have changed from the first lyric-hearted enthusiasm. But it was a dour and inveterate will. At the worst most of the men fully meant to go down killing for all they were worth. And there was just a hope that in Germany such default as they saw on our side was the rule; it was perhaps a disease of all armies and countries, not of ours alone; there might be a chance for us still. On that chance they still worked away with a sullen ardour that no muddling or sloth in high places could wholly damp down.'

When Montague was in Cologne with the occupying army Field Marshal Sir Douglas Haig came and made a short speech to his unit. Most of it was routine. 'But once he looked up from the paper and put in some words which I felt sure were his own. "I only hope that, now we have won, we shall not lose our heads, as the Germans did in 1870. It has brought them to this." He looked at the gigantic mounted statue of the Kaiser overhead, a thing crying out in its pride for fire from heaven to fall and consume it, and at the homely British sentry moving below at his post.

'But,' Montague concluded sadly, 'no one heeded his words.'

A German view of the war was vividly described by Erich Maria Remarque (1898–1970), who was conscripted into the German army in 1914 at the age of eighteen, was wounded several times, but survived to write *All Quiet on the Western Front* (1929) and *The Road Back* (1931). Remarque's unemotional realism shows that the life of the private soldier was probably much the same in every army:

'One morning two butterflies play in front of our trench... What can they be looking for. There is not a plant or flower for miles... The birds are just as carefree, they have long since accustomed themselves to the war. Every morning larks ascend from No Man's Land. A year ago we watched them nesting: the young ones grew up too.

'There is always plenty of amusement, the airmen see to that. There are countless fights for us to watch every day.

'Battle planes don't trouble us, but the observation planes we hate like the plague; they put the artillery on us. A few minutes after they appear, shrapnel and high-explosives begin to drop on us. We lost eleven men in one day that way, and five of them stretcher-bearers. Two are smashed so that Tjaden remarks you could scrape them off the wall of the trench and bury them in a mess tin.

'Although we need reinforcements, the recruits give us almost more trouble than they are worth. They are helpless in this grim fighting area, they fall like flies. Modern trench warfare demands knowledge and experience; a man must have a feeling for the contour of the ground, an ear for the sound and character of the shells, must be able to decide beforehand where they will drop, how they will burst and how to shelter from them.

'The young recruits of course know none of these things. They get killed simply because they can hardly tell shrapnel from high explosive, and miss the light, piping whistle of the daisy-cutters....'

All Quiet on the Western Front is a classic because its story is that of all soldiers.

CHAPTER 14

Was the War Avoidable?

These words are being written as we approach the eightieth anniversary of the outbreak of the Great War. The fact that its name was later changed to the First World War may seem sufficient answer to the question. Twenty-one years after the outbreak of the Great War, and in spite of numerous efforts to remove the causes of war, a second, even greater, world war began.

At the end of the First World War the victors decided to punish the aggressors and while doing so to establish free, democratic governments of ethnic groups which would, supposedly, have no reason to go to war. A League of Nations was established with the main aim of confronting potential aggressors with overwhelming force, and with the secondary aim of eradicating possible causes of war such as injustice and economic hardship. But it failed.

Although it has been said that no country really wanted war in 1914, this is manifestly untrue of Germany, which for half a century had been establishing itself as a great industrial power by the encouragement of heavy industry including, in particular, arms manufacture. Having come late into the nineteenth-century rush for colonies, she had only acquired the least favourable ones. She looked enviously at India, Burma, Malaya, Australia, South Africa, New Zealand, Canada, the last four of which were virtually independent but still, in Germany's eyes, colonies. Belgium had the Congo, Holland the East Indies, France Indo-China, Morocco and Algeria. Germany realised that the big prizes could only be acquired by force: other areas might be acquired by astute diplomacy – perhaps.

Every foreign policy move made by Germany alarmed Britain, who saw it as a threat, which it usually was. This led to a naval arms race and considerable military preparations.

France had been beaten decisively in the 1870–1 Franco-Prussian War but had recovered so quickly that Germany feared a revenge attack. In consequence, she had prepared the way for a first-strike (the Schlieffen Plan) and also made alliances with Austria-Hungary and Italy.

Russia had colonial ambitions too, but also feared Germany. Her fears were soon to be justified.

The Austro-Hungarian empire contained a number of different ethnic groups, was badly administered, and disliked both Russia and Russia's potential allies, the Serbs.

These were merely the most important factors leading to a possible conflict. Karl Marx and his followers believed that capitalist countries would inevitably go to war because, as they expanded their industry they needed more markets (in colonies) and sources of cheap raw materials (also from colonies). America showed subsequently that it is possible to capture markets and sources of raw material by economic penetration without resorting to war, but used force when it seemed necessary.

America had leased and fortified a Canal Zone on the Isthmus in the 1890s, built the Panama Canal and then established a protectorate. She had also fought the Spanish in a dispute over Cuba in 1898. As a result Cuba was made a protectorate, Puerto Rico was annexed, and the Philippine Islands in the Far East were made into an American colony. In 1898 America had also annexed the Hawaiian Republic, which contained the valuable Pearl Harbor base, and much potential wealth, to prevent Japan acquiring it. This was called 'manifest destiny', but in theory America was vehemently opposed to military imperialism.

However, America demolished Marx's theories of capitalist countries competing for ever smaller markets by demonstrating that markets and sources of raw materials expand, rather than contract.

Fear, envy and greed were possible reasons for a war in 1914, but there were other influences too. Germany longed to test her new strength; Britain was quite happy to teach Germany a lesson, on the High Seas, if nowhere else, and paid the penalty for being complacent. Germany was alarmed by the agreement between Russia and France, which those two countries saw as a defensive move, but which Germany saw as a potential threat. Germany also feared that Russia might acquire Turkish territory to the detriment of Germany's expansionist aims in the Middle East.

Finally, there was the human factor. The world had been free of a great conflict since the 22-year-long Napoleonic Wars ended in 1815. There had, of course, been small colonial wars, and the Crimean War of 1854–6, which had been localised. The British had fought the Boer War in 1899–1902, but this had concerned no other European power, although Germany had expressed strong sympathy for the Boers, and sold them some effective guns.

None of these factors need have led to war. Germany could have been 'appeased' by a share of colonial territory if the Kaiser had been less aggressive but, as the 1930s showed, placating autocrats by giving them concessions only tends to stimulate their appetite and encourage them to produce even more threatening behaviour.

Perhaps the reason why war came in 1914 was that it was regarded as inevitable. Human beings are naturally aggressive, more so in some areas than in others. Ancient animosities and feuds linger on, and every attempt to avenge real or alleged wrongs leads to worse reprisals – eventually. In the 1990s the world is shocked by the brutality and atrocities of the fighting in the Balkans: it has deep roots. In 1914 we spoke of 'gallant little Serbia'; few would do so today.

It is nearly 50 years since the Second World War ended and in that time there has been no major war, although Korea came close to it. The avoidance of major war between the great powers, with their mutually assured destruction, seems to have achieved some success. But in 1914 and again in 1939 the world leaders had to learn their lesson. That made war in 1914 unavoidable.

The other question is: could the war have been stopped at an earlier stage? This has been partly answered in the text. Although neither the Allies nor the Central Powers had spoken of 'Unconditional Surrender' (as they did in the Second World War), this was the only ending they visualised. In 1916, when peace negotiations (described earlier) were discussed, both sides still believed they could win.

In the years since the end of the First World War there have been many changes in attitude towards disturbance of the peace in society. A long process of social reform has modified the drastic penalties inflicted on law-breakers in the past. Medieval penalties for stealing usually involved some sort of mutilation and penalties for greater crimes were often death, in public and painfully. In the nineteenth century, transportation and hanging for minor offences was abolished. It seemed that human nature was gradually improving and criminal behaviour was a disease which should be treated rather than punished.

After the Second World War the reform process went further and faster until in the 1990s every effort was made to 'cure' criminals, rather than punish them. Unfortunately this seems to have been linked with a very considerable rise in criminal behaviour of all kinds. It would appear that deterrents as well as reformist policies are needed, inside as well as outside nations. In the past much crime was ascribed to the effects of poverty, but this no longer seems the motive. The modern criminal is as likely to commit crimes because of boredom as a medieval baron was likely to attack his neighbour or engage in some other form of anti-social behaviour. 'Mindless aggression' is a popular phrase nowadays: it could have been applied to many kings, statesmen and soldiers throughout history. Wars of aggression were launched because of greed and boredom. They ended in victory, defeat or mutual exhaustion. Once wars started, it was difficult to stop them because the person attacked usually wanted revenge if he had managed to avoid defeat. Often the original aggressor was driven by a megalomaniac desire to take his own side to the point of destruction rather than surrender. This applied to the Kaiser in 1914–18, to Hitler in 1944, and to the Japanese in 1945. In this context it is clear that there was no chance of ending the First World War before November 1918.

As Tacitus expressed it in AD 98:

'They make a desert and they call it peace.'

Wars, it seems, can only be prevented by curbing and punishing aggression.

Pale Ebeneezer thought it wrong to fight.
But Roaring Bill, who killed him, thought it right.

246

Seeing for Yourself

Students and others wishing to know more about the First World War are advised to visit former battlefields and museums. Tours of former battlefields may be made with the help of books mentioned in the Further Reading section, or with the many battlefield tours which are advertised. The most comprehensive museum is the Imperial War Museum, Lambeth Road, London, which has weapons and realistic displays, and which has a policy of being extremely helpful to students. Nearby is the National Army Museum in Chelsea, which also has displays. Many British towns have regimental museums containing relics and weapons of the First World War.

In France, in Péronne, is the Historiale de la Grande Guerre, in Belgium there is the Musée Royale de L'Armée in Brussels, and a small display at Ypres. At Poperinghe, the original Toc H building is open to the public, and there is much else to see. In Austria; in Vienna, is the Heeresgeschichtliches Museum referred to in the text.

Farther away are the Canadian War Museum at Ottawa and the Australian War Museum at Canberra.

Further Reading

Aldington, Richard, *Death of a Hero*, Penguin, 1936.

Bairnsfather, Bruce, *Bullets and Billets*, Richards, 1916.

Barnett, Correlli, *The Sword Bearers*, Jane's, 1963.

— *Britain and Her Army 1909-1970*, Allen Lane, 1970.

Baynes, E. H., *Animal Heroes of the Great War*, Macmillan, New York, 1927.

Bean, C. E. W., *Official History of Australia in the War*, Vols 1–12, Angus & Robertson.

Beesly, Patrick, *Very Special Admiral*, Hamish Hamilton, 1980.

Binding, Rudolf, *A Fatalist at War* (Trs), Allen & Unwin, 1928.

Blake, Robert, *The Private Papers of Douglas Haig, 1914–1919*, Eyre and Spottiswoode, 1952.

Blunden, Edmund, *Undertones of War*, Cobden-Sanderson, 1928.

Bond, B. (Ed), *The First World War and British Military History*, Clarendon, 1991.

Boraston, Lieutenant Colonel J. H., *Sir Douglas Haig's Despatches 1913–1919*, Dent, 1919.

Brown, Malcolm, *The First World War*, Imperial War Museum and Sidgwick & Jackson, 1991.

Bülow, Prince von, *Imperial Germany* (Trs), Cassell, 1914.

— *Memoirs*, Putnam, 1922.

Campbell, P. J., *In the Cannon's-Mouth*, Hamish Hamilton, 1979.

Chambrun and Marenche, *The American Army in the European Conflict*, Macmillan, New York, 1920.

Chapman, Guy, *A Passionate Prodigality*, Buchan and Enright, 1985.

Coombs, Rose, *Before Endeavours Fade*, After the Battle, 1983.

[This is the definitive guide to the main battlefields and monuments in France and Belgium, each of which is explained. Rose Coombs was Special Collections Officer of the Imperial War Museum, London.]

Coppard, George, *With a Machine Gun to Cambrai*, Papermac 1980.

Crozier, Brigadier-General F. P., *A Brass Hat in No Man's Land*, Cape, 1930.

Dane, Edmund, *British Campaigns in Africa and the Pacific, 1914–1918*, Hodder and Stoughton, 1919.

Edmonds, Charles, (C. E. Carrington), *A Subaltern's War*, Davis, 1929.

Edmonds, J. E. (Ed), *Military Operations France and Belgium: Official Histories*, HMSO, 1948.

Ellis, John, *The Social History of the Machine Gun*, Hutchinson, 1975.

Falkenhayn, General E. von, GHQ *1914–1916 and its Critical Decisions*, Hutchinson, 1919 (Trs).

Falls, Cyril, *The First World War*, Longmans, 1960.

Farrar-Hockley, A., *The Somme*, Eyre and Spottiswoode. 1964.

French Official History: *Les Armées Françaises dans la Grande Guerre*, Imprimerie Nationale, n.d.

German Official History: *Der Weltkrieg 1914 bis 1918*, Mitler und Sohn, 1936.

Gilbert, Martin, *First World War Atlas*, Weidenfeld & Nicholson, 1970.

Glover, Jon and Silkin, Jon, *The Penguin Book of First World War Prose*, Penguin, 1990.

Glubb, John, *Into Battle*, Cassell 1978.

Gough, Sir Hubert, *Fifth Army*, Hodder and Stoughton.

Graves, Robert, *Good-bye To All That*, Cape, 1929.

Horne, A., *The Price of Glory: Verdun 1916*, Penguin 1978.

Hough, Richard, *Former Naval Person* [Churchill], Weidenfeld & Nicolson, 1985.

Joffre, Marshal, *Memoirs* (Trs), G. Bles, 1932.

Jones, A., *War in the Air*, OUP, 1938.

Junger, Ernst, *Storm of Steel*, Chatto and Windus, 1924.

Kannengiesser, Hans von, *The Campaign in Gallipoli*, Hutchinson (Trs), 1928.

Kluck, Generaloberst von, *The March on Paris*, Arnold (Trs), 1920.

Kuhl, H. von, *Der Weltkrieg 1914–1918*, Berlin, Weller, n.d.

Laffin, John, *The Western Front Illustrated 1914–18*, Alan Sutton, 1991.

Lawrence, T. E., *Seven Pillars of Wisdom*, Penguin, 1977.

Liddell Hart, B. H., *Foch: Man of Orleans*, Penguin, 1937.

— *History of the First World War*, Cassell, 1971.

Lloyd George, D., *War Memoirs*, Odhams, 1936.

Livesey, Anthony, *The Viking Atlas of World War I*, Viking, 1994.

Ludendorff, General von, *My War Memories* (Trs), Hutchinson, 1919.

Lushington, F., (Writing as Mark Severn), *The Gambardier*, Benn, 1930.

Macdonald, Lyn, *1914*, Penguin, 1987.

Macpherson, Sir W.G., *History of Great War Medical Services*, HMSO, 1923.

Martin, Owen, *Poor Bloody Infantry*, John Murray, 1987.

Marwick, A., *Women and War 1914–18*, Croom Helm, 1977.

Messenger, Charles, *Trench Fighting 1914–18*, Pan/Ballantine, 1972.

Middlebrook, M., *The First Day on the Somme*, Fontana 1975.

Mitchell, David, *Women on the Warpath*, Cape, 1966.

Montague, C. E., *Disenchantment*, Chatto & Windus, 1922.

Moore, William, *See How They Ran*, Leo Cooper, 1970.

Owen, H. C., *Salonika and After*, Hodder and Stoughton, 1919.

Peel, C. S., *How We Lived Then (1914–1918)*, Lane, 1925.

Pitt, Barrie, *1918: The Last Act*, Macmillan, 1984.

Portway, Donald, *Militant Don*, Robert Hale, 1964.

Prior, Robin and Wilson, Trevor, *Command on the Western Front*, Blackwell, 1992.

Remarque, E. M., *All Quiet on the Western Front* (Tr: A.W.Wheen), Mayflower, 1960.

Repington, Colonel, *The First World War*, Constable, 1920.

Robbins, Keith, *The First World War*, Oxford, 1984.

Roberts, Cecil, *Spears Against Us*, Hutchinson, 1933.

Roberts, F. J., *The Wipers Times* (facsimile), Everleigh Nash and Grayson, 1930.

Robertson, Sir William, *From Private to Field Marshal*, Constable, 1921.

Rommel, Erwin, *Infantry Attacks*, Greenhill, 1990. [Became Field Marshal in the Second World War.]

Rupprecht, Crown Prince of Bavaria, *In Treue Fest, Mein Kriegstagebuch*, Munich, Deutscher Nationalverlag, 1919.

Sassoon, S., *Memoirs of a Fox-Hunting Man*, Faber, 1942.

— *Sherston's Progress*, Penguin, 1948.

Sanders, Liman von, *Five Years of Turkey* (Trs), US Naval Institute, 1927.

Scott, Michael, *The Ypres Salient* [Battlefield Guide], Gliddon, 1992.

Seligman, V. J., *Macedonian Musing*, Allen & Unwin, 1918.

Smithers, A. J., *Cambrai*, Leo Cooper, 1992.

Stone, Norman, *The Eastern Front 1914–1917*, Hodder and Stoughton, 1932.

Taylor, A. J. P., *The First World War. An Illustrated History*, Penguin, 1963.

Terraine, John, *To Win a War*, Papermac, 1978.

— *The Smoke and the Fire*, Sidgwick and Jackson, 1980.

— *White Heat: the New Warfare 1914–18*, Leo Cooper, 1992.

Trevelyan, G.M., *Scenes from Italy: War*, Jack, 1919.

Tuchman, Barbara, *August 1914*, Macmillan, 1987.

Turner, E. S., *Dear Old Blighty*, Michael Joseph, 1980.

Vaughan, E. C., *Some Desperate Glory*, Papermac, 1985.

Warner, Philip, *The Battle of Loos*, Kimber, 1976.

— *The Zeebrugge Raid*, Kimber, 1978.

— *Kitchener*, Hamish Hamilton, 1985.

— *Passchendaele*, Sidgwick & Jackson, 1987.

— *Field Marshal Earl Haig*, Bodley Head, 1991.

Winton, John, *Jellicoe*, Michael Joseph, 1981.

Index